# THE BEST OF
# VERITY STOB

*Highlights of Verity Stob's Famous Columns*
*From EXE, Dr. Dobb's Journal, and The Register*

Grade Twelve Computer
Science Award

Dept. Head and teader:
( Mr. Kevin Deslauriers
↳ (Integrated Technology)

# THE BEST OF
# VERITY STOB

*Highlights of Verity Stob's Famous Columns*
*From* EXE, Dr. Dobb's Journal, *and* The Register

VERITY STOB

Apress®

**The Best of Verity Stob: Highlights of Verity Stob's Famous Columns from *EXE*, *Dr. Dobb's Journal*, and *The Register***

Lead Editor: Chris Mills
Technical Reviewer: Shelley Powers
Editorial Board: Steve Anglin, Dan Appleman, Ewan Buckingham, Gary Cornell, Tony Davis, Jason Gilmore, Jonathan Hassell, Chris Mills, Dominic Shakeshaft, Jim Sumser
Project Manager: Kylie Johnston
Copy Edit Manager: Nicole LeClerc
Copy Editor: Ami Knox
Production Manager: Kari Brooks-Copony
Production Editor: Kelly Winquist
Compositor: Dina Quan
Proofreader: Linda Seifert
Indexer: Kevin Broccoli
Artist: Kinetic Publishing
Cover Designer: Kurt Krames
Manufacturing Manager: Tom Debolski

Library of Congress Cataloging-in-Publication Data

Stob, Verity.
  The best of Verity Stob : highlights of Verity Stob's famous columns from EXE, Dr. Dobb's Journal, and The Register / Verity Stob.
      p. cm.
  Includes index.
  ISBN 1-59059-442-8
  1. Computers—Social aspects. 2. Computers—Humor. I. Title.

  QA76.9.C66S878 2005
  303.48'34—dc22

                                                    2004029021

Printed and bound in the United States of America 9 8 7 6 5 4 3 2

Distributed to the book trade in the United States by Springer-Verlag New York, Inc., 233 Spring Street, 6th Floor, New York, NY 10013 and outside the United States by Springer-Verlag GmbH & Co. KG, Tiergartenstr. 17, 69112 Heidelberg, Germany.

In the United States: phone 1-800-SPRINGER, fax 201-348-4505, e-mail orders@springer-ny.com, or visit http://www.springer-ny.com. Outside the United States: fax +49 6221 345229, e-mail orders@springer.de, or visit http://www.springer.de.

For information on translations, please contact Apress directly at 2560 Ninth Street, Suite 219, Berkeley, CA 94710. Phone 510-549-5930, fax 510-549-5939, e-mail info@apress.com, or visit http://www.apress.com.

*For the dear peeps at Dotted and Dotless,
who laughed first*

# Contents

**PART II**

# THE RASP OF THE MODEM *(1995–19100)*     55

## PART III

# AFTER THE APOCALYPSE *(2000–2004)*                  171

# PREVIOUSLY UNPUBLISHED 295

# Foreword

It's hard to believe now, but there was a time when writing jokes about multi-dispatch inheritance in dynamically typed languages simply wasn't the glamorous, highly paid profession that it is today.

Before Slashdot, before *User Friendly* and the *Joy of Tech*, before *Futurama*, before Old Man Murray, before Dilbert, and before "1001 Surefire Gags about C++ That Will Wow Your Klingon Wedding Guests," funny for geeks was a criminally underserved market sector.

Biro-drawn cartoon strips were the typical fare, all called something like *Just Byting Around!* or *Giga-giggles!* These would run for a few months in *Practical Computing* or *PC Handholder* or some such magazine. After recycling gags revolving around hard drives and floppy disk entendres, these wretched specimens died for lack of inspiration and, I would hope, some vestigial sense of shame.

And then there was, thank God, Verity Stob.

I remember the first time I read the Stob column. It was 1988, and I was hiding in a fluorescent-lit dungeon in the heart of my university, strumming futilely through the lower-rent academic journals and controlled-circulation tech mags.

The first few lines—some throwaway comment about Lisp, I think—had my snorts echoing across the library.

I was hooked. I remember at the time having a light bulb appear above my head: thinking, yes, this is how it should be done. In the end, I ploughed through all the back-issues the library held, cackling like all the functional programming crazies that sat in the corner of that particular institution.

Not that I had any idea about how Stob managed it. I'm still somewhat in awe of the tricks Stob pulled off. Unlike everything else in the tech world then, Stob's jokes were subtle, original—and also often rather *hard*. Even as I laughed out loud at the gags I understood, I could sense there was dozens buried underneath that I was missing. And, somehow, the tricksier the references they were, the funnier they got.

I think I ended up learning Turbo Pascal and dBase mostly just so I could get the jokes in Stob.

The erudition didn't end with the technical trivia of a coder's life.

There were references here that hinted at great books to be read, poetry to be learnt by heart, an overall literacy that completely belied the cultural desert-nomad, and near-autistic galoot image that all the other "computer funny" pages reveled in.

Everyone else who even tried to be amusing in the tech world sounded like the pub bore; Stob sounded like the Algonquin Round Table's tech correspondent.

Stob would write parodies that would delight me so much that I'd find myself digging out the originals. Not only are Stob's columns the only back page pieces worth re-reading; they made everything she referenced worth re-reading, too.

And, if that wasn't enough, from the antiseptic world of eighties tech, to the delusional hype of the nineties, to the shell shock of the twenty-first century, Stob columns glowed with a rare humanity. The stories she told weren't Sysadmins From Hell revenge fantasies, or sneering putdowns of people who were so foolish they didn't even know what a non-maskable interrupt *was*. Instead, she wrote about what was really going on. Bittersweet battles with the human condition: little palliative essays that were more about soothing the pain of everyday life than in turning it into some carnival of grotesques.

I know, I know. I'm laying this all on a bit thick. I'm sure even Ms. Stob herself would be gracefully demurring right now; smiling sweetly as I go on, all the while eying the exits, waiting for the moment I start quoting biblical prophecies which mention her by name.

But the truth is, even now, when we're drowning in comedy and geek culture is an ocean or two wide, I'm delighted to get the chance of re-reading these columns. And seeing, once again, how it really should be done.

Danny O'Brien
Co-editor of NTK
http://www.ntk.net
October 2004
San Jose, California,
at the International House of Pancakes

# About the Author

**Verity Stob** has been a programmer for 20 long years, and has extensive experience in many disciplines of the profession. Programming languages known in-depth include C++, Delphi, Visual Basic, plus scripting languages such as JavaScript, PHP, and—in a real crisis—Perl. Can bluff her way in C# and Java, but there again who can't, eh? Ditto UML, XML, HTML, and any other -MLs you care to lob at her. Except for ML itself, of course. Mostly Windows, bit of Linux at a push, Mac no way. (I'll bung in a few methodologies here later, bulk it up a bit.) Although currently living and working in London, prepared to be flexible . . . Definitely a team player . . . Very many *good* hobbies . . . Sorry, who is this for again? When's the interview? I tell you, I'm not going if they use those damn Microsoft quizzes.

# Author's Preface

## HOW THE ARTICLES CAME TO BE WRITTEN

In the late 1980s, the personal computer industry finally got over the cheerful, pioneering era of start-up companies run by skinny teenagers who soldered together their inventions overnight, and embarked upon the dull, grey era of carry-on companies run by fat fortyagers who used phrases like "total cost of ownership" and "state of the market." Apple had let go its twitchy, visionary co-founder and entrusted its future into the hands of—as S. Jobs Esq. himself famously put it—a former salesman of sugared water. Bill Gates, of whom my Mum had not yet heard, finally stopped modelling the Peter Pan look and switched to the bespectacled, be-clean-shaven Bilbo Baggins look he uses to this day. Britain's own Sir Clive Sinclair, creator of my country's first real personal computers, had sadly taken his eye off the digital ball and now was best known for an important national joke: the C5 electric tricycle.

The glory days may have been over but, with every little business from greengrocers to horse dentists buying its first computer, it was a boom time for publishers of monthly computer magazines. Dozens of titles were launched, all over the world, most of them pretty similar. Each gave off an agreeable odour of modernity and affluence, and contained bland articles comparing the top 25 acoustic hoods for dot matrix printers as measured *in our own labs*. Each issue ran to several hundred pages, nearly all advertising matter, and was built like a young telephone directory. There was a widely circulated rumour that an airdrop delivery of *What PC World Today Shopper* to a subscriber living in remote parts had hit and killed a sheep. The publishers of WPWTS demurred; they claimed it was a horse that was killed.

The British publication *.EXE* magazine was different. Despite boasting a notably glossy cover and applying various other trick effects that magazines use to suggest prosperity and authority, it always retained a lean and hungry look. It had the same defiant vigour of those bushes that somehow seed themselves into cracks in vertical walls and live out precarious lives, literally eking out an existence in a niche. Programmers were the magazine's intended audience, but programmers are rarely big spenders, and if the publishers kidded themselves that things could be otherwise, the advertisers generally knew better.

But .*EXE* was also different in that it addressed itself to real working programmers; specifically those who, like me, used microcomputers. I suddenly felt less alone, part of a community. It seems ridiculous now, in these en-webbed days, where the most obscure scripting language and most specialised library of code have their own lively discussion fora on SourceForge, to speak of a sense of isolation. But isolation is what it was, and .*EXE* broke the spell.

It was such a relief to discover that there were other C coders out there writing MS-DOS programs. Most books I could find assumed that, if you were using that noble programming language, you would be coding for Unix on, at the very least, an Apollo workstation. They ignored or glossed over the sticky issue of mixed 8- and 16-bit pointers; none would deign to tell you, as .*EXE* did, how to use the serial port UARTs in interrupt-driven mode, or discuss a dozen different ways to make your program Terminate and Stay Resident (an obsession of the magazine at that time). Nowadays this sort of information is to be had for a few moments' googling; then we fell upon it like urban pigeons on stale breadcrumbs.

Most magazines put something light on the inside back pages, and .*EXE* conformed to the norm with a regular article in this slot, squeezed below a half page list of advertisers. These efforts showed signs of being filled at the last minute by a staff writer with other, pressing duties on his mind. In 1988, inspired by the pro-programmer culture of the magazine, and with the luxury of more time and inclination to devote to the exercise, I thought I might do better. I was a fan of that granddaddy of all funny programmer articles, "Real Programmers Don't use PASCAL," which in those pre-Net days was circulated as a dog-eared photocopy. I wanted to write new stuff in a similar vein.

As it happened, a significant proportion of the mag was contributed by its readers—probably necessarily so, given the unwillingness of regular journalists to spend months writing a device driver for a return of about £150 (say $200)—so it was easy to make an offer and get a tryout. The piece I submitted is the first article in this book; the .*EXE* people liked it well enough to allow me back the next month.

The resulting column continued, with one 18-month interruption, until the now dotless *EXE* was eventually blown out of its niche by the first cold winds of the dot-com failure of 2000. In the twenty-first century, the venerable US magazine *Dr. Dobb's Journal* and the deliciously vicious and vivacious Brit website *The Register* have, on occasion, kindly given the orphan column a home.

## HOW THIS BOOK IS ORGANISED

This selection of articles is presented in chronological order, enabling the fanciful to think of it as a social history of modern geekdom, from 1988 to 2004. A bonus chapter at the back of the book contains some previously unpublished material. By including this stuff, my intention is partially to enable grizzled programmers with attics full of dusty boxes of *.EXE*s and *DDJ*s to purchase this volume without feeling too cheated, and partially in the hope of cynically exploiting any completists who may be out there. Buy now, boys! Don't wait until the last existing perfect first edition copy in the world has been bid up to $12,000 on eBay!

Where Old Aunty Time has rendered the subject matter of a piece particularly obscure, I have inserted a few explanatory notes to the article in question, shown

[in square brackets and in this font]

These should assist those who have somehow forgotten the great OS/2 API return code debate of 1991 or—worse—have the impertinence to be far too young to have taken part in it. I am convinced that, with the aid of these notes, the material reads as tautly and topically as the day it was first printed. Probably more so, I should think.

At the suggestion of my Technical Reader, a glossary of British terms unfamiliar to US readers is included at the end of the book. I had somehow, unrealistically, hoped that this would list choice words from the golden age of Brit Comp like, I don't know, Sir Tony Hoare's private pet name for his newly devised sorting algorithm, or a term for efficient synchronisation from the model of parallelism that the Transputer people used. In the event, it seems to be mostly slang words for kinds of drink. Anyway, it's there for you if you want it.

—V.S.

## PART I

# LIFE BEFORE GUIS
## (1988–1994)

*"Hey hey 16k*

*What does that get you today?"*

—MJ Hibbett, *"Hey Hey 16k"* *

*Elderly techies are highly recommended to google this song up and enjoy a nostalgic weep. Get the version with Rob Manuel's excellent Flash animation—see everything.

## OCTOBER 1988, *EXE MAGAZINE*

[The first Stob column, which originally appeared in *EXE* magazine October 1988.

Even at this early date, you'll note, we were already enjoying the benefit of viruses. Dr. Alan Solomon was one of the earliest to identify their key benefit to the vendor of anti-virus software: the lovely way that it rapidly goes out of date.

Other items of useful background information that might or might not help make sense of the piece: the Atari ST was a not particularly popular home computer of the time; the popular program WordPerfect eschewed the F1 key in favour of, as I remember it, F3; most PC computers still lacked battery-backed clocks and reset their calendars to midnight 1/1/1980 when switched on; Int 21h was the interrupt vector entry point to most of MS-DOS's application functions; programs written using Microsoft Basic printed the not terribly helpful error message "?Redo from start" if a user put so much as a comma out of place; the makers of the chocolate bar Marathon had not yet renamed it to the hateful internationally-friendly name Snickers; I admired the cop show *Hill Street Blues* whence came the catchphrase "dog breath"; and Ada had been mandated as the programming language for heaps of defence projects but was believed by many programmers (as opposed to their managers) to be a big white turkey.

What? You knew all that already? Excellent. I won't bother again.]

# How Friendly Is Your Software?

1. Your program is running, and the F1 key is pressed. Does it

   a) Immediately bring up a screen full of relevant information?

   b) Immediately bring up a screen full of information relating to the Atari ST version?

   c) Immediately print a message, "Help file not yet available"?

   d) Beep, because F1 is an illegal key? The correct help combination is ALT-?-H-F3, as the operator would know if he had troubled to read the help info.

   e) Format driver C: (to teach anybody fooling around a damn good lesson)?

2. Your program requires a disk to have been put in the floppy drive, but it hasn't. What happens next?

   a) A coloured box pops up with the message "Excuse me, there seems to be a slight problem with the diskette drive. Put it right in your own time, and then press a key. Only when you're ready, mind."

   b) A box pops up with the message "No disk in drive. Correct fault and press a key to continue."

   c) A message appears on the status line: "NO DISK DOG BREATH."

   d) A message appears on the status line: "P FAULT D/12—tf WAGWAG."

   e) The program crashes out into DOS, leaving dozens of files open.

3. Your program needs to know today's date. Does it

   a) Check for the existence of a battery-backed BIOS accessible clock, and only trouble the operator if there isn't one?

   b) Always prompt using the correct date format as determined by an MS-DOS Int 21h call function?

   c) Always prompt in American (mm/dd/yy) format, because let's face it the US is where the money is?

**d)** Always prompt in Japanese (yyyy/mm/dd) format, because it's easier to code a date-sort that way?

**e)** Always assume the date is 1/1/80?

4. Your program requested the total number of widgets in the warehouse, and the operator has replied -234.8 (instead of 2348 as he intended). When he presses the ENTER key the program

**a)** Plays a little tune to indicate a mistake, and a coloured box pops up with the message "Oops! I don't think we meant to do that! Let's try again, with a positive integer value please."

**b)** Makes a raspberry noise, and flashes "POSITIVE INTEGER INPUT" on the status line.

**c)** Prints "?Redo from start" over the function key crib and scrolls the "Number of widgets?" prompt off the top of the screen.

**d)** Crashes out into DOS, leaving dozens of files open.

**e)** Displays "2348" (because "-" and "." are illegal characters in an integer field). However, it uses the value "-234.8" in the calculation of net widget production.

For each question score a)10, b) 8, c) 6, d) 3, and e) 0.

## SCORING

0–10: Well done! Your software is unfriendly bordering on vicious. Write a letter to Dr. Alan Solomon, and he may give you a grant to help you turn it into a virus.

37–150: Your programs are a bit like a Marathon bar: soft on the outside but with some hard bits in the middle. Let's try and step up the peanut input.

200–300: Careful! Your programs are too friendly. Rewrite it in Ada and send it to the MOD* to become a defence program. They'll soon have it firing missiles and frightening the children.

---

*British Ministry of Defence

**NOVEMBER 1988, *EXE MAGAZINE***

[Although it omits some biggies, this list gives a reasonable indication of the popular microcomputer languages at the time, before the OO tsunami struck—this was truly the era of the classless society. Now these languages are all pretty much gone from regular non-niche use, excepting C.

The "Good Book" is K&R, natch.]

---

# The Programmers' Guide to Programmers

*Spot 'em a mile off! Here is .EXE's programmers' guide to programmers.*

## BASIC

BASIC programmers are paranoid because any 16 year old could do their job, if asked. To try to secure their positions, they deliberately write code using the double-spaghetti method, never using a FOR...NEXT loop where four or five IF...THEN...ELSE constructs might do. Since they taught themselves programming on a ZX81 rigged up to the family telly, they have quixotic gaps in their computing knowledge. BASIC programmers ring up technical support centres to ask questions like "What are those funny numbers with letters in them?"

## PASCAL

Despite an early reputation for gambling (you've heard of Pascal's Bet), these days Pascal programmers are all deadly enthusiastic. They are proud of the ability of their language to define a type representing, for example, different flavours of crisps. This enables them to write useful code where `tomato = succ(salt_n_vinegar)`, and `ord(roast_beef)/2>ord(prawn_cocktail)`.

Pascal people all know exactly how programming Should Be Done, and enjoy casting their pearls of wisdom among the swine who write in lesser dialects.

## FORTRAN

FORTRAN programmers learned their craft at college in 1935. They are convinced that theirs is the language of the future, pointing out that in 1966 it was selected as the ANSI standard for writing Snoopy calendar programs. FORTRAN programmers are not altogether at ease with modern peripherals such as VDUs (which they revealingly refer to as "glass teletypes"). They are the only people in the programming community to use flow-charts, which they draw with loving care using the special WH Smith's* stencils. These diagrams are then filed away with the source code, ignored for the life of the program, then finally thrown away unread; because even FORTRAN is easier to read than a flow-chart.

## ASSEMBLY LANGUAGE

Assembly Language programmers are closer to the machine than anybody else: emotionally as well as in programming terms. This symbiosis can be taken too far: programmers who faint when the reset button is pressed should perhaps consider switching to C or even chartered accountancy.

---

*WH Smith is a chain of stationery and newspaper shops in the UK. William Henry Smith II, son of the eponymous founder, was a notable Victorian who became First Lord of the Admiralty and was lampooned by WS Gilbert in the opera *HMS Pinafore*. Cor! S'nearly as good as Wikipedia, isn't it?

Assembly programmers often pretend to be able to patch their code in hex as they go ("I think you'll find that C4 F2 D1 at offset 24A2 will fix the problem, Nigel"). They manage this by introducing deliberate errors into their programs, pre-assembling the "patched" result secretly and concealing the results in tiny writing on their shirt cuffs.

# C

Traditionally the programmer was a bearded bore who would corner you at parties and breathe garlic and Unix all over you. All this has now changed. These days C programmers are clean-shaven bores who corner you at parties and breathe lager and the advantages of OS/2 all over you. They can still be trusted to have a witty quote or two from the Good Book to liven up a dull conversation; my personal favourite is "A primary expression followed by an expression in square brackets is a primary expression."

Notwithstanding these faults, it should be noted that some C programmers are incredibly together people, who turn over an honest penny writing articles for computer magazines.

**DECEMBER 1988, *EXE MAGAZINE***

[This article celebrates the fine city of Newcastle-Upon-Tyne, situated in northeast England, and its gentle inhabitants, the Geordies.

My compatriots may be interested and enchanted to learn that Newcastle Brown Ale is currently being marketed in the US as a fashionable drink for the elite. I recently found an advertisement for it in the pages of the American satirical rag *The Onion*, in among advertisements for BMWs and other swanky gear.

US readers, in turn, will be reassured to hear that our image of the drink in its own land entirely fits this description. Oh yes. Nothing like a pint of dog to establish oneself as a suave sophisticate.]

———————

# Larn Yasel Programmin!

*Once a decade, a single product redefines the parameters of programming practice. That moment has now arrived. From our extensive software laboratory, located high above Chiswick on the 25th floor of .EXE Towers, comes a new concept in programming languages.*

## THE BACKGROUND

You will recall that Kernighan and Ritchie developed the C language from BPCL to simplify the construction of the UNIX operating system. Our language was developed one evening from ten pints of brown ale. The idea was to distract the author from a strong feeling of nausea that was afflicting him (didn't work). From these humble origins, the product has matured to the point where we feel able to release it onto an unsuspecting world.

## THE LANGUAGE

GEORDIE—the name is an acronym for "Gulping Excessively Often Ruins Decent Indian Edibles," in memory of another incident the night the language was born—is surely the most versatile and powerful of programming languages. It is adaptable to nearly all applications from authoring to astronomy, and from systems to simulation. Like BASIC it's easy to learn, like Ada it has facilities to handle interrupts and multitasking events, and like FORTRAN it has seven letters in its name.

Consider this fragment of pseudo code, part of a real-time fire-prevention system:

```
IF fire-detected THEN
DO take-fire-prevention-action
```

Here is the same fragment coded in GEORDIE:

```
If ya ganna smork ya tab in ear,
ah'll belt ya from ear to Geeatsheed, mun
```

Like COBOL, GEORDIE was designed to be as similar to natural language as possible. We have made very few concessions to the compiler writers, although the symbol mun is used as a statement separator—equivalent to the semicolon in Pascal. Nobody would really speak GEORDIE, but we think it's a darn close run thing!

## THE COMPETITORS

GEORDIE beats its rivals hands down. Consider this pseudo code:

```
FOR each item in Shopping List array
DO print item
```

Here is the same program coded in Cockney Rhyming BASIC:

```
10 FOR MINCE PIE = 1 TO MAXLIST
20 MURRAY MINT SLIST$(I)
30 SORELY VEXED I
```

Finally, here it is in GEORDIE:

```
Tell us whaya gerrin in for dinna, hen
```

Need we say more?

## THE PACKAGE

You get a lot more than a simple compiler with GEORDIE. There's an interpreter so that applications can be developed interactively. Forget obsolete prompts like "ok" and "READY"; when you see the line "What fettle, petal?" you know you're working with the market leader. Also free with the compiler comes a complete programmer's environment—and we aren't talking about a text editor and a manky MAKE utility. GEORDIE is bundled with a copy of Scott Dobson's definitive work "Larn Yersel Geordie," a black-and-white scarf, and a couple of crates of the aforementioned electric soup.

To get your copy of GEORDIE, send a cheque for a lot of money to V Stob, c/o .EXE, Chiswick. GEORDIE. It's champion, man.

**MARCH 1989, *EXE MAGAZINE***

[It seems incredible now, that in the late twentieth century one could still phone up a technical support line and speak to a human being, right away. Young persons reading this may suppose that I am pulling their legs, but truly: it did happen.

I should explain Bobby Robson was the manager of the England football\* team, an important ceremonial post in British religious life. The popularity of the incumbent of this post traditionally follows a fixed trajectory, an *Arc de no Triumph* as it were. Initially his stock soars, as he is welcomed as a fresh-minded replacement for his incompetent predecessor. Then he loses a game or two, and/or becomes involved in a scandal, and finally, to the loud jeering of the newspapers, his fall from favour rapidly accelerates into a non-recoverable dive.

This article was written towards the end of Mr. Robson's England career, as it plunged towards the sea.]

---

\*That's "football" as in "soccer" of course. All nations call their local form of officially sanctioned fighting "football," as though their form were the only proper kind, in the same way that all nations colour themselves red on their own maps. It's just one of those things.

# POET'S Day

*The story so far . . . Verity Stob has been having trouble with the software she bought from WADS (Will'n'Dave's Software) Ltd. Last Friday afternoon, at 3:30 pm, she rang technical support, and spoke to Dave himself.*

*(Phone rings 17 times)*

" . . . Arsenal don't stand a chance. S'oright, Will, I've got it. Hello, this is WADS, what can I do for you?"

"A bug in WADSbase? I'd be most surprised if it is, Miss, 'cos it's what we call a wossname, a tried and tested ERK, 'scuse me, product. I'll just see if our expert is available."

*(Puts hand over mouthpiece)*

"When you left the Goose and Paperclip, was Terry showing any signs of moving? He was getting in another round? Brilliant! He won't be able to fly a compiler this afternoon. No, it's just some bint on the dog wants technical support. Yeah, she has got a sexy voice, hur hur hur."

*(Takes hand away from mouthpiece)*

"I'm sorry, our expert is currently tied up in a meeting at the moment. Can I have him ring you back later, Miss?"

"Oright darlin, keep your hair on. I'm sure I can sort you out. Now, what sort of a machine have you got?"

"Now that's not really what you call your genuine compatible, is it, I think we may have found out the root of our problems there. What exactly are the symptoms?"

"Let's get this straight. You asked WADSbase to give you a printout of all your customer records, and instead it went through the whole file inserting BOBBY ROBSON MUST GO into the customer name field. If I could just put you on hold a moment, I will consult with my colleague."

*(Nine-minute musical interlude: a selection from the LP* Geoff Love and His Orchestra Murder the Beatles*)*

" . . . Blimey she's still there. Hello? I'm afraid that we are having some trouble locating . . . Ah! Look what the cat's brought in! Our expert has just got back from the, er, meeting room. I will just put him in the picture."

*(Phone muffled once more)*

"Tel, someone else has that Bobby Robson bug. I've warned you about pratting around before . . . Are you listening to me, Terry? Terry, you don't look very well. What are you doing? Terry, don't do that!"

*(Various background noises and cries of "Oh Terry!," followed by loud thump, as of body collapsing on floor)*

"Nar, leave the plonker there to sleep it off. Look at my keyboard! God knows how I'm going to get that out from between the keys."

"Listen, we have just suffered a major hardware failure. I'm afraid that we really are going to have to get back to you another time. What was that? Thanks very much for our help? Oh, it's nothing Miss. It's what we're here for, really."

**APRIL 1989, *EXE MAGAZINE***

[Unisys at this time was not thought of as the former owner of the LZW patent and despoiler of GIFs, but as the merged remnant of two of the great names from the Robbie-the-Robot era of computer history: Sperry Rand, maker of the mighty Univac, and the Burroughs Adding Machine Co.

Pointless titbit: Burroughs' marketing slogan used to be "Burroughs dares to differ" and, to prove the point, the company created a range of not 8-, 16-, 32-, or even 64- but *51*-bit processors. This fact, used tactically at the right moment, has been known to kill dead all conversation at a medium-sized dinner party.]

---

# The Maltese Modem

*"To enhance Scotland Yard, the Metropolitan Police has ordered Unisys 2200/404 systems" boasted a recent Unisys press release. Verity Stob wondered what Dashiell Hammett and Raymond Chandler would make of it.*

It was one of those shabby tower block estates on the Isle of Dogs, East London, that the yuppies hadn't yet gotten around to stealing. Mr. Patel's grocery shop was located at the base of the tallest concrete tower. It was noon, but there were graffiti-covered steel shutters over the windows, decorated thus:

> *Patel poisons people*

and

*Johns are bigger than Buster Gonads\**

I needed some cigarettes, and a break from the drizzle, so I pushed open the door of the shop.

Inside, fluorescent lighting fought a flickering battle with the shuttered twilight. At the far end, past shelves filled with dusty biscuit packets and battered cans of diet lemonade, a skinny, tired-looking blonde stood behind the counter. Her hair was a little greasy, but no more so than if she had just rinsed it in chip fat, and her make-up was a little thick, but nothing you couldn't get off with a cold chisel, given the inclination.

"Yeah?" She screwed her face into what was probably a pout, underneath.

"Twenty Camel filters, please." She reached behind for the cigarettes, and went to ring up the sale.

Some till. It was none of my business if Mr. Patel chose to keep his luncheon vouchers in an Acorn R140 UNIX workstation, but it looked to me that 4 MIPS and a 32-bit RISC processor were going to waste adding up the price of soap. A drawer opened where a 5.25 inch Seagate should have been, and the girl started scrabbling change.

A shop bell jangled behind me. Framed in the doorway was a tall bearded figure, wearing a bright orange anorak of the type that railway men call "train-proof jackets," because they're not. He was in his early forties, his thinning black hair streaked with grey. He looked gaunt and hollow-eyed, desperate. The girl groaned when she saw him. The visitor was about as welcome as a dose of salmonella in a Marks and Sparks sandwich bar.

"Give me a line. You've gotta give me a line!" The man's voice was pleading.

"I've told you before. There ain't no data processing facilities here, Mister. You've come to the wrong place."

"Perhaps I can help."

We all swung around. In a far corner there was a glass-fronted counter, in which were displayed spherical brown objects that looked

---

\*A famous character from *Viz* magazine. Don't ask me. See Google for details.

like onion bhajis but didn't move like onion bhajis. Behind the counter stood the speaker, an elderly Asian man, presumably the eponymous owner.

"If Sir would please to show me his terminal?"

Orange Anorak groped in a large shoulder bag he was carrying. As he pulled out a black plastic box, I glimpsed a Unisys badge. The girl must have seen it as well, for she shrieked "He's a cop!" and reached under the counter. Something hard hit the back of my head, then a bottle of ink broke inside my eyeballs and I decided to take a nap . . .

*Who is the mystery assailant? How much further will we have to read before the love interest appears? Will Orange Anorak be able to log in at once, or will there be all that fooling around with baud rate, parity, and gender benders like real life? Find out etc., etc.*

**MAY 1989, *EXE MAGAZINE***

# Late One Night

*Despite extensive unpaid overtime, Verity Stob has not been able to track down an elusive bug.*

*"Poc!"*

That's all I need. The central heating going off. Life support systems failing fast. Mr. Scott, can you do anything? I'm sorry Captain, but the Dilithium crystals canna take much more of this.

It's nine o'clock. Nine o'clock on a Friday, and I'm staring at two hundred lines of stupid poxy rotten rancid smelly manky schmanky C code. But I'll have to leave soon. I'll just look through it once more.

"If you *could* see your way to fixing the transaction module tonight, Verity," said the manager, his smile beaming platitudes, his eyes full of remember-it's-your-pay-review-this-month, "then I'll be able to look the Customer in the eye at our Monday meeting. I would stay myself, but there's a do on at the Masons." That was three hours ago. He'll be rolling up his trouser leg by now.

It's such a stupid bug. Look. Balance of account, Smith P, £478.23. Credit transaction £8.29. Revised balance of account, Smith P, £47894637284512.03. Finding it should be easy-peasy.

Oh look, now it's 9:23. By the way, this isn't my code. This code was written by Graham, 30 secs before he left for a cushy job in the city. You remember Graham: beer gut, nasty leer, couldn't program his way out of a paper bag. Graham, who used to pat me and say, "Structured programming limits the imagination." Until the day I replied, "Graham, if you touch me again I'll bite you," which limited his imagination still further. I hope.

Yes, of course I've tried putting in lots of `printf()` statements. The `printf()` statements now outnumber the original code by about 2:1. 'Struth, it's 9:58. I'll go in a minute.

So Graham's in London earning £30k and I'm stuck here, up the creek, with a coffee to which warmth is but a distant memory, debugging Graham's imaginative code. I s'pose we could complement each other, me and him; I'm the de, he's the bugg

*"Poc!"*

What was that? We've already had the heating go off, it must have been the refrigeration unit cutting in. Either that or an armed psychotic burglar, come to steal my incredibly valuable Amstrad.

I wonder if it's the machine. Probably a Taiwanese microprocessor, made by a Taiwanese peasant lady, slaving over a hot microscope twelve hours a day, monthly salary 23p. I see it now. She contracted hay fever, and, what with antihistamines costing 24p from Boots (Taiwan branch), sneezed all over my CPU. One tiny globule of snot, less than one micron diameter, settled on an obscure transistor junction: two years later Stob has to work late to 10:32, correction, 10:33.

This is ridiculous paranoia, get a grip on yourself. It's got to be a software fault.

Perhaps I'll just try it out on Steve's machine. Oh God, it's not booting up. Oh God, I've broken it. Well, that certainly wasn't my fault. I'll just turn it off, and feign ignorance on Monday. I'm not getting involved with dangerous screwdrivers and electricity at 11:00 in the evening. I really, really must go home now. I'll just look through the listings once more . . .

JUNE 1989, *EXE MAGAZINE*

[I'm rather dubious about the natural history underlying this item. Could all these (suspiciously edible) species really be found together, apart from on the fishmonger's slab? I implore the gentle reader to work extra hard to suspend disbelief.]

———

# The Kraken Sleeps

*"Could you work in Japan?"*
*"Certainly. I like raw fish and am beginning to understand how they work. What I like is the way they set themselves objectives and then apply themselves totally to achieving success."*
 —Interview with economist and businessman John Ockenden,
Corporate Computing, *March/April 1989.*

"Of course," said the cod, "the secret of achieving success, in a business context, is not to confuse the objective with the means."

"He's off again," whispered the red mullet to a shoal of whiting that was drifting lazily past. "It'll be the efficient-market hypothesis next, you mark my words." The whiting tittered politely.

"And our objective in this case, fellow fishlings," continued the cod, ignoring the interruption, "is to ensure that Mr. Ockenden is accorded the warmest possible welcome when he arrives."

"'Does it actually say that he will be coming down here?" enquired a plaice in adenoidal tones.

"It doesn't actually say it *explicitly*, no." admitted the cod. "With a man of John's calibre, you have to exercise a bit of your discretion. If *Corporate Computing* printed that John was coming to see us, why, he'd have *Sunday Sport* reporters following him around, trying to catch him near a beach. **LOONEY BUSINESSMAN FLEES TO FISHY FRIENDS, HE LEFT ME FOR A HADDOCK WEEPS JILTED WIFE,** there would be no end to it. That and all the junk mail he'd get from wetsuit manufacturers."

"Why does he say 'raw fish'?," asked the red mullet, pointing to the waterlogged fragment of paper clasped between the cod's dorsal fins. "I would have thought the docility of cooked fish would appeal more to his sort."

"Thank you, brother mullet, there's no need for that sort of humour here. Remember the bereaved among us."

"But what can an economist do for us?" asked a jellyfish.

"Good question, brother," muttered the red mullet. "What we need down here is control of the resources by the workers, with major decisions taken on a one fin, one vote basis; not some money-grubbing businessman droning on about responsible accounting."

"Any more lip from you," the cod growled, "and I shall have to ask Kevin to remove you from this meeting." This was no idle threat, as Kevin was a hammerhead shark. The red mullet shut up.

"He will further our cause in the world Up There," said the cod, resuming his oratorical thread. "He can encourage Water Authorities to flood the seas with tasty, but non-fish harmful, sewage, so that humans stop eating us. He can persuade industries to produce more and more carbon dioxide, so the polar glaciers melt and raise the sea level. He can—what is it now?" The cod, whose voice had risen to a shriek with the excitement of his declamation, was interrupted by a nudge from the plaice.

"Excuse me," said the plaice, "but we were wondering what 'Japan' was?"

The cod's brow furrowed, as he studied the text once more.

"I think it's something that they eat Up There," he said.

["ANSI and ASCII" at this time were acronyms mostly associated with terminal configuration. The ASCII character set contrasting not with the not-yet-invented Unicode but with IBM's horrible EBCDIC—the latter fondly remembered for its curious sequencing of letter codes, which only nearly make sense when viewed in BCD through the bottom of a beer glass: "a", "b", "c", "d", "e", "f", "g", "h", "i", miss out seven, "j", "k", "l" . . . ]

---

# Twenty Things (Almost) You Didn't Know . . .

*It is once again that time of year when lazy computer hacks, desperate to fill yards of empty columns, compile lists of computer terms that you already knew. Here is Stob's contribution to the genre.*

**ANSI and ASCII.** Two characters from the first draft of the Brothers Grimm fairy tale, Hansel and Gretel. In this version of the text, after the two children have been heartlessly abandoned in the middle of the dark forest, Ascii, the little girl, kills and eats her brother Ansi. "There's no point in us both starving," says practical-minded Ascii.

**BASIC.** Acronym. Stands for "Blimey Andrew, Still Into C?" The sneer of the programmer who has just acquired a C++ compiler.

**cross compiler.** What you get if you pour boiling water down a compiler hole. NB: Anybody who thinks that this should be a *hot* cross compiler is a clever clogs, and must stand outside the class until the end of the lesson.

**dongle.** Suspicious black plastic object, found concealed in a colleague's drawer the night after an Ann Summers party.

**dot matrix printer.** Parasitic creature characterised by harsh screaming mating call. Despite its antisocial habits, it is extremely gregarious. Left to its own devices, it rapidly becomes lonely, and will try to throttle itself with paper, or even set fire to itself.

**handshake.** Describes the small, yet exquisitely painful, static shock that you get from metal objects (such as door handles) if you work in an air-conditioned office and wear rubber-soled shoes. (cf. dog-owner's usage of "He's only saying hello," addressed to person who is being bitten.)

**Mandelbrot set.** The group of half-starved nerds found in every Computer Science class, who spend all their free time writing graphics programs.

**power user.** An American salesman, who wears a double-breasted suit, bright-coloured braces, and large spectacles with red plastic frames. He uses a 33 MHz 386 machine to run Lotus 1-2-3. He believes that he is working on the leading edge of technology. Makes you sick, eh?

**Radix.** A kind of bath salts that runs Unix.

**SOOPS.** Acronym for Sex Object Oriented Programming System. An algorithm, which, when applied to the office environment, determines (among other things) who fetches the coffee.

**specification.** Pretentious name for the back of a cigarette packet.

**SPOOL.** Acronym for Simultaneous Peripheral Operation OnLine. Before spoolers, you had to wait until printout had finished before continuing with your work, because the act of printing locked up your PC. Now that we have this wonderful software, you have to wait until printout is finished before continuing your work, because you need the listing to go on, and anyway it's impossible to concentrate with that machine screeching away. (See *Dot matrix printer*.)

**Virtual Memory.** Describes a new RAM card that, when fitted in your PC, remains unrecognised through all possible permutations of DIPswitch settings.

**WIMP.** Acronym. Name given to a type of user-friendly OS environment. The user-friendliness is achieved by keeping the CPU tied up with complex manipulations. The consequential slowness of programs gives the user more time to think.

**WYLIWYG.** Spurious, meaningless word devised by PR department of ailing word processor manufacturer. It was hoped that the public would confuse the word with the acronym WYSIWYG. Unsurprisingly, nobody did.

[Historical perspective needed here. I should point out that a 40 MB hard disk was huge at that time. And that AST was an incredibly smart brand of PC, only given to key personnel. And that Sprint was a clever word processor from Borland that went nowhere at all. And that a 6MB .dbf was a colossal thing; bigger than any database file in the known world. No question about "could have been"; I **was** a contender.

. . . Mind you, I didn't win . . . ]

# Few Lend (but Fools)

*"I had a little pony, his name was Dapple Grey / I lent him to a lady, to ride a mile away / She whipped him, she slashed him, she rode him through the mire / I would not lend my pony now for all the lady's hire"*

*—Anon.*

Had some complaints about the frivolity of this column, so this time I am offering a fierce, closely-reasoned attack on last month's *Banks' Statement* in *PCW*. I worked out the bones of the thing at home; it's just a matter of typing it into the faithful office AST. I'll be with you in a minute.

So why is faithful AST standing upright on floor, eh? I hate PCs being on the floor; you have to crawl around in the dust to plug things into their ports. Oh I know why, I told Steve—yes, that is the Steve of the "You turn my software into hardware" coffee mug—he could borrow it over the weekend, while his machine is garaged for a RAM upgrade. Steve likes It on the floor, Verity prefers It on the desk, fnarr, fnarr. He might have put my PC back where he found it. Simple courtesy. No time to put that right now: lean down into orifice between desk and wall (dislodging nearly empty can of Tennant's Pornographic Lager that someone has abandoned on my desk), grope grope grope for Big Red Switch, got it, click.

While that warms up, time to rehearse the sinking of my scarlet claws into Banks' (Banks's? Banks's's's's?) soft white hide. It is surely a fantastic overestimate of his own importance and intelligence when

Beeeeeeeeeeeeeeeeeeeep

The machine is going beep and printing over and over: VERITY STOB HAS GOT AN ENORMOUS BOTTOM. An endless loop in my AUTOEXEC. Well ha ha ha. I'm sorry but that just isn't funny. You know me, good old Verity. I know how to take a joke against myself. But that is not funny. I've seen funnier things on Christmas cracker mottoes. I've seen funnier things in *Punch* magazine. I've seen funnier things on Michael Barrymore's *Saturday Night Out*.

Right; Ctrl-Break in, fix that later, got to get on, power up word processor. I've got it completely macro-customised, you'll like this, all I do is Alt-V and instantly, with no interference from me, nothing happens. The sod has wiped my macro file. OK, do it manually. Verity says create new file, Sprint replies Beep! Disk Error. Verity shrieks What? Sprint retorts 512 bytes free on disk, matey.

That's 512 bytes on my 40 MB hard disk which, as long ago as last Friday, had just 34 MB free. That makes me mad. You won't like me when I'm mad. Let's have a look in this subdirectory. Two dBASE files, 6 MB each, Steve's secret database of girls' phone numbers, I don't think. DEL *.*. Are you sure? Am I sure? I should cocoa. Copy Sprint dictionaries over the top, delete. Right, Steve, let's see you Norton your way out of that.

While we are here, let's edit that big-bottomed AUTOEXEC. What's this? GOT YOUR ATTENTION, EH VER! MY MACHINE CAME BACK EARLY. SENT OFF YOURS FOR UPGRADE. COPIED MOST OF YOUR FILES TO THIS MACHINE, REST ARE ON FLOPPIES. BE CAREFUL OF DBASE FILES—CONTAIN CUSTOMER ACCOUNTS— THEY WERE TOO BIG TO BACK UP. SEE YOU LATER. CHEERS—STEVE. P.S.: YOU HAVEN'T REALLY GOT A BIG BOT.

Ah. I'll just go and lock myself in the ladies for a few days. By the way: you haven't seen me. I wasn't here. After all, it wasn't my fault. Serves Steve right, really. Few lend (but fools)/Their working tools.

---

# The Best Improve with Age

*"Isambard Kingdom Brunel, 1806–1859. If he was [sic] alive today, he'd probably work for us."*

—*Advert for Keen Networks*
*in* Infomatics *magazine*

I sat in Keen Networks' entrance lobby, leafing through a magazine, and wondering what was in the large glass aquarium, which hummed and bubbled quietly by the door. A receptionist, who, as usual, looked a shade too much like Angela Rippon for her own good, was pretending to hack around in WordStar. As she typed, she kept glancing at me, just in case I got the urge to make off with some of the glossy mags that were lying on the coffee table. *.EXE*, of course, *Modern Computers, Business Networks, Arthritis Today . . .*

I was on the point of getting up for a closer look at the tank when a middle-aged man in a grey pinstripe appeared at the door. "Miss Stob? Hi. I'm Mike Keen. I understand you've come to meet the genius IKB?" We shook hands, and he led me out of reception down the corridor.

"What is he working on?" I asked, as we arrived at an important-looking door.

"Oh, this and that. You know. With a man of his capability, you just give him an office and some equipment, and let him get on with it.

"Isambard!"—this shouted through the door—"Isambard, you have a visitor."

As he opened the door, I caught a whiff of the hospital smell: disinfectant, sweat, vomit. The small office seemed empty, except for a large Keen Networks computer in one corner and a kidney dialysis machine in the other. Then there was a whine of an electric motor, and a wheelchair appeared from behind the computer. In it was seated a wizened husk of a man, wrapped in a dressing gown. The wrinkled skin of his bald pate and face was a light grey, and a feeble claw operated the controls of the wheelchair. The sealed ends of his pyjama bottoms, neatly pinned flat, spoke forlornly of amputation. He was dribbling slightly from the left side of his mouth slit. He looked like Davros-creator-of-the-Daleks on an off-day.

Brunel's remaining watery, venous eye peered at me. Suddenly his hand twitched, and the wheelchair lurched towards me. "Seven foot and a quarter inch! Seven foot and a quarter inch! SEVEN FOOT AND A QUARTER INCH!" he cried in a thin, mad voice, as he accelerated. Keen grabbed me by the elbow and pulled me out the door, slamming it to behind us. There was a sickening crunch, and a horrid wail.

"I'm sorry, Miss Stob. IKB is not himself. He's terribly cut up about the adoption of 4ft 8in as standard gauge. He's only just discovered that they used it in his Rotherhide-Wapping tunnel," explained Keen.

"Surely," I said, determined to make some use of the research I had put in, "Surely the tunnel was built by Isambard's father Marc, who . . . "

"Who is in room 182. Would you like to meet him, Miss Stob?"

I wanted to meet some fresh air. "That's all right, Mr. Keen, I really must be getting on." I backed off towards the exit, with Keen calling after me: "But you haven't met Sir Isaac—I've had his iron lung polished specially for your visit."

I broke into a trot at the door to the reception, but as I passed the aquarium, I tripped on its wire and pulled the whole thing crashing to the ground . . . In the puddle, amongst the broken glass and electric wires, something coloured porridge grey flopped nastily.

The receptionist peered over her horn rims, then called back to Keen: "Now she's done it! Archimedes is out of his bath."

**DECEMBER 1990, *EXE MAGAZINE***

[One of the lowest of the many low points in the short and troubled history of Software Engineering was surely reached by the fashion for code walk-through meetings.

They do superficially sound like a good idea: all programmers know the value of a fresh eye on a coding problem; one would suppose that the prospect of colleagues scrutinising one's code must surely drive standards up.

In practice it didn't work like that at all. As Parity shows in this article, the system was a licence for the small-minded to enforce petty standards whose *raison d'etre* they often didn't understand. Furthermore the philosophy that one was invited to embrace—that one should emotionally detach oneself from one's code and designs, and not take any criticism of it as personal—was a sure-fire recipe for driving talented programmers away and building up a workforce composed entirely of the idle and the second rate. If you take pride in your work, you are not wanted here, thanks very much.

Happily, this sort of thing mostly went on in large corporations, where, as we know, the quality of work doesn't matter much anyway. No, no; don't worry about me. I'll have a chocolate biscuit and then I'll be all right again.]

# STOB versus the Software Engineers

*Parity Stob, Verity's smarter elder sister, works in the defence sector. She has a poor opinion of certain software engineering practices.*

## HOW TO SURVIVE A CODE WALKTHROUGH

### A) Wrong

Submitted code:

```
#include <stdio.h>

main()
{
    printf("hello, world\n");
}
```

*Minutes of Review:* Attending: Parity Stob (Programmer), Bill Dull (Token Peer Group Representative), John Straight (Testing), Ron Little (Design/Chair), Cheryl (Minutes).

1. Bill Dull said that Parity Stob had forgotten to do an opening comment. Ms. Stob replied that she didn't think that it was necessary with so short a program. Mr. Dull said, "It may be obvious to you what it does, Parity, but it won't be so blooming clear to the poor man that's got to maintain it. I haven't been an AP/2 for 15 years without learning anything."

   The meeting actioned Ms. Stob to add an opening comment.

2. Ron Little noted that the "hello, world\n" string was not capitalised, as it was in his design document pseudo code. Ms. Stob pointed out that it was not capitalised in the master design document, from which Mr. Little's document was derived. Mr. Little stated that the master design document fell beyond Ms. Stob's remit.

   The meeting actioned Ms. Stob to capitalise the "hello, world\n" string.

3. John Straight enquired if `printf()` returned a value. Ms. Stob believed that it returned the number of bytes written to `stdout`. Bill Dull observed that it was company policy (and had been for 15 years) to collect all return values. Ms. Stob enquired what the Dave Allen she was supposed to do with this return value once she had collected it. Ron Little reminded Ms. Stob that the purpose of the meeting was to discover errors, not to correct them.

The meeting actioned Ms. Stob to record the return value from `printf()`.

4. Ron Little asked, "What if `printf()` fails?" Ms. Stob replied . . .

(Minutes continue in this vein for several pages)

. . . actioned Ms. Stob to obtain a printout on nice green and white stripey paper.

The meeting adjourned. Ms. Stob has 74 actions against her, plus one oral disciplinary warning (level 1). The code is to be formally re-reviewed, when Ms. Stob has actioned the actions.

# B) Right

Submitted code:

```
#include <stdio.h>
man()
{
   printf("hello, cheeky");
              }
```

*Minutes of Review:* Personnel as before.

1. Ron Little said, "Talk about Freudian slips; isn't it `main()`, not `man()`, hur-hur-hur, eh Parity?"

Ms. Stob replied, "Yes Ron, you're right, what was I thinking of?"

John Straight said, "You were still distracted when you typed the string!"

Ms. Stob couldn't think what had come over her.

Bill Dull said that the } was out of alignment.

Ms. Stob was covered in confusion.

Ron Little said that, technically speaking, the meeting should minute actions against Ms. Stob, but—hold on a sec. Cheryl love— since it was Our Parity, we'd say no more about it.

2. Bill Dull said he would go ahead and get them in at the EEPROM and Eaglet. A pint of best, a monkey-juice for John, and two halves of cooking lager top for the girlies, all right?

Ms. Stob said that the girlies would have vodkas and tonics, thanks Bill.

3. The meeting adjourned. On the way out, Ms. Stob winked at me.

**FEBRUARY 1991,** *EXE MAGAZINE*

[After this article appeared, a colleague asked me what the *aide memoire* was that I used to determine the sex (I am rather afraid that her actual choice of word was "gender") of RS-232 plugs. My answer falls outside the scope of this book, but I would like to say to any reader who also harbours doubt that it would be a good investment of your time to research the matter and clear it up to your own satisfaction.

For complex tax reasons, it is important that this book offers at least one genuine computer tip. Here it is. A reader wrote in with a less facetious suggestion regarding coffee-soaked keyboards: swish them under the tap with heaps of cold water (she wrote) then leave to dry on the radiator for two days. Works for me.]

# Auntie Verity's Hardware Help

*"Wouldn't it be a great idea," mused the Editor, "if somebody wrote us a little hardware column." In the ensuing general rush for the door, Verity was the one who tripped up on the editorial carpet.*

## PROJECT 1—ADDING EXTRA RAM TO YOUR PC

1. Inspect the machine's rear panel, ascertaining the number and type of screws securing casing. You should find eight (8) flat-bladed-type screws, many with those crinkly washer things.
2. Inspect your only screwdriver. It is a large Philips-type with all the pointy bits burred off.

3. Borrow your assistant's Swiss army penknife and, using the end of the bottle-opener, remove screws 1 to 3.

4. Screw 4 was put on with a hydraulic screw tightener. Spend several minutes ruining its top. At the critical moment, as you give it one last go, the penknife will suddenly fold itself up, nipping the flesh of your right hand. Drop penknife.

5. Borrow the toolset from your Manager's BMW. Use the screwdriver found therein to extract remaining screws. Remove cover, placing screws and washers in a safe place, viz the spider plant's water collection saucer.

6. Unscrew a metal blanking strip at the end of a free slot. The point at which the strip may be eased clear is reached when the screw you are turning drops out of its hole and falls somewhere inside the machine.

7. Attempt to retrieve screw using Philips screwdriver and a blob of Blu-Tak.

8. Attempt to retrieve screw and blob of putty by holding machine upside-down and gently shaking it. Screw and VGA card fall out. Screw rolls out of sight.

9. Replace VGA card.

10. Insert RAM card in slot, and secure using a screw from spider plant's dish. This may be quite hard, as the screw is too big for the hole, so be prepared to be firm.

11. Turn on machine. Power On Self Test (POST) reports error in CMOS equipment configuration. Spend 20 minutes hunting for the floppy disk containing SETUP program.

12. Replace case and remaining six screws (another casualty lost down back of radiator) plus any crinkly washers that you can be bothered with. Switch on reassembled machine. Nothing: no power supply fan, no screen, nothing. Chuck it in for the day.

# PROJECT 2—CONNECTING TWO RS-232 DEVICES

1. Examine devices, and determine that you need a 9-pin male D-type plug to a 25-pin female D-type plug serial cable.

2. Examine your stock of spare cables. You have three (3) mains power cables (none with plugs), one (1) PC to Centronics parallel cable (the printer end is bust, and the wires inside are spilling out like multi-coloured intestines), one (1) telephone cable (from that modem that John bought that never worked properly), and one (1) car jump lead (source unknown).

3. Give assistant a tenner from petty cash and send him out to Shop to acquire requisite connectors. While he is gone, cut connector off the end of a power cable. Peel back 20 mm of outer insulation. Separate inner strands, and baring 3 mm of copper.

4. One hour later, assistant returns with one (1) 9-pin female plug and one (1) 25-pin male plug. Ask him what he thinks he is playing at. He explains that he always has a difficulty keeping track of which is which.

5. Deliver to assistant short, sarcastic lecture about Birds, Bees, and D-type connectors, which includes a useful *aide memoire*.

6. Suddenly remember that Bill, who has the same setup next door, is out this afternoon. Sneak into his office and steal his cable.

# PROJECT 3—REPAIRING A KEYBOARD WHICH HAS HAD A CUP OF COFFEE SPILT ON IT

1. Exercising extreme care, remove the four retaining screws from the bottom of the keyboard.

2. It's important to keep your workspace tidy. Sweep up the assortment of springs, clips, and rubber bits that have fallen out and throw them away.

3. Phone supplier and order new keyboard.

[When I reused the detail about the Basic code in the Dick Francis book in a more recent article, I received several emails challenging me on the technical point that the assignment is never executed. As a result of this, I did a little bit of testing. My assertion holds true for Microsoft's GWBASIC and a couple of others, and nobody could produce evidence of a dialect where it didn't. I mean, come on guys, if a Basic doesn't execute a "goto" at the first opportunity, how is it to maintain its self-respect?]

# Underground Liff

The Meaning of Liff *is a book by Douglas Adams and John Lloyd, in which useful words are coined from the names of towns. Stob the plagiarist has applied the technique to programming terms, using London Underground stations as her starting point.*

**bank** *n.* A bank of memory is a block of RAM which can be switched in and out of the processor's address space. Gosh, that was easy, wasn't it? I wish there were a few more like this. Perhaps London Transport could open a Virtual Base Class East station on the proposed Jubilee extension, and we'd be through in a minute.

**Dollis hill** *n.* Named after Professor Esther Dollis of the Computer and Domestic Science Department, University of Chiswick and Fashionable West London. When on the track of a particularly elusive bug, a programmer, if he is not careful, will start to climb a Dollis hill. First he will blame his compiler, which must be producing incorrect code; then he will become convinced that there is a mistake in the library; next he will wonder if something is wrong with his machine, and so on. The peak of a Dollis hill is to suspect a fault in the electric main. Needless to say, 87% of Dollis hills are caused by operations on unassigned pointers.

**fairlop** *n.* A fairlop is an annoying pause or delay, caused by circumstances outside the programmer's control (but often blamed on him). A real-time animation that pauses every few seconds for a garbage collection is said to "burp a fairlop." The hourglass "please wait" icon used by GUIs signals a blatant fairlop.

**Goodge Street** *n.* Those of you who spotted that "oo" will have already dived for cover to dodge the incoming acronym. "Goodge" stands for Gnomic Object-Oriented Designers Get Everywhere; if you are down the pub and everybody around you is saying things like "Windows programming is so much easier with a few C++ classes," then you are definitely on GOODGE Street.

**holborn** *n.* A holborn is a mistake in a work of hi-tech fiction which indicates the depth of research undertaken by the author. A classic example may be found in a Dick Francis novel about a "get-rich-quick" computer program that predicts the winners of horse races. We are only vouchsafed a few lines of this wonderful BASIC program, but one of these goes something like this:

```
560 IF I < P THEN 730: I5 = 40
```

We trust I5 is nothing important. A good episode of *Dr. Who* may contain as many as five distinct holborns.

**loughton** *v.* To loughton is to attempt to create a system using manifestly unsuitable tools. Trying to write a C compiler in dBASE language, or a simple database in assembly language are examples of loughtoning. Loughtoners are typically individuals who are fanatical about the system that they use, or are just stupid, or both.

**pimlico** *a.* An ornate style of program code commenting, probably incorporating many sloane squares *(qv)*. If it takes less time to fix a bug in a routine than it does to alter the accompanying comment, then your coding is definitely too pimlico.

**sloane square** *n.* A program comment contained entirely in a box of *******s. A leicester square, incidentally, is a bastard sloane square where all the verticals are out of alignment as a result, for example, of the printer having the wrong tab value.

**stepney green** *n.* A programmer who expects his code to compile first time.

**turnham green** *n.* A specialised graphics-fill routine which enhances the verdure of screen entities. Wow.

**virtual base class east** *n.* Just seeing if you were still awake.

MAY 1991, *EXE MAGAZINE*

# The Games We Play

*Object-oriented programming, AI, and virtual reality techniques should make the arcade games of the future much more exciting for the player. And the program, predicts Ms. Stob.*

"Better get your skates on, Dave; you'll be on in a moment."

Dave glanced through the CRT nonchalantly, then leaned back again, garbage-collecting his local heap on a chunk of static RAM.

"Neah. No worries. He hasn't got past Screen 3 yet. Neville'll sort him out when he tries to get through the whirlpool."

"I wouldn't be so sure, Dave, if I were you. He got me before I had time to draw my laser."

Dave looked at him sadly. "With all due respect, Cyril, my son, everybody gets you before you have time to draw your laser. Even the old grannies who put their money in by mistake, thinking it's a fruit machine, and spend half the game trying to fire with the coin return button, even they get you before you have time to draw your laser."

"Now, now, Dave," said a third alien, waving an admonishing tentacle, "you're forgetting that our Cyril here serves a purpose. He is our loss leader, as it were. Punter gets on machine, shoots Cyril to smithereens, thinks, This is a piece of pisciculture, and spends the rest of the evening with us, barring the odd journey to the bar to crack a fresh £20 note for change."

"I jolly well could give them a run for their money, if it wasn't for that wretched Iron Maiden pounding out all the time," said Cyril, scratching his status bits. "I don't see how anyone can be expected to shoot straight with that racket going on."

"Oh I am sorry," said Dave, with heavy irony. "Hi am sorry Hif the music is putting Sir off. I was under the impression that we were providing an all-action, machismo fantasy scenario, not some sort of girlie PacPerson thing for the ladies to toy with while their gentlemen drop bits of cheese-and-gherkin crisp into their dry white wines. Perhaps Sir would prefer it if we had a little discrete Jive Bunny-Rabbit, or maybe a sweet love-ballad by Andrew Lloyd-Web—"

A tremendous explosion rocked the machine. A tattered dragon, with three of its fire-breathing heads and its nuclear-missile launching tail shot off, staggered out of bit-mapped video RAM.

"Blimey, he's a sharp one," said the dragon, reloading its missing pieces from ROM. "Kept dodging behind the triffids before I could get a clear shot at him. We could be looking down the wrong end of a free game here."

"Now that's defeatist talk, Bill," said Dave. "If we start giving away free games, the takings'll drop faster than personal taxation in a pre-election promise, and we'll be out in the back yard with a pin-ball machine in our place before you can say Power On Self Test. Anyway," he continued, having taken a fresh peek at their human combatant, "I still don't rate him. He's got his hand on his girlfriend's knee. You can't get past Neville and have a fumble at the same time."

"Since you're such an expert, Dave," said Bill, "I might ask: just how many times have you been on."

Dave check-summed his instance data, which is the way an artificially-intelligent object blushes. "Well, obviously, coming in behind a fighter of Neville's calibre, I can't boast as much experience as . . . "

JULY 1991, *EXE MAGAZINE*

[If you aren't familiar with the film *Brief Encounter*, try to think of *The Seven Year Itch* instead. That way, at least you'll get the music right. Waddayamean you've never seen *The Seven Year Itch* either?]

———————

# A Chance to Meet You

*Stob is seeking alternative employment.*

I arrive at Dismalton, Essex, with three quarters of an hour in hand (having set off well in advance to cater for Network South East timetable eccentricities), so I purchase an unwanted coffee and perch uncomfortably in the station caff, pretending to read newspaper, so as not to turn up at WayAhead Computers Ltd. too early. Sitting here in my interview gear, trains rushing past while I'm indulging in treachery, feel like Celia Johnson in *Brief Encounter*. Mustn't think about *Brief Encounter*, not when I'm this nervous. Might break into *Brief Encounter* dialogue mid-interview, "Oh darling, I can't tell you how heppy and carefree and gay I feel." Worse yet, I might start humming Rachmaninoff's Second Bloody Piano Concerto. Too late. I **am** humming RSBPC.

Let's go now. I'll only be thirty-five minutes early. That's not early, that's just really prompt. Surely this hideous concrete and aluminium monstrosity is not the place? Come on Verity, wrong attitude, think positive.

Hello Miss Reception Girl, yes Mr. Shuffle is expecting me; look, there I am in the diary *11:15–Verity Stab*. Take a seat alongside three other candidates, engineer a sincere smile. "Yes, the weather is grim isn't it?" Why is this man making conversation? I don't want to talk to him. I don't want to talk to anybody, least of all him. I want him to explode.

I bet I get called in last. I'll have to sit here, getting ever lonelier, the last green bottle on the wall, while all the others get in there and make their fiendish Good Impressions and witty light conversation, coming out smiling and shaking hands and pencilling in a provisional starting date. I won't get it. Everybody knows the last candidate never gets it.

"Miss Stab, will you come through now?" Oh God, I'm first. Why am I first? They're just getting the trash over with first, that's why. Oh God, the back of my neck has gone all cold. Now, up you get, don't trip over the high heels of your interview shoes, well done, another warm smile, stop humming Rachmaninoff, here we go.

"Nice offices you have here." Oh, good shot Verity! Straight out of the Interviewee's Book of Ingratiating Phrases. We're on our way now. What's this? He's testing me on assembler mnemonics. Well there's a low-down trick. I'm glad I'm not going to be working for you, Mr. Shuffle, because I don't like people who play tricks like this. What do you think reference manuals are for, propping up the uneven legs of your horrible office furniture?

"HOCCF? Er, yes, that means HOld Carry Count Flag, I think." Or Halt On Computer Caught Fire. Beep-bi-beep-beep-beep, and at the end of that round, Miss Stob, you have scored two points. You passed on 15 . . . I wish I wasn't here. I wish I were back in my dull little, safe little office, curled up with a cold coffee and Microsoft C.

"Music? Yes, well I really like Rachmaninoff." Rachmaninoff? *Rachmaninoff?* Just as well he didn't ask you your favourite author, you'd probably have said Shakespeare. Aha, it's over now is it; no, thank you for your time, you greaseball, I'll see myself out, bye-bye Mr. Shuffle, bye-bye Other Candidates, bye-bye Miss Reception Girl, there's the door, try not to run, aaaah—fresh air and liberty.

Well, how do you think I did?

**OCTOBER 1991, *EXE MAGAZINE***

[Yet another British institution, I'm afraid. Nigel Molesworth was the creation of Geoffrey Willans and Ronald Searle in the 1950s. Molesworth was a pupil at a preparatory (== private, pre-teen, single sex) school—not a public school as some British websites that should know better suggest; he is too young—who chronicled his experience in four books, the best known being *How To Be Topp*.

Nigel was an unwilling imbiber at the drinking fountain of learning, suffering from chronic bad spelling, a poor attitude toward those elders ("beaks") who attempted to share their wisdom with him, and a brother who, in accordance with the rather ungentle educational practices of the time, he thought of as "molesworth 2." "Chiz" was Nigel's constant cry of exasperation.]

———————

# Wot Any Bule Kno

*Stob wondered how Nigel Molesworth would cope with the modern computerised classroom.*

Comp is just like Fr, Lat, Geog geom ect ect eg it is totaly wet and weedy. It is tort by maths masters, who say now boys, we are going to do something v exciting, compleetly different from alg, and then rite
    LET A+B=2*C
on blakbord, chiz, chiz.
    Most comp is about Bule, who was so cleva he invented bule alg (sick) 200 yrs *befor ther was any use for it.*

Scene: brekfast table of Mr & Mrs Bule, 1791

**Mr Bule:** IF it is raining, THEN I shall NOT take the dog for a walk.

**Mrs Bule:** Pass the marmalaid please dere.

**Mr Bule:** Oringe XOR lemon-and-lime flavor?

**Mrs Bule:** I do not mind, sweethart.

**Mr Bule:** This IMPLYS you like oringe AND you like lemon-and-lime.

*(Enter 2 men in wite coats with strait jaket)*

**Mrs Bule:** Hes over there.

*(The men grab Mr Bule and carry him away kicking and screaming)*

**Mrs Bule:** Piece at last.

Sometimes we have a comp practikal. The skool comp is a BCCI B, three trillion years old and hav about half the power of Grabber's calc and game watch. (Grabber is hed of skool, v rich and winer of the Mrs Joyful prize for al gore rhythms). The quay bord is full of chooin gum, bungy ect, so when you try and tipe it go

```
FORRRRRRRRRRR I = 11111111 to 3
```

Not even the master can work it, evry time he program it, it sa

```
SYNTACKS ERROR LINE 3
RELODE DISK AND TRY AGAIN
YOU ARE A TOTAL FAILURE
```

and we all yell Yah Booh Sucks! sir couldn't program a fiver out of a cashpoint. One time molesworth 2 got this grate game called gulf war 3 which was smashing **NEEEEEOW ZOOOM dagadagadaga BOOM** but the beak confiskated the disc, chiz.

The only good thing about comp is that it enable you to **IMPRESS GROWN-UPS.** Mater sa: nigel, could you set the vid to record the new mini-series with david mcullom and that girl from dallas, yes, he is cleva isnt he, your so lucky to do comp at skool, nigel, and could you pro-gramme the micro wave to heat up the leftovers please daling?

If it goes on like this, by the year 2000 no grown-up will be able to open a door. And what will they all do then, pore things?

## DECEMBER 1991, *EXE MAGAZINE*

[The first article to pay serious attention to Windows deserves a serious note. Below I have listed all the key clichés and phrases required for such a note; the task of providing linking words to turn the thing into a cogent bag of wind is left to the reader.

"By 1991 Windows was really making an impact . . . all programming done in C . . . giant switch statement . . . GetClassWord() . . . a worser OS/2 than OS/2 . . . little did we realise . . . 16-bit pointers, so near and so far . . . Charles Petzold's book . . . ugly, ugly code . . . breakthrough with VB . . . Apple still led by Sculley . . . short filenames . . . MM_ANISOTROPIC . . . running the resource compiler separately . . . dawn of a new era . . . Windows '95 set the seal on it."]

---

# About . . .

*Understandably, many of you have been writing to Ms. Stob, known in her hairdresser's as "the Petzold of Hounslow," to ask her to solve your Windows problems.*

Dear Verity,

The enclosed photograph shows an icon that I found on my desktop. It does not seem to be attached to any particular application, and I cannot make out what it is supposed to represent. When you click on it, the hard disk runs for a couple of seconds, but there are no other observable effects. Please can you help?

RN, Epping

Unfortunately RN's photograph was not up to the high standard that .*EXE*'s production department requires, so I will draw you a word picture. Imagine a two-dimensional half-brick, done in green, on the back of a doughnut, rotated through 30 degrees counter-clockwise, on a grey background. This is an escapee from one of those floating blocks of incomprehensible button icons that are now *de rigueur* in Windows apps. It is clearly a visual metaphor for "transpose the current spreadsheet relative to the current marked block" or, if you haven't got a spreadsheet, it could be "reload default monochrome palette from network drive without discarding current drawing." Anyway, RN, it's not doing you any harm, so stop being a bully and leave it alone.

> Dear Verity,
>
> Over recent months I have read many articles describing OLE, and have formed the distinct impression that nobody knows what it is, or what it's for; although many journalists expend a lot of effort trying to pretend that they do understand. May I rely on you to do better?
>
> HU, Witham

Yes. Next please.

> Dear Verity,
>
> For many years we have been making a good living from a very poorly designed program which does little and is difficult to use. We also make a lot of money by selling very expensive support contracts. Now we are very worried. GUIs are going to make the function of programs clear, and their usage straightforward. Does the increasing popularity of Windows spell the end of the road for us?
>
> JL, Southend

Stop panicking, JL. It is absolutely no trouble to write difficult-to-use programs under Windows. Here are a few ideas to set you on the right road.

1. All your drop down menus should contain at least nine items. Six of these should always be greyed out.

2. Provide full Windows Help, but include only a page-and-one-half of not-very-helpful text. (You might think that this is being too positive, but remember that Windows Help takes five seconds to load, and messes up the desktop.) If you are feeling especially daring, you may even like to open the help file of a completely different program, e.g., the rotten Solitaire card game.

3. If you are aiming to get up the nose of the punter, you could do far worse than write an MDI app. Child windows can easily be placed extremely awkwardly within the parent, and the profusion of maximise/minimise corner icons soon baffles the punter. See the Windows 3.0 File Manager for an e.g.

4. Add a free-floating icon bar thingy® as described in my answer to RN.

Dear Verity,

Have you noticed how many Windows-type acronyms consist of three letters; e.g., GUI, OLE, UAE? Don't you find this rather exciting and more than a little sinister?

TE, Basildon

No.

Dear Verity,

Sorry, I have to pick you up on this. In the answer before last, you cast aspersions on the excellent Windows Solitaire game. My wife and I have enjoyed many very pleasant evenings playing this clever game. Why were you rude about it?

PP, Chelmsford

Because, unlike real Solitaire, you can't cheat.

## FEBRUARY 1992, *EXE MAGAZINE*

[For the benefit of whippersnappers, it's perhaps worth explaining about the "QEMM" program, which stood for the Quarterdeck Expanded Memory Manager.

The memory map of the original PC reserved 0xa0000 upwards for the likes of video memory and BIOS. This meant that, after you had subtracted a few bytes for an interrupt vector table at address 0x00000, you had a bit less than 640 KB in which to stick your operating system, any drivers, and your actual program. This was really frustrating by the end of the MS-DOS era, as most 386/486 machines shipped with at least 4 MB of memory . . . which was invisible to 16-bit programs. One was constantly running out of "real memory," as it was called. To find out how much you had left, you ran the disk-checking program. Obviously.

QEMM worked by loading as many as possible of the drivers into "extended" memory, and doing wildly clever but dangerous things with the memory map to bring them back into 16-bit addressing space when they needed to be there. In its ongoing quest for a few spare bytes, it would even do things like poke its fingers up the holes in the reserved address space between video cards and ROM chips.

It was possible, if one spent hours coaxing QEMM and fiddling with the order in which one loaded network drivers and rebooting after each attempt, to end up with as much as 630 KB available at the MS-DOS prompt. Remember, you had to reboot after each attempt, so it was a time-consuming exercise, and the resulting machine was often rather unstable. No wonder we never had any time for programming.]

# Not Fairies' Footfalls

*"Backing up? Why, backing up is for punters!" (Traditional)*

Finish typing in amended comment and hit Alt-V for Verity's Compile, Link, Save to disk, and Run (it only took me about eight hours in macro programming to set this up, which quite justifies the two minutes it must save me each week). The server is right behind me, so I can hear the familiar rhythm of the 300 MB hard disk as the compiler shifts up through the gears, you know, I bet I could identify most of the software on our network blindfolded, I'm so familiar with the different sounds . . .

Hold up. Put smallthought on Pause a sec. It's not making the usual noise. Instead of fairies' muffled footfalls on drum, we have distant scream like inexpertly wielded bluntish drill bit skidding on car wing. Listen. There it is again.

Now, Verity, don't panic. Ignore cold feeling on nape of neck, suppress urge to hiss "If you have lost this file I will bite you" into server's A: drive. Be calm. Be rational. Ctrl-C. There; that's broken out of the macro. Attagirl. File. Save As. C:\PLEASE.CPP. And, with careful finger, press ENTER key, so that, in a second, in a second, QEMM has detected an attempt to execute an illegal instruction in the program you were running. Press E to end the program, or R to reboot the computer. Or how about "B" to tell QEMM to Bog off and mind its own bloody business.

Well, that's three hours' work down the drain, ha-ha (no, that was a light laugh, no, not at all like that woman in *Casualty* whose head exploded), so I suppose we may as well find out what's up with server. DIR C:\, two trillion things flick by at the speed they do on a 486, fine. DIR D:\, same thing. DIR E:\, someone switches on the power drill again, we have a General Failure Reading Drive E:\, guess which drive someone has entrusted with all her recent work, General Failure Verity's Temper; Abort, Retry, Ignore, Scream.

Look at backup log, to discover who made most recent weekly copy of server. Dave. Uh-huh. You remember Dave—the man with two talents: he can solder an IC chip holder onto a bit of vero while squinting through the smoke of a Silk Cut Menthol, and he cheats on his wife every Thursday night—she believes it has taken a year to repaint the TA hut. Dave's just the chap to be entrusted with my life's, OK week's work.

Oh, hi Dave, you couldn't just lend me the tape of the backup that you made last Friday. What's that? You didn't do a full backup? So what sort of backup did you make, you old sock-smeller? You made a partial backup of C: and D: did you, you old sock-smeller. Well you know what, you old sock-smeller, you're not fit to back up a 1969 Mini on a disused airstrip, never mind a computer, you old . . .

*And so, as we leave Verity swearing at her colleague, Betty the Backup Bunnie says: "Remember, Readers, a few minutes spent backing up your work is more than just a few minutes lost drinking time."*

*This edition of Stob was sponsored by the HM Government Department for Getting People to Do Sensible Things for Their Own Good. For a free leaflet, please write to the Abandoned Fridge, Unreported Gas Leak Road, East Condom, Cholesterolshire.*

JULY 1992, *EXE MAGAZINE*

[My headline celebrates the now obsolete practice of games manufacturers of copy-protecting their products by printing curious codes on the pages of their non-photocopyable manuals. When the game started, you had to type in one of these codes, as directed. Bulletin boards and the Internet quickly put the kibosh on this pleasantly low-tech system.]

———————

# FLGMJLLGHQ

*In which Ms. Stob discovers that her life has been taken over.*

I wake up, and I'm hot and sweating, and the alarm clock radio says AM2:0E, which is how it has portrayed 2:08 am ever since a couple of its LED segments failed. Insomnia on a warm summer night: one of my favourite things, together with brown paper parcels and kittens tied up with string. Nothing for me here but the long, dreary, sticky wait for dawn and sweet exhaustion.

But, hold up, there's something moving. A panel has opened in the ceiling, a line of luminous little figures, like little men, each a couple of inches high, is dropping out onto the shelf. (If you are wondering about the high quality of animation in this dream sequence, by the way, it was done by the same people that did *Roger Rabbit*.) Now the front of the column has dropped onto the duvet, and is marching up the bed towards my head. Now the front figurine is standing on the pillow, his feet among my golden tresses. Now he has produced a miniature pick-axe, its razor sharp point sparkling green-ly in the glow of the clock, and is aiming a tremendous blow at my face . . .

I woke up properly then, and everything was the same as before, except clock now said AM1:4E. Cautiously clambered over sleeping-snoring Loved One, shuffled through toe-stubbing darkness to kitchen, treated myself to a glass of greasy, bitter, blood-temperature Thames Water water, sat down on kitchen chair to take the weight off my adjectives.

*Lemmings* is the name of the game, and if you haven't already encountered it, this probably isn't going to make a lot of sense. It came into my life a month ago, as an innocent substitute for listening to Dave and Phil talk motors through the lunch hour. The scenario is simple: you guide a column of the things, which march nose-to-tail like the ants in *Tom and Jerry*, across a sequence of garish landscapes. Unlike T&J's ants, which were indestructible, Lemmings are emphatically uninde-structible, forever blowing up, falling off cliffs into boiling oil, etc. If you don't save enough of them, you lose, and get to go on playing *Lemmings*. If you do save enough of them, you win, and get to go on playing *Lemmings*. For the true addict, like myself, there is no pleasure in playing, there is just the relentless pressure (which motivates the Lemmings themselves) to move ever onward to the next screen.

So after I had been skipping lunch, and pub-time, for a few weeks; and had lost the ability to concentrate on programming (What if I turn him into a blocker? Could I release him later on by tunnelling under-neath?); and my social life had become comparable to Rudolph Hess's; after I had struggled to level 103 of 120, and could look forward to a return to humanity in the near future, what happened? Some git in the office bought the sequel entitled, I believe, *More Bloody Lemmings*, and now I'm only at level 102 of 220.

And then I thought: use the pickaxe first—I've dreamt the answer. So of course, I had to try it out at once.

Which is how you came to find me, Officer, at 4:00 am on a Friday morning, dressed in my night attire, trying to break into my place of work. Of course I'll come quietly. If I could just have a few moments alone with this PC . . .

*Verity Stob was reviewing* Lemmings *and* OH NO! More Lemmings, *published by Psygnosis Ltd.*

**APRIL 1993, *EXE MAGAZINE***

[It's a funny thing about PCs and sound and other multi-media. Somehow, they have never quite been at home together.

Even to this day, if a program is *really* rude and ill-mannered, chances are it's a PC multi-media program. If it doesn't grab nearly all the file associations every time you run it, chances are because it is too busy sending your personal information back to its creator, or ratting on you about use of some digital rights. Compilers, databases, editors, games very rarely behave like this.

Anyway, the rot set in early.]

-----------

# In Glorious VerityVision

*Verity Stob answers your questions about the technology of the future.*

### So what is multi-media all about?

It's a new exciting technology which allows ordinary people to get more out of computers, creating a stimulating, exciting world which will bring Mankind one step nearer the state of Utopia.

### No, what's it really all about?

It's about hardware spivs flogging Soundblaster-type cards and CD-ROMs to the gullible and the under-brained.

### So who do you know who's bought a sound card, then?

Well, the Editor of *.EXE* for a start.

**What does he use it for?**

He uses it to annoy everybody else in the office. He has configured Windows to play various .WAV files. It plays the Tardis taking off when he starts Windows up, Marvin the Paranoid Android being depressed when he shuts it down, McCoy from *Star Trek* telling Jim "He's dead" when his compilations fail, and Monty Python shouting "Bloody peasant" every time he tries to backspace past the beginning of a file.

**I can see that that selection might pall. Why doesn't he get some other .WAV files?**

There are no other .WAV files.

**Is there anything that sound cards are good for?**

Well, they certainly improve *Lemmings*. Incidentally, I would like to take this opportunity to point out to the manufacturer of the just-released *Lemmings 2* that I am certainly not one of those snooty journos who is above giving blatant plugs for "review" software I have received. Oh no. I have a 3.5-inch disk drive, by the way.

**That's quite enough of that. What about CD-ROM drives? What has been your experience of them?**

The previous Editor of .*EXE* had one of those. He found it could handle ordinary compact discs, and used to sit there all day listening to the Carpenters on headphones.

**That would explain the ornithological manifestations whenever he is in the vicinity. We don't seem to be getting very far. What about the really new stuff, you know, the things you see at trade shows?**

You mean those cards which, for as little as the price of Sony's very best 21" couch–King Edward unit, can deliver a sort of animated postage stamp of a picture running jerkily on your Windows screen?

**Yes, those. What do you think they will be used for?**

I think they will be used by late-working programmers to watch repeats of *Dr. Who*, *Star Trek*, *Monty Python*, and *Red Dwarf*. And old Carpenters concerts.

**What about the exciting interactive stuff—you know: the image capture off-air and whatnot.**

The search for a really good background bitmap of Davros will be over.

**Verity, you really are being an old sourpuss about all this. What about these exciting new applications which will let estate agents show prospective home-buyers around properties at the double-click of a database icon?**

I'm sorry, I didn't realise you were so concerned about the lot of estate agents.

**Point taken. So what multi-media invention really would impress you then?**

A system that provided taste sensations would be pretty smart—if it could be managed in a hygienic way, of course.

**And what sort of things would we get to taste?**

Klingons.

## PART II

# THE RASP OF THE MODEM

## *(1995–19100)*

*"I'm thinking of doing the unthinkable and not renewing [her MSDN subscription] . . .*

*"It could just be my age . . . Maybe an old programmer is like an old Mick Jagger. Past a certain age, it just won't do to keep sticking out your tongue and singing 'Satisfaction.'*

*"Then again, the problem may be just too many updates to Microsoft Windows."*

—*Ellen Ullman,* Close to the Machine

**JUNE 1995, *EXE MAGAZINE***

[When *EXE* magazine lost its beloved dot, it gained, as a sort of useless compensation, the ability to print colour on the inside back page, where this column lived. The following article, which documents the early impact of the game Doom on office life, was written to exploit the trinket of coloured fonts.

Sadly, we are not able to reprint the piece in all its glory here, and have had to resort to crude monochromatic labelling. To compensate, my Editor, off his own bat, has supplied an emergency joke, adapted from inept early BBC TV commentary of a pool-like game called snooker. If you just hang on a moment while I unwrap it:

"For those of you reading in black-and-white, Mr. Green is the one in between Mr. Red and Mr. Brown."

(Thanks Chris. I think that came off beautifully.)]

---

# I Want to Die

*The problem with Doom, according to Ms. Stob, is not the appalling violence, the effect on the younger generation, or even being no good at it. It's being stuck in a room with four people playing the network version . . .*

*(Scene: the offices of a small software house. The time: 5:43 pm.)*
[GREEN] Who wants to die?
[RED] I want to die!
[BROWN] I want to die!
[GREY] I want to die! Wait for me!

[GREEN] Hey Mr. Red—can I use your machine? My machine is always green. It's not fair being green—everyone can see me more easily. Can we swap please? Pretty please?

[RED] Nope.

[GREY] Sing if you're glad to be grey!

[GREEN] Shut up, Mr. Grey.

[GREY] What shall we play? Hey not too rough or Hurt me plenty?

[BROWN] Hurt me plenty!

[RED] Hurt me plenty!

[GREY] OK, let's go . . . Oh no, not here. I hate this level!

[GREEN] Are we playing teams?

[BROWN] I don't want to play with Mr. Red. He always shoots you in the back!

[RED] No I don't, you always stand in the way.

*(Booomph-whoooosh . . . Aaaargh!)*

[RED] Sorry.

[GREY] Hey, Mr. Red, where did you get that rocket launcher?

[RED] That would be telling.

*(A telephone rings.)*

[GREY] Quick—put the game on hold. Hello . . . Hello darling. No, not for an hour at least. No, I'm not playing Doom . . . We've got an important meeting to discuss version 2.0 . . .

*(A strawberry: ROOOAAAAR!)*

[GREY] . . . Yes, some of the others are playing . . . Well, no, not the ones in the meeting, obviously . . . Come on, there's no need to be like that . . . What do you mean you don't like my tone? Of course I do but . . . Huh! Bloody woman's hung up. Which idiot took the game off pause?

[RED] Sorry.

*(Blattta blatta blatta blatta Aaaaargh!)*

[GREEN] Thank you very much, my partner Mr. Grey. It wasn't my fault Mrs. Grey rumbled you!

[GREY] I feel much better now, thanks.

*(Yaketty yaketty yaketty yaketty)*

[BROWN] Uh oh. Here comes the spider.

*(YAKETTY YAKETTY YAKETTY YAKETTY Aaaaargh)*

[RED] He got me! He got me!

*(YAKETTY YAKETTY YAKETTY YAKETTY Blammerammerammmeram Booomph)*

[BROWN] Ha ha! Got him! Ha ha! Got him with the BFG*! The supreme talent of Mr. Brown triumphs again! I am indeed the king of Doom, the most devious lurker, the chief fragger of them all. All bow down before my stupendous powers. You are not worthy to play in the same game with me. Come on you losers, do your worst, I could beat all of you blindfolded.

*(Pant Pant Pant Pant Aaaaaargh)*

[BROWN] I fell in the soup! I fell in the soup and now I've got -1 frags.

[GREEN] Serves you right.

*(A telephone rings.)*

[GREEN] Hello? Oh, hello sweetie pie. No, Daddy can't come home now. No, Daddy's got to stay at work to earn some money. No darling, you go to bed like Mummy says, and I'll come and see you when you are asleep. Night-night darling. Bye. Hahahahahaha—got you with the pistol and I only had 13% health!

[RED] Don't let good fortune go to your head. I'm taking us through.

[GREEN] Not now, I've only got 13% health!

[RED] You should have thought of that before you shot me.

*(Bam! Blattablattablattablat!)*

[GREY] Eeeeeyes! And Mr. Grey wins the frag race again. On we go.

[BROWN] OK, let's go . . . oh no, not here. I hate this level!

*(The telephone rings . . . etc., etc. Continues thus until 11:00 pm, or until the network crashes, or until a spouse turns up with a real machine gun, whichever is the latest.)*

---

*In Doom, the BFG is a powerful weapon that can despatch monsters and rivals with a single, well-placed shot. The BFG FAQ at http://www.gamers.org/docs/FAQ/bfgfaq notes that "general consensus is that BFG stands for Big Fragging Gun." Of course it does.

JULY 1995, *EXE MAGAZINE*

# Dear Bill

*We have heard little of Microsoft employee Melinda French since her marriage last year to Bill Gates. Presumably she is safely installed in the Gates' Xanadu-like underground palace, with its computer-controlled doors and myriad other gadgets. But Verity is concerned . . .*

## TUESDAY

The shower went wrong this morning, so I called out a programmer.

It was my fault. I rebooted the john, owing to how it wouldn't flush, but was stuck on a modal dialog saying *Now wash your hands OK/Cancel* and thought I would freshen up while I waited for it to finish its login sequence. So I stepped into the cubicle and waved my hand over the virtual faucet, and of course I got a stream of boiling mango-scented gel down my right boob, *Yipe!*, because, as Bill explained later in his email, the Net DDE link with the boiler had gone down when I rebooted the toilet.

Then I got mad, which was kind of silly, because this sort of thing must happen to other people most days, and I pressed the emergency reboot button for the whole bathroom, which of course you mustn't do while the toilet is rebooting in case it picks up a stray interrupt and goes into its emergency back up routine. Which it did and it did.

I wouldn't have minded so much except of course I couldn't wash it off in the shower because the shower was still spurting molten mango goo, and I wasn't really in a fit state to call out the 24-hour programmer over the vidlink. So in the end I emailed him priority Urgent. It took him ages to get here, because of course you need LoveNest security clearance level to get through all the doors to our *en suite* bathroom, and he had to literally hack his way in, so it was 4:00 pm before I got to fix myself up and have a blueberry waffle.

I do wish that Bill were here, instead of on an evangelising mission persuading the Native Australian Aborigines to use NT for boomerang design. He is such a practical man to have about the house.

# WEDNESDAY

And it's my birthday! Sadly, Bill couldn't make it back from Down Under owing to how he had to fly to Rio to get them to use Windows '95 in all their snowmobiles. But he hadn't forgotten; I was woken up in bedroom suite #3960 (which is where I am sleeping until they fix up the LoveNest bathroom properly) by the email thing going off with a new message. The macro substitution hadn't worked out quite right, but it was still real Special. It said

```
Dear <Employee First Name Tag>
Happy Birthday. We look forward to another year of excellent work
from you.
Yours sincerely
<Friendly Line Manager Tag>
This message autogenerated by Microsoft Scheduler™ for Windows '95®.
```

And to think most girls have to put up with flowers!

In the evening, I held a virtual dinner party to celebrate my birthday. I asked Bill's parents, who are called Mr. & Mrs. William Gates II. We ate and I had matzo balls and I said, Isn't there any other part of the matzo you can eat? which is from Dinnerania™, the Microsoft CD-ROM of dinner party jokes. Only nobody laughed because they were having pot roast and they couldn't see what I was having what with them being 400 miles away and when I tried to explain they shut down the link. Which was kind of sad because Dinnerania is in alpha and this is the only joke in the database and I had matzo balls special because as Bill always says, someone has got to do the alpha testing.

# FRIDAY

I am a bit down this morning. Partially this is because, according to the house Newsnet system, Bill has had to go on to Red China, on account of them needing to be told how to use Microsoft Dictator™ for Windows—I guess this must be our new voice recognition add-on for Office. Also I am still worrying about the joke in Dinnerania: what about all those dear little matzos that get hurt just so that persons can have dinner parties?

But mostly I am unhappy because the whole house crashed last night and when it came up again it had to go to its weekly backup security database, which means it thinks I am in LoveNest when I am actually in bedroom suite #3960, which means I cannot open the door as I do not have correct security clearance. Also, there is no phone in here, as Bill thinks guests should be discouraged from using obsolete mainframe technology, and no windows, because the house is built under the hill, and as Bill says who needs windows in a room when you have got Windows®?

However, no need to worry! There is a terminal in here and I have emailed Bill to send help and look! I just got a reply. I just click on the little envelope and

```
Dear <Guest in bedroom suite #3960 Tag>
Thank you for your message. While Bill is always keen to hear from
his guests, you will appreciate that he is a very busy man, and he
can't always reply to his email straight away. Your patience is
appreciated.
William Gates III
```

[It used to be the common practice of software craftpersons to sell their expensive applications with a special security device, a dongle. If you forgot to plug it into your printer port, the app would say, "Oi! Missing dongle! You are a thief!" and close itself.

Mind you, if you did plug it into your printer port, the app would quite often say, "Oi! Missing dongle!" anyway, because the technology sometimes depended on non-standard signal lines that weren't always connected, and ports that fully conformed to the 1981 IBM PC specification, and the app shipped with the wrong version of the dongle driver for this operating system, and so on. And as for being able to drive a printer *through* a dongle, well, I *never* saw that work.

All this was quite annoying if you had shelled out a non-trivial amount of wonga on the software, and it is a relief that parallel port dongles seem to have mostly fallen from fashion.

These days, dongles are generally USB-based and work much better. Or they would do, if they weren't always being swiped, owing to their resemblance to those natty USB RAM drives . . .]

---

# Modem Tales

*"Kids' stories, that's where the money is," Ms. Stob was advised. With the following consequence.*

Once upon a time in Brixton, it rained dongles. When the children came out of school, there were brightly-coloured puddles of small plastic objects all over the playground that went scrunch! when you trod on them. A little girl bent down and picked one up and, sure enough, it had a two-way 25-pin D-type parallel connection on each end, with a nearly uncrackable encryption algorithm embedded in the EPROM within. "They're dongles!" she cried happily, and all the children cheered, and started running around gathering up as many as they could. One of the boys discovered that you could fit a whole lot of dongles together into a wobbly kind of stick, and in another minute the biggest pretend-sword fight you ever saw broke out, with everybody waving clipped-together dongles in the air.

Soon lots of grown ups came out to see what the noise was all about, and they too began to gather up dongles. Women collected armfuls of them, and put them in bowls around their houses and tied them up with colourful headscarves into pretty bundles. The old people brought wheel barrows and took away tons of them to hoard for winter fuel, which was a silly thing to do as dongles don't burn that well, and give off noxious fumes when they do. The local gay population discovered that some of the precipitation comprised "gender-benders" rather than dongles—they hunted these out specially and proudly hung them through their pierced noses and nipples.

Everybody had such a splendid time that by evening there were hardly any traces of the rainfall left, except the occasional piece of splintered plastic casing or blob of epoxy resin in the gutter. And although, to this day, it is a buyers' market for software protection devices in Brixton, I don't believe that they have ever had such a marvellous rainfall again, nor have they in Southend, nor Gateshead, nor Aberdeen, nor even Truro.

\*       \*       \*

"Let's make up operating systems!"

"Yes let's! How about this: George 3, George 6, George 9, Michael 7, Simon 20, C/PM/PM/PM, OS tutu."

"Too old fashioned, try these: Windies 514 for 3, Windows for Playgroups, Bournemouth/586."

"Which operating system must you never take to sea? Lilonux!"

"And what do you call a very stupid operating system? Unintaligent!"

"Oooh, that's dreadful. Let's make up some more Unixes, and then stop."

"OK: Asterix, Obelix, QuickFix, Catholix, Protestantix, Graham Hix, University of Romford Essex, Quentin Tarantinix."

*         *         *

There once was a man who took courses. He was trained in Basic C, and C++, and Advanced C++, and C++ for Unix, and Object-Oriented Design, and Object-Oriented Analysis, and Powerbuilder, and Open Systems, and British Computer Society Part II, and Relational Database Management, and Theory of Image Enhancement, and Implementing ISO 9000 in a Small Company, and FoxPro.

He lived in a software house with five friends, and whenever they said to him, "Hey, let's sort out that bug in the print preview routine," he would say, "Sorry, I'm off to a SQL Windows for Engineers course this week," and when they said to him, "Please could you put together a rough spec for the Waterhouse job," he would say, "I'd love to, but I'm keeping my nose buried in this Prolog book—remember I'm off to Cirencester next week for Advanced Artificial Intelligence."

As time went by, his five friends understandably became rather hacked off with this, and in fact ceased to be his friends. One day they said to him, "Gordon, if you don't stop going on courses, and start doing some actual work, we are going to sack you." The man went red in the face, and said, "If that's your attitude, then I'm off," and he resigned in a huff.

The man went and applied for a job with a big corporate, and because the big corporate had a stupid personnel department—unusually stupid even by the standard of such departments—and because the man had a huge number of certificates and qualifications and whatnot, he landed a plummy role at more than £60k, for which all he had to do was sit around in his office reading the paper, and occasionally do yet more courses.

Meanwhile his old company, dragged down by excessive training costs, went under, and the five ex-friends ended up working under the man at the same corporate, only for one quarter of his wages, and with no car allowance.

*Moral*: Some buggers seem to be able to get away with it.

With apologies to Gianni Rodari.

**OCTOBER 1995, *EXE MAGAZINE***

[As Microsoft's publicity people well know, chutzpah is a type of East European sweet on which one can easily choke.

Full marks to the opposing team from Apple, however, whose effort on the same occasion read, simply, "WELCOME.W95."]

---

# Around and Around

*"First Fire, then the Wheel, now Windows 95"*
*—Microsoft advertisement in* The Times

Bilga struggled slowly up the hill, muttering curses into his beard at every step, making for the big cave just below the ridge. Every few paces he stopped to rest his burden, an unwieldy wooden frame structure held together with lengths of inexpertly tied weasel gut. By the time he reached the mouth of the cave he was completely whacked, and was obliged to stand panting in an undignified manner while a classy blonde—he could tell she was superior stuff, she had at least six teeth and almost no faeces in her hair—eyed him coolly over the mud daub work in which she had been engaged.

"Go right in Mr. Bilga," she snapped, "Mr. Olgmat is expecting you."

Bilga shouldered his bundle and staggered into the smoky depths, where he found three fat men, squatting on their haunches by the fire, snacking on a pig's head that was sizzling on a hearth stone.

"Ah, Bliga," cried the fattest of the three, getting up and offering a hand well-bespeckled with porcine cerebellum, "glad you could make it."

"The name's Bilga," said Bilga, grasping the squelchy handshake.

"Bilga, Bilga, of course. How is the invention coming along? You know, I'm surprised at you being late—I'd have thought with your new *wheel* you'd be able to get here in short order."

Olgmat's companions guffawed and dug each other in the ribs.

"The cart got stuck in the bog," admitted Bilga, "but I have brought along a beta for you to look at." He indicated the frame at his feet.

"That's very kind of you," said Olgmat, giving the wheel a contemptuous prod with his toe and causing one of the spokes to fall off, "but I think it would be more pertinent to the marketing effort if you could just enumerate the benefits of this model over Wheel 3.11."

"Well, it's got 32 spokes instead of just 16 . . . "

"Spokes don't just grow on trees, you know" said one of Olgmat's companions in a stage whisper, and the pair collapsed in fresh merriment.

" . . . and I have introduced new circular rim technology," said Bilga, pressing on regardless, "and of course the new design is much more robust than the old system." By way of demonstrating this last point, he picked up the wheel and shook it. Another spoke tinkled to the ground.

"I suppose," said the executive who hadn't spoken before, "that all these extra doodads make the wheel heavier? That Mr. and Mrs. Grunt will have to buy a new, bigger cart in order to use it?"

"In most case, owners of modern cart technology will be able to bolt this on to existing hardware. It is possible that users of outdated carts will need to upgrade."

The executive rolled his eyes heavenwards. "This is going to be the biggest dodo since that idiot fire guy came up with the idea of burning all your food before you eat it," he muttered to his companion.

"What we need," said Olgmat, who all this time had been tugging his beard and pacing up and down the cave, "is a good tag line. Something not too technological—we don't want to frighten them. Something that expresses the freedom, the ability to travel, the world of possibilities that Wheel 95 will give your customers. Something that . . . " His voice trailed off in thought, his tiny brow furrowed in concentration.

"How about 'Where do you want to go today?'," ventured Bilga timidly.

Olgmat's eyes bulged, and for a moment it seemed as though he was choking.

"Don't be ridiculous!" he gurgled.

**NOVEMBER 1995, *EXE MAGAZINE***

[Many Computer Science courses now no longer include even a single unit of Monty Python Studies. This is a disgrace. The recipients of this inferior education do not even know their Basic Pythonic Responses.

There was a time if a high priest of software were to remark, as they often did remark, to the world in general:

"I think there is something wrong with Mr. Paslow."

Then all good software apprentices present would at once chorus:

"Ah yes his head has been ripped off."

Then the master might assert:

"He nailed your wife's head to a coffee table?"

And receive the reply:

"He was a hard man. Vicious but fair."

"Shut up, will you?"

"Now we see the violence inherent in the system."

And so on, for hours on end. No wonder the 1980s sped by so fast.]

# Four Yorkshiremen*

*The following is a verbatim account of a conversation that happens every night in the snug at the Duck & Dongle. The names of the participants have been changed to protect their identities.*

*Michael Chapman*: . . . put some more five-and-a-quarter inch disks on the fire and lets have a bit of a blaze. These kiddywinks today, with their multi-media four-way data-sensitive CD-ROM Windows 95 for Playgroups multi-gigabyte gloves and triple-soft easy-to-use Inter-bloody-active Development Environments, they don't wouldn't know how to make a computer program if you gave them chapter 1 of *K&R* and typed in *Hello World* for them.

*Graham Jones*: Not like in our day. Four PC/ATs between the five of us, with those old EGA cards that flickered like strobe lights and a hard disk so small, if you could fit more than one project on it at a time, you were in clover. The compiler crawled, you knew you could smoke a whole fag every time you typed BASCOM, so it paid to keep the compilation errors down. The only debugger we had was a copy of SID someone had pirated, and that didn't work properly because an overlay was missing. And you know, the software we wrote was just as good as what you get now, 'cept a darn sight quicker and more reliable. *(Wipes away foam moustache with back of hand.)* And easier to use. Still use the accounts package myself.

*Terry Palin*: Hard disk? Debugger? *(Puts on an effeminate voice.)* Listen to 'im with 'is lickle hard disky-whisky and debugger-wugger. *(Normal voice.)* Now we had to do *proper* programming. Three 256 KB PC/XTs between the six of us, running MS-DOS 1.0 mark you, so no subdirectories to muck you up, not that we had room for subdirectories in 180 KB. A compilation took 20 minutes, and you had to do at least twelve disk swaps, so there was no chance of us snatching a sneaky fag in the rec

---

*For those unfamiliar with the original version of this sketch, it can easily be found on the web by googling "Four Yorkshiremen".

room, my son. If you did, the "Please insert disk 3 into drive A:" would burn into the screen's phosphor, and the Systems Analyst would give you a thrashing with an Epson MX80. Three syntax errors cost you half an hour, so we chose—and you may think this is old fashioned—we chose to bash in our programs correctly first time. As for debugging, we used PRINT statements—none of this namby pamby special tool stuff. And we never had any complaints—and I know for a fact they still use some of our stuff at the Edinburgh branch of the North of England and Basingstoke Building Society.

*Graham Idle*: You pair of wet girls' blouses. PCs? Compilers? *(Belches.)* We did our coding on a real machine, a Commodore Pet. Keyboard like a pub piano, screen as bright and readable as a LCD display in the mid-summer sun, disk drives in a separate unit as big as a Dansette Gramophone—weighed 50 lbs and took an hour to format a disk. Not that we needed disks—we were writing in six-five-oh-two *assembler*, like God intended, and you had to load our assembler from this cassette tape. Now that *were* programming. As for debugging, we never needed any special tools—if the program crashed (and it never did) you just switched the machine off and on again—the RAM was that slow, your program would still be there, and you could work out what had gone wrong by PEEKing it from BASIC. And do you know, big organisations like Creaky and Croaky Solicitors to the Elderly are still using it every day.

*Michael Chapman*: Well, while you boys were poncing around with your personal rubbish, some of us were working. *(Thumps table, knocking ashtray into Palin's lap with upswing.)* I started off with half-an-hour a week on a teletype. You punched a paper tape—the punch for hole 5 was unreliable, so we used to have to literally bite in corrections—and shipped it off to the bureau, who would send you back the printout in as little as a month. The code ran on an old English Trivalve-Norton 201: 55-bit words with four 11-bit registers, and 613 words of store (and that's proper magnetic core store, mark you). As for an assembler, we did write our own assembler (in T-N 201 machine code) from a design suggested in the *Annual Review of Automatic Programming*, but I could never see the point of it. When you're doing financial stuff—pounds, shillings, pence, farthings, and groats—you need to be right, you need to be in contact with the machine. And do you know, they still use our application every day at the Bank of England, to work out the overnight drop in the pound's value against the dollar.

*Graham Jones*: And if you tell the kids of today that, they just don't believe you.

*All*: Aye, aye, very true, whose round is it? etc., etc.

## JANUARY 1996, *EXE MAGAZINE*

[It is with great regret that we must report that, since the original publication of this article, the X.400 email system has for all practical purposes passed away. Isolated, standardised by the ITU, and blessed with an address format from hell (an old X.400 FAQ records this:

```
G=Harald; S=Alvestrand; O=sintef; OU=delab; PRMD=uninett;
ADMD=uninett; C=no
```

as the equivalent of SMTP's harald.alvestrand@delab.sintef.no), the X.400 email system worked by the power of paradox. The only reliable way to get hold of somebody's address was to have them send you an email; the only way they could send you an email was if they could get your address reliably. Shortage of bandwidth was rarely a problem.

Despite or maybe because of these features, the system lingered for many years in such organisations where the phrase "good enough for government" still means something—for example, the British National Health Service.

X.400, we salute you.

Mind you, they never got any spam.]

# Email and Femail

*What criteria should you consider when selecting an electronic mail system? Verity Stob is our well-wired woman.*

**What are the main types of email?**

That depends on whether you work in a large or small organisation. A large organisation will have seven independent email systems: the system that runs on the mainframe, the system that works on the old proprietary mini, the Unix package, the groupware package, the strategic cross-platform package, the freebie that came with the PC operating system and "The Solution That The Technical Department Prefers™."

**And a small organisation?**

A small organisation will have nine independent systems: the Windows stuff, the cut-down copy of cc:Mail that Jim picked up for a song at a show two years ago but which won't run on Dave's machine for some reason, the program that does the CIX connection, the freeware that we pulled off the cover disk of *PC Today! Today!* originally written for the Mac by Germans whose knowledge of English and the PC is in question, the program that does the CompuServe connection, the useless bit of freeware that came with the Internet provider's package, the rather better bit of freeware pulled off the Net to replace the former which occasionally ignores a message so we have to revert, and the cut-down copy of Notes that Jim picked up for a song at a show a year ago but which won't run on Christine's machine.

**Hold on—you said nine. That's only eight.**

There is also "The Solution That The Technical Department Prefers™."

**There you go with this "solution" business again. What distinguishes it from all the other packages?**

TSTTTDP has the ability to append random homilies, sometimes known as "cookies," to the bottom of each message. Stuff like "Thought for the day: A man is as old as he's feeling, A woman as old as she looks—Mortimer Collins."

**Cracking stuff! But why the need for a preferred solution? Surely all these packages can communicate with each other?**

I thought you were allowed to go to the bathroom by yourself these days.

**OK, OK—just kidding. Do you have any guidelines, Verity dearest, on what we should be looking for?**

The first rule of good email is that it is nothing to do with X400.

**Look, if you are going to burn up column inches stating the bleeding obvious, I still haven't read last week's *Mole* yet.**

The second rule is that it must have some mechanism for handling attachments.

**This sounds more like it. Double-ewe tee eff are "attachments" about then?**

Attachments allow the user to "attach" a binary file to a message.

**And what, I suppose this allows you to send programs and things wherever you like?**

No, it allows you to mailbomb people you hate with successions of huge messages containing complete gibberish and get away with it. A independent expert recently estimated that only one in five uuencoded messages are ever successfully uudecoded, one in eight MIME messages are EMIMed, and that nobody has ever, ever hexbinned anything.

**Hmm, that's impressive. Where did you get those statistics?**

I just made them up, silly. The third rule is the usability of an email system is inversely proportional to the amount of money it costs.

**Wow—that's almost good enough to be a cookie!**

I can't remember why I thought I liked you.

**Two more before you go. What means "consolidation of email systems"?**

It means purchasing another piece of software that interacts with existing email systems in such a way that they all fail in exciting new ways.

**And how do you stand on RFC822?**

A not unpleasant RFC, although it lacks the power and clear narrative structure of the earlier ARPA document RFC733, which it obsoleted. And there's not enough sex in it.

# Morse Code

*"Help in catching malicious programmers may be at hand from Ivan Krsul and Eugene Spatford at Purdue University, Indiana, who are developing 'forensic' techniques for examining software and identifying its author."*

—New Scientist

The strains of *Eine Kleine Nachtmusik* (von Karajan, 1974 recording) were deafening even outside the door, so Lewis didn't bother knocking, and just walked straight in.

"Sir?" Then louder: *"Sir?"*

Morse looked up from the sheaf of printouts—the line printer kind on green and white paper that nobody else used anymore, and which had to be printed off specially for him—and switched off the CD player with a gesture of impatience.

"Well, Lewis?"

"I've got the listing of Deadly Brain Killer III, sir." Lewis placed a fresh sheaf of listings respectfully on the edge of the desk.

"Deadly Brain Killer III!" Morse snarled contemptuously. "I wish these people would show a modicum of imagination."

"It's not going so well then, sir?" Over the years, Lewis had become expert at interpreting his chief's moods

"It looks like Traffdon's work, it smells like Traffdon's work, but there's something *wrong*, Lewis." He reached out a much-scribbled-on printout from the bottom of his pile. "Take a look at this."

"It looks like the load module, sir."

"Yes, yes, Lewis, even I realised that. Tell me what you *see*."

Lewis took a deep breath. "Well, it's good quality K&R, old style function declarations, four character indent with lined up curly brackets . . . "

" . . . *braces*, Lewis, you're not in Gosforth night school now . . . "

" . . . lined up braces, some attempt to use Hungarian variables but he got teed off and gave it up, a tendency to use do/while constructions, 80-character line wrap, minimal casting, poor C++ style commenting with spelling mistakes."

"And your conclusion?"

"I'd say it's Traffdon's work. Unix programmer, only came to C++ and Windows quite late, doesn't use classes unless he has to, hates long variable names, just wants to get the job done."

Morse put his head in his hands. "But there is something not right, and I can't put my finger on it."

Lewis shifted uncomfortably. "I'm sure you'll work it out, sir. Err . . . is it all right if I go home now? The wife's gone up to see her mother in the RVI, and I don't like leaving the baby-sitter."

"Yes, yes, Lewis, you go home to your hearth and children."

Lewis paused as he turned to go, and pointed. "Oh look—he's got a nasty bug in his switch statement. Missed out a break."

Morse followed the direction of Lewis's digit, then stood up in excitement. "By God, Lewis, you've got it!"

"I have, sir?"

"No Unix C programmer would ever leave out a break, unless he meant to drop through deliberately. Now this man, Lewis, has forgotten that he needs a break at all, which tells us that he trained in a language which doesn't need them. A language which has a repeat/until construct, which he has to simulate with do/while. A language which . . . "

"Pascal!"

"Right. So the programmer must be . . . "

" . . . Simpkins in A-block! Of course. I'll get onto it in the morning."

"Goodnight Lewis. And, thanks . . . "

As Lewis walked down the corridor, he thought he hadn't seen the Old Man so cheerful in months. Which was a good thing: after the years of success in Oxford, the dismissal for alcoholism and appointment as Code Quality Inspector at Barclloyds Bank had come as a bit of a blow . . .

**APRIL 1996, *EXE MAGAZINE***

[When Sun Microsystems first introduced Java in the mid 1990s, it also unleashed a tsunami of hype and turgid prose in praise of its new technology—although none of this prose was quite as turgid as the original Java runtime itself. Sun couldn't reasonably be blamed for the rash of coffee-named add-on products that appeared at the same time, although that didn't prevent me from doing so.]

---

# I Prefer Tea

*Ms. Stob has decided that it is time to deliver one of her world-famous "leading edge of technology" briefings.*

**Hi Ver! What's it all about this month?**

Don't call me "Ver." I thought it was time I gave you my thoughts on "Java," the new and little-discussed Internet tool from Sun Microsystems.

**Coo, so we can look forward to 500 words of adoration with terrible coffee-oriented single entendres every other paragraph?**

Yup, as required by the Sun licence agreement for writing about Java. What's the problem—coffee puns *not your cup of Ness-caff*? I could try to *filter* them out, they can get to be a bit of a *grind* if you aren't feeling *full of beans* (and I should *cocoa*).

**Mercy! Do some of the adoration bit.**

All right. The Java programming language is completely platform-independent, thanks to a p-code system . . .

**P-code system? Are you sure that you haven't got this muddled up with that old Pascal press release we used to wedge the CD-ROM drive in place?**

No. Unlike *that* p-code system, which was the very much third-place competitor behind MS-DOS and CP/M 86 to be the standard PC operating system but failed owing to glacial speed, *this* p-code system runs like . . .

**. . . like a spilt café-au-lait across a rich aunt's best tablecloth?**

I'll do the coffee references, thank you. Anyway, it runs jolly fast; probably as fast as a Visual Basic 4 16-bit application.

**I find that easy to believe.**

Yeah, yeah, sneer away. Even language snobs like you will like Java. Although some say it's a blend of Eiffel and . . .

**A *gold* blend surely?**

I won't tell you again. A blend of Eiffel and C++, it's really mostly based on the latter, only with all the nasty bits, that cause Honest Programmers to Make Mistakes, taken out.

**You interest me despite myself. So Java is some kind of C++-a-like, where the basic cout << "Hello World\n" still works, and one still has dear old pointers to give you a bit of speed, but they have done something about the assignment = and equality == operators?**

Errrm, well . . .

**What? Which one of those things doesn't it do?**

It doesn't do any of them. Operator overloading has been dropped because it's obscure and never used; pointers have been dropped because they are not suitable for a secure system like Java, and the standard C/C++ symbols for assignment and equality have been retained for the sake of maximum leverage of existing code skills.

**Terrific. What sort of applications do you actually write with Java?**

Less of the "application," thank you, we call them "applets." It's a much more '90s word, more caring. There is a whole range of exciting things you can do, from noughts and crosses, to amusing animated "Page under construction" creature with a pneumatic drill, to a flying toaster, to a Mickey Mouse whose eyes follow the mouse cursor, to a . . .

**I get the idea. Truly an awe-making gamut. Anything else you want to say before I go?**

Yes. Don't forget to pick up a copy of my new bestseller from Manuals for Pirated Software Publishers Inc. It's called *Learn Yourself Java— 59 minutes*, and is not to be confused with the many hundreds of similar titles appearing this week.

**Presumably this book is freely adapted from your old bestseller *Learn Yourself* C++, and a help file you found knocking around the Java site. And what, pray, is the significance of the "59 minutes"?**

You need to ask?

SEPTEMBER 1996, *EXE MAGAZINE*

[Robert X Cringely in his fine book *Accidental Empires*, my primary source for Gatesisms, reported that Bill Gates' people used to send the representatives of local charities away with fleas in their ears and the excuse that billionaire Gates was "too young to be a pillar of his community."

Love it.]

---

# Junior Makes Three

*What's it like in the Gates household, now that the stork has visited? No need to speculate: Verity Stob has once more managed to hack into the diary of Mrs. William Gates.*

. . . Dear Bill couldn't be there, owing to how he was explaining the advantages of NT 4.0's new interface to the New Jersey PowerPoint User Group. However, he had arranged Steve Ballmer's deputy's PA's gardener to give me a lift to the hospital, but as it turned out it was five guys from the MFC development team who took me, as they wanted to video the birth. They explained that it would make a really cool test AVI file to go with Visual C++ 4.3.

The Maternity Unit of the hospital is special because it is just one of many local public works named in honour of Dear Bill's charitable activities. When we arrived at the West Redmond Built With No Money From Bill Gates The Tight Git Birthing Facility, my contractions had stopped coming, which was a worry. But Randy Dreedle, who Dear Bill says has done some really great work on the exception handling stuff, figured I was so dilated that I had better be induced under anaesthetic, so that's what the doctors did. A beautiful girl was born at around three o'clock. I had hoped to preserve the umbilical chord in dolphin spit, as recommended in the *Californian Woman's Practical Guide to Modern Birthing*, but while I was under gas the guys took it, as they wanted to use it in their water pistol fights with the Visual Basic team.

**Wednesday**—Dear Bill hasn't managed to get here yet, owing to how he is explaining the Internet Strategy to the New Birmingham Women Guild's Campaign for Colorful Winterwear. But he has sent a lovely email to celebrate the birth of our darling daughter:

> Dear {Female Microsoft Employee's first name}
>
> Congratulations on {the successful launch of a new Microsoft product | the birth of your {son | daughter}}. At this {happy | critical} time, we hope that you will {take some time off to celebrate your achievement | not forget your duties to the company}. After all it's not everybody who can {boast having created a Microsoft product | take nine months paid leave and still come back to a job}. So this message is to remind you {of how proud we all are of your efforts | that there are plenty of young men out there who would give their eye teeth for your position}.
>
> Sincerely
>
> {Microsoft Line Manager's Name}

I guess they still haven't quite fixed the macro expansion in that new beta of Exchange.

We have been transferred to the Redmond General Not A Cent From You Know Who Post Natal Clinic, and the guys came round this afternoon for a visit, which was sweet, especially as they are having a tricky time with the new collection templates. Randy was most interested and helpful at feeding time, and warned me that I should be careful because persons with large areolas are liable to chaff; but the other guys were stupid, and said I was being cruel making the baby drink something which wasn't even chilled, never mind carbonated.

**Friday**—We can go home today, although I will have to go to the Washington State No Thanks To Billionaire Bill Outpatient Facility next week to have the stitches out, but this is OK as Randy and the sweet guys from Visual C++ have offered to go along, even though they are having a tough time with their WOW thunking right now.

Dear Bill managed to put in a video call from New Newcastle, where he is lecturing the AA on in-process OLE objects. I asked him what he thought we should call the baby. He said, "We must call it William, of course." I said, "But Bill, it's a girl." He seemed puzzled. "So why can't we call it William?" he said.

**Sunday**—Bill has delegated the business of choosing a name for the baby to the Visual C++ team, which has decided to call her `grlSarah`, in accordance with Hungarian notation. Suddenly feel overwhelmed by PND . . .

[Yes, yes; this article was written in late 1996.

A brief message to anyone who invested heavily in Corel stock on the basis of my predictions: What can I say? I really **really** liked the little balloon that used to be on the front of the CorelDRAW box.]

---

# Don't Look Back

*Contrary as ever, Ms. Stob marks EXE's first decade by predicting the events that will accompany its second.*

1997—The Java revolution continues. Foyles allocates a whole floor of its Charing Cross Road premises to Java and Javascript books. Of the 2300 software packages and products released this year, 1245 have names derived from coffee or beverage drinking.

However, one crack appears in the facade. While watching a demonstration of a new Java application at the JavaTwo conference in June, a small boy is heard to cry, "But it's so slow!" He is hastily carried out.

The *Observer* newspaper follows up its intelligent and campaigning 1996 Internet coverage with an article about CERN research centre, where the World Wide Web was invented. Since most pornographic material is carried by the HTTP protocol, the *Observer* argues, CERN should be held at least partially responsible for its widespread availability. The article is headlined "King of Filth."

1998—Security continues to be a big issue. An independent consultant based in Redmond, Washington, claims to have found a hole in Netscape Navigator by which applets are able to determine and broadcast the colour of a browser-user's knickers. Netscape's stock plunges, and in September the company is acquired by Corel for a song. Corel sorts out Javascript, and in recognition of the faded attractions of the word "Java," renames the scripting language "Malcolm." Microsoft announces that it will implement the new language with its own extensions—these will be known as MalcolmX.

Borland alarms and puzzles industry pundits by making a profit for six consecutive quarters.

1999—Corel is in the news again with its surprise acquisition of Novell, which has been ailing badly under the onslaught by NT. Corel-Novell publishes a new open networking standard that it is claimed will enable cheap and useful integration of embedded processors, such as those found in cars, toasters, and industrial plants. Microsoft endorses the standard, and implements its own version of it, including proprietary extensions that only work with Visual Basic.

Microsoft also announces two new versions of Windows that will succeed NT 4.1 and '97. Following the company's tradition of using city names for future Windows releases, these are codenamed Eldorado and Atlantis. They are expected to be released in spring of 2000.

The most fashionable programming language of the year is Roughtalk, a non object-oriented version of Smalltalk. RT's success is attributed by its designers to the fact that " . . . computing isn't about objects; it's about doing things. By stripping out the object framework, we allow the programmer/designer to concentrate on function, and, incidentally, improve the performance of the compiled code."

2000—The oft-predicted century rollover disaster is something of a damp squib. Great excitement when a woman living in Southsea receives a bill for £32,767, but this turns out to be ordinary post-privatisation utility sharp practice rather than any computing error. However, Jeremiahs are cheered up when on February 29th the clearing banks' ATM networks go down. It is subsequently established the cause is a bit of PL/I written by a NatWest programmer in 1978 who, in order to shoehorn his calculation of leap years into 3 KB, applied the divisible-by-4 and not-divisible-by-100 rules, but not the divisible-by-400 rule. (This is not funny, but does establish my techie credentials.)

In September, a worldwide shortage of RAM causes the price to rocket past the $3/MB mark. Microsoft denies that the still unreleased 3D versions of Windows—now renamed "My Happy Workspace" and "My Happy Playspace"—will require 2 GB per workstation to run.

The Free Software Foundation releases a RDBMS called Freeziqual. The product is pooh-poohed by the commercial database vendors, who predict that no company will entrust its data to a system that isn't outrageously expensive for what it is. Freeziqual downloadings from the Net are brisk.

2001—A huge legal battle rages all year over who has the trademark right to the name "Hal" to describe a computer product. The protagonists completely fail to notice that nobody else gives a damn.

All flavours of UNIX finally converge; on the Linux standard.

2002—"My Playspace," as it is now called, is finally launched with a 4GB VFRAM (Very Fast RAM) requirement and a furore of publicity. Stunts include painting Wales yellow (the official Playspace colour) and a misguided attempt to bring the Rolling Stones back to life. Sales are steady, despite a draconian copy protection scheme which requires the purchaser to have a serial number laser-branded onto the back of his retina.

My Playspace incorporates not only a wordprocessor, spreadsheet, drawing package, games, financial and tax calculation applications, virtual reality suite, air traffic control, etc., etc., but is also supplied with a "free" Microsoft PC, desk, and chair. Unlikely bedfellows Compaq and Ikea press for action from the anti-trust people, but without success.

A hacker breaks into the Pentagon and changes all the internal codes, so that the US is unable to fire off its missiles. He is caught and charged with maliciously preventing nuclear war.

2003—Corel acquires ailing Oracle-Sybase.

Several companies announce products based on speech and smell recognition, claiming that this technology has finally matured. As usual, it soon becomes painfully obvious that they have not, but not before Microsoft has announced new speech and smell recognition APIs for Playspace.

2004—Following the reintroduction of the death sentence for software piracy in several Midwest states of the US, the Free Software Foundation announces that it has developed a My Playspace compatible product. It is promptly obliged to retreat into hiding before an army of lawyers.

**2005**—With the IT sector no longer growing at the huge rates of former times, thousands of programmers are out of work. There is a knock-on effect; other businesses in the dumps include the manufacturers of CD-ROM cases, T-shirt printers, and pizza bakers.

New industries have moved into the limelight, and terrible indignities are inflicted on former software giants. Corel is bought out by the Geno, a firm of genetic engineers that specialises in household pets (their first and runaway success product being a dog genetically engineered not to smell its own private parts).

*Wired* magazine publishes its first ever comprehensible editorial.

**2006**—At the East Kilbride offices of a chemical conglomerate, a junior executive is fired for buying Microsoft.

## DECEMBER 1996, *EXE MAGAZINE*

[It seems to me that Borland has never really recovered psychologically from the days when, under the leadership of Phillippe Kahn, it thought it was going to beat Microsoft and own the world.

Its relationship with its customers is a bit odd. They are like the supporters of a not-very-successful sports team, clinging by its fingertips to a high league. They react emotionally to every move that the company makes; they swear that Borland's stuff is technically by far the best, yet weep with fury if the company puts up the price a few dollars; they are in love with the product and despise the management. The management, for its part, would dearly like to shed its fan base of tearful techies in exchange for less whiny corporate customers who would pay much better and not moan . . . but can't quite work out how to sell to such people.

The company's ongoing cycle of minor catastrophes, as this strained relationship wobbled along, seemed curiously reminiscent of the tribulations of the Israelites. This article records the first of those disaster-ettes.]

# Book of Anders

*"[Look for the] Reader-friendly Waite Group 'Bible' format"*
*—Blurb on the back of a programming book.*

*"Anders Hejlsberg is leaving Borland for Microsoft."*
*—The Internet*

And it came to pass *that* the sons of Kahn, who dwelt in the valley of Scotts, in the land of Cali-fornia, fell upon hard times. For they were hard plagued by the Mic-rosoftees who dwelt in the north, yet ruled all the lands around, and forced all to bow down and pay tribute before *their* god Vi Su-Albahsic. And there was much wailing and gnashing of teeth in the valley, *and* also much careful reading of the Situations Vacant columns.

2. And then An-ders, an elder in the tribe of the sons of Kahn, *dreamed* a dream. And he called together all the tribe and spake unto them saying: Brothers—last night I dreamed that everyone in the world paid tribute to the god Vi Su-Albahsic. And the Mic-rosoftees did come down *into* the valley of Scotts, and forced all men who dwelt there to worship Vi Su-Albahsic. And the sons of Kahn gave in and became programmers like Jerripur-Nel, the scribe of Bytemag, *who* toileth still upon Roberta's Basic flash-card program; yea, yet he hath toiled upon it for seven and four-score years or more, as it seemeth to me.

3. And An-ders spake, saying: Do you want *this* to happen?

4. And the sons of Kahn replied as one saying: Indeed, we sodding well do not.

5. And so the sons of Kahn looked once more upon Tur Bhopas-kal, and into the void *which* was called Owl. And they saw *that*, while calling it a void was a tad unfair, there was plenty of scope *for*

improvement. And An-ders and Gar'ee and Zackur-Lockur and Giant I and many others girded up their loins, and toiled long and hard. And together they fashioned TObject.

6. And TObject conceived, and begat TPersistent. And TPersistent begat TComponent, and TComponent begat TControl, and TControl begat TWinControl, and TWinControl begat TCustomControl, and TCustomControl begat TCustomGrid, and TCustomGrid begat TDrawGrid, and TDrawGrid begat TStringGrid.

7. And TObject also begat Exception, and Exception begat EMathError, and EMathError [That's enough begatting.—Ed.]

8. And so it came to pass *that* the fruit of TObject's loins were indeed fruitful, and the whole multiplied much. And the tribe of TObject's children was known as Veesee-ell. And Tur Bhopas-kal was henceforth named by the name of Delphi, by decree of the department of market, who had once spent a happy fortnight in Corfu, and was wise in the ways of the Greeks.

9. When the sons of Kahn looked upon Veesee-ell and Delphi, and they saw that Delphi micturith upon the head of Vi Su-Albahsic, as though from the top of the mountain of Rockee.

10. And the sons of Kahn were glad within their hearts, indeed they were well chuffed.

11. And there was much wining and celebration and slaughtering of fatted calves in the valley of Scotts, *with* plenty of alcohol-free and meat-free alternatives laid on for those who cannot partake of strong drink or murdered animals for reasons of medication or creed or obstinacy, or because *their* girlfriends won't let them. And by all a good time was had.

12. And it came to pass that two seasons came and went. And the first season was rich and fruitful for the sons of Kahn, and their bellies grew round and plump with milk and honey.

13. But the second season was thin and lean, and was a time of famine. For verily the department *of* market *of* the sons *of* Kahn was not unpractised at snatching defeat, yea even from the very jaws of victory. And the sound of weeping and wailing was heard once more in the valley.

**14.** And one day An-ders journeyed *to* the wilderness, and wept and wailed and cried out unto the Lord, saying: Shall I spend the rest of my days tinkering *with* a Pascal compiler I wrote 15 years ago? Couldn't I have a go at something else? Shall I never have stock options which consistently increase in value? Can I not be on the winning side *for* a change?

**15.** And it so happened *that* nearby stood a scout for the tribe of the Mic-rosoftees, disguised as a juniper bush. And he heard An-ders cry out. And he came forward to An-ders, saying: Can I be of assistance?

**16.** And one thing led *unto* another.

**17.** And when the sons of Kahn heard what had happened, they put *upon* the matter a brave face saying: An-ders hath worked *but* a little on recent releases, we will be on time with Delphi 3.0, we are sorry to see him go, of course, but this will not impact any of our technology.

**18.** But friends of the sons of Kahn remembered the wisdom of M'andee-rice Davis. And *such* men were sore afraid *for* the sons of Kahn.

**FEBRUARY 1997, *EXE MAGAZINE***

# The Black Eye of the Little Blue Techie

### Vitaï Quakerama

There's a roar and a screech in the office tonight—
Ten frags down and 8% health,
No decent weapons to level the fight—
Trapped in the open, no chance of stealth.
A scrag at his shoulder, a vore at his side
A chainsawing ogre slashes to maim.
Then up pops the message: "Are you here for the ride?
Play up! Play up! And play the game!"

Reception is locked, there's a cat in the hall
The heating's cut out, the lights are all dim.
He's turned off the switchboard for fear of a call
From his wife (but she long since has giv'n up on him).
With fierce concentration he Quakes on untired
But looks up astonished when his boss speaks his name:
"Now Alan I've warned you—this time you are fired!
So play up! Play up! And play the game!"

### Not Thunking but Looping

He double clicked the old DOS app
Treacled NT was crawling:
"Must be 'cos it's 16-bit." He's wrong—
Not Thunking but Looping.

Never was a speedy app
We should have ditched it years ago
It's just got worse since Windows 4
It's 32-bit that makes it slow

Oh no no no you silly folk!
(Still NT was crawling)
The bloody thing is written wrong
Not Thunking but Looping.


I Saw a Jolly Trek Flick

I saw a jolly Trek flick
Best so far it's reckoned
Picard's team came jolly first
Borg came jolly second.

Though Data is a jolly 'bot
It's hard to understand
Why jolly Data enters data
All by jolly hand.

An RS-jolly-232
Would jolly things much faster.
It's not like jolly Doctor Who
And jolly friend—The Master!

*Chorus:*
Klingons on the starboard bow, starboard bow, starboard bow, etc.


The Naming of Parts

Today we have the Naming of Parts. Last week we had
booting up with and without the F8 key depressed. And next week
we shall have Special Config Secrets of the Windows 95 Gurus,
and then connectivity to Sun. And outside Sun shines, and birds sing
          For today we have the Naming of Parts.

Our photo shows the printer port, and this is the port
for the joystick (which in your case you have not got),
and here is the power supply, and the ribbon cable
for the floppies. It has both male and female connectors
        Which in your case you have not got.

[Now turn to page 30, Issue 7]

Freely adapted from *Easy PC Magazine*


## The Black Eye of the Little Blue Techie

There's a battered H-P Inkjet down by the Ladies' loo
And a Compaq Pentium 90 sans its case.
There a broken-hearted techie mourns the ghost of OS/2
And he's got his CV ready—just in case.

He was known as "Little Blue" by the "We-love-Windows" crew,
His faith in IBM was unconstrained.
His workmates liked to goad, but they couldn't fault his code,
So for his C++ he was retained.

The girl who stole his heart: she wasn't awf'lly smart,
But in her presence he'd just sit and gawp.
He asked her which OS would she like on her PC?
He very nearly wept when she said "Warp."

To make the setup clean, he dismantled her machine,
The installation took the whole weekend.
Monday, when she got in, he was waiting by her desk
To present his work and beg to be her Friend.

She upbraided Little Blue in the way that women do,
She said she'd asked for Warp just as a joke.
But then she got a fright for his lips went paper white
And he gurgled as if he were going to choke.

He grabbed the Compaq's case, and he hurled it at her face,
It missed and smashed a printer to the floor.
She swung her handbag high and she caught him in the eye
Then beat a hasty exit through the door.

There's a battered H-P Inkjet down by the Ladies' loo
And a Compaq Pentium 90 sans its case.
There a broken-hearted techie mourns the ghost of OS/2
And he's got his CV ready—just in case.

VS apologises to Sir Henry Newbolt, Stevie Smith, Charles Causley, Henry Reed, and
J. Milton Hayes.

[Douglas Coupland's novel *Microserfs* made me laugh like a drain, and is heaps more readable than his *Generation X*. All techies should read it.]

# Mr. Jobs Works Next Door

*"Like John Lennon returning to the Beatles," shrieked* The Guardian, *reporting Apple's recent acquisition of its own cofounder Steve Jobs. Verity Stob wonders how other Apple employees are coping.*

Marcie screamed, "It's him!" and of course the whole hut piled over to the window; but when the man on the BMW bike took off his helmet he had frizzy blond hair, so we trooped back to our places. This sort of thing happens two or three times a day since The Second Coming.

We call it a "hut," but it's just 700 square feet of '80s-style open plan on Floor 2 of 4b Infinite Loop. Officially we are working on a new laptop—well that's not going to happen, but we have been together through three re-orgs now (is this a record?), so I think we must have been blurged from some company database. At any event, it's nice working together with people for five months solid. Especially I like Marcie: we have exchanged private PGP keys (total total mutual trust factor 10).

After a while Randy said, "What if it was him, but he was wearing a wig?"

Randy is definitely going random. Everybody knows super-heroes don't wear wigs.

We all have secret personal projects (remember, nearly all the big breakthroughs started as secret projects). Randy, who is a hardware guy, has a project which is a digital alarm clock that can be set to go off at a different time at weekends. He has assembled a prototype from $400-worth of components.

"It can be set also for three- and four-day weekends for semi-retired people and part time workers."

"For Woz's sake Randy, this is Apple Computer, not Radio Shack!"

"I hope you are not making the Xerox mistake, Malcolm."

The Xerox mistake. Randy considers his weekend alarm clock to be on a par with the desktop metaphor for personal computing. You've got to admire the guy's confidence.

Randy calls his alarm clock "Bart," because Bart is Lisa's kid brother. Groan ^ 4.

First contact! Marcie (it would be Marcie) was in the lobby of building 7, waiting to meet her friend from the Photoshop liaison division. They have two elevators there, but elevator B is broken and sits at lobby level awaiting this week's CEO's permission to call in an engineer. Since the doors to elevator B are stuck open, people go in and press buttons, then get mad when nothing happens.

Marcie was leaning on the desk, watching about four groups of people get trapped by the dead elevator, when she hears this growling noise behind her, so she turns round and it's Steve! She nearly pukes with fright and awe, and her vision is going blurry with the reality distortion field, then he says,

"Why doesn't someone stick an 'Out Of Service' Post-It® by the door?"

(So direct!

## So brilliant!

# So Steve!)

Marcie says,
"That's a great idea, sir. I'll see to it at once."
And He nods.

When Marcie got back to the hut, I plugged my old Yamaha Amp into my Powerbook and brought up this shareware drumkit program that I pulled off the Net; then we all took off our shoes and socks and did our Steve dance.

Here is our Steve dance:

> [Oooomph Crash dee-Boom-Boom Crash]
>
> *Marcie*: What do artists do?
>
> *All Except Marcie*: Real artists ship!
>
> [Oooomph Crash Oooomph Crash]
>
> *Marcie*: Good artists copy!
>
> *AEM*: GREAT ARTISTS STEAL!
>
> [Stomp Stomp Oooomph Stomper Stomp Oooomph]
>
> *Marcie (shrieks)*: ARE WE GREAT?
>
> *AEM*: **INSANELY GREAT!**
>
> *Everyone*: Steve Jobs is my hero, Steve is number zero!

If you think this is silly, try making a dance from the sayings of Bill Gates:

» A computer on every desk and in every home.

» OS/2 will be the operating system for the 1990s.

» The Internet is just a passing fad.

See?

Java (uh oh Chungo—it's Jarrr-varrr!) for me from now on. Marcie won't let me program in C++ any more. She says that it's masculine and spiky and aggressive and homophobic (huh?) and (strongest possible insult in Marcie's repertoire) *IBMish*. Besides which she says it always causes memory leaks sooner or later.

Marcie has a thing about memory leaks. She says that if all the memory leaks in all the C++ programs in all the world could be eliminated, then the Taiwanese shrimping otter, which apparently lives downstream of the mega-polluting biggest RAM chip factories in the world, could be saved from extinction. She says that giving up C++ is a way of being more eco-sensitive, without having to give up Captain Crunch or whatever.

Randy says this theory sucks rocks. Although he has a point, I don't like siding with Randy, besides which Randy hasn't had an Encounter of the First Kind and he doesn't have my private PGP key. So Java it is.

Last night I woke up from a nightmare that IBM had bought Apple, and all us software people were sucked into Lotus and made to work on Notes add-ons. I couldn't sleep after this.

Tell us it ain't so Steve. Help us Steve. Save us Steve.
    Steve, please don't let it be too late.

[I understand that they have now admitted, those standards boys, that the ISO 900x: 1994 standard did nothing useful for software development. As admissions go this strikes me as on par with admitting that World War I did little to improve the landscape surrounding the river Somme: it's both true as far as it goes and missing the point. In due course, I predict that they will admit that the year 2000 update of this standard—it's all about measuring something, *anything*, to prove that your work is improving—is similarly hopeless. (It is.)

Opinion: the difficulty with management methodologies like ISO 9001 is that they attempt to provide a mechanical substitute for thought. But programming *is* thought, and it can brook no substitutes.]

---

# Quality Street

*Contemplating going for a quality standard? Want to put an ISO 9000 logo on your letterhead and garner a few of those Big Company contracts? Verity Stob would like a word.*

**Verity, what exactly does ISO 9000-and-thingy involve?**

Nothing at all. That's the beauty of it. You just continue doing exactly what your are already doing, going about your business. Occasionally you may make a little note. Which takes a few seconds at most.

**What, really?**

Good grief, what time yesterday did you fall off the Christmas tree, angel? *'Course* not really. ISO 9000 is the millstone around the neck of the weary traveller as he attempts to wade the quagmire of bureaucracy, it is the packet of dry roasted peanuts offered to the parched and blackened lips of the man dying of thirst in the desert of paperwork, it is . . .

**OK, so you don't like it. But the nice consultant-man we are paying 600 smackers a day has given us a leaflet . . .**

This would be the DHS-style leaflet written in baby language with embarrassingly badly drawn cartoons and a passage explaining how to encourage employees to "think quality" during their lunchbreaks?

**I admit the artwork is perhaps not up to snuff, but that's hardly a reason to dismiss the whole thing out of hand. After all, as soon as we get up to speed, we will soon feel the benefit from the improvement in our working practices. Time benefits, cost benefits.**

Nonsense. ISO 9000 does nothing at all to improve working practices. It just adds more work to your existing working practices. If you have good working practices, then you will have less time to do the work because you have to spend all the time documenting them, and having meetings to review the documentation, and further meetings to review the documentation procedures. If you have ho-hum working practices, you will be so completely up the creek that your boat will be touching north and south banks simultaneously.

**Surely you are not really claiming that filling in the odd form as you go about your work is so time consuming?**

No. Filling in "the odd form" as you go along is pretty unbearable, but the real killer is forging retrospectively all the documentation that you didn't have time to fill in when you were supposed to. And don't pretend that you won't find yourself in this position, because you will.

**You're such a kidder Verity. Since we are to write our own quality manual, we will control what has to be done. There will be none of this bureaucracy.**

Ah, now there you have put your finger on one of the Big Lies upon which the quality racket depends. This "you write your own manual" business is a trap. What happens is they give you *their* manual as a template and have you write your company's name on the front, and add *your* working practices expressed in *their* language. In the warm glow of producing a fat A4 folder entitled "Joe Blogs Ltd. Quality Assurance Manual," you completely fail to notice the home-spun web you are entangling yourself in.

**So, what are you saying, Verity: that it is bad to keep proper records?**

Not at all. Keep records where you need to. Don't where you don't. Work for yourself, not *Them*.

**You keep mentioning Them. You have a conspiracy theory explaining ISO 9000?**

Oh yes. There are essentially two types of human being: the real person (like you and me—well, me anyway) and the middle manager . . .

**And I suppose the quality fad is an attempt by middle managers to regain their control over the likes of programmers, who as a consequence of their quicker wits and the emergence of a technology that requires thought in order to use it, have displaced large numbers of management in the social and economic hierarchy?**

I see it's all clicking into place for you too.

**Verity, I just want you to sit there calmly still while I pick up this phone and call an ambulance.**

Just one more thing.

**What?**

Your cost code for reading this article. It's VER/13382-970472!EXEMAG.

**Oh, thanks.**

JULY 1997, *EXE MAGAZINE*

# You May Start

*Ms. Stob has been imposed upon to acquire some Microsoft qualifications.*

. . . the base qualification, the BSY ("Bill Says Yup"), may be obtained by taking and passing any single examination from the Learn Microsoft Good range of qualifications for IT professionals. However, real developers, as opposed to low-status tech supporters and those whose job mostly comprises installing things from floppy disk, will want to obtain the higher qualification, the BSYI ("Bill Says Yes Indeedy"). This requires that candidates attempt and pass TWO examinations from the operating system papers, i.e., More Than You Ever Wanted To Know About Windows Part 1 and More Than You Ever Wanted To Know About Windows Part 2, plus TWO elective language papers, choose from: Visual C++—A Fine and Friendly Compiler, FoxPro the Way to Go, Visual Basic—Not Just for Stupid People, MS Access Your Little Database Chum, SQL Server—How Do You Spell "Oracul" Anyway?, and Difficult OLE Stuff for Real Keanos.

I'm in an exam. I'm in an exam! I'm thirty-four. They shouldn't be able to make you do exams after you are twenty-five, except the ones you take in your dreams. I've retaken my finals about two million times, haven't we all? Somehow always discovering that the exam was to be held this very morning and here's me, not having done any revision, because I didn't know it was today.

I've had that dream the last four nights now, I suppose because I knew bloody well that it is today. No more dreaming, here I am in a real exam, just like I swore I never ever would be again; palms sweating, stomach churning, underwear mysteriously fitting in an odd way which makes it impossible to get comfortable, despite two supervised visits to the cloakroom to try to put my house in order. The supervisor is convinced I have concealed Inside OLE 2 Inside Stob's Knickers. Consequently his halitosis is condensing on my NEC Multisync as he watches my every move with an intensity that would be unnerving, if I had any nerve left to un.

Of course, things have moved on since the prime of Ms. Verity Stob. The exam is computer based, in fact it's multiple choice. Oh yeah, I know what you're thinking; you're thinking Chemistry O-Level: Which of the following is NOT an element? A) Iron, B) Sodium, C) Neon, D) Oxygen, E) Banana flavour. Calculators may be used; sporty-type candidates are encouraged to copy from brighter neighbours.

But this isn't like that at all. Have a look at this one here:

**Question 7: How does Windows NT detect errors? A) By having its API functions return an error code, B) By having its API functions return illegal values—the programmer then calls a second function to obtain the error code, C) By throwing an exception which the program can trap if it chooses, D) By allowing independent third parties to write device drivers which run at ring 0 protection on Intel platforms.**

OK, so I have more or less eliminated D) from my enquiries. D) is the banana. Probably. But how the hell is one supposed to choose between A), B), and C)? What does "How does Windows NT detect errors?" mean for God's sake?

**. . . successful completion of the exam, the newly qualified BSY will be sent their special Learn Microsoft Good Pak. This contains 1) A mass-produced certificate with facsimile signature of Bill Gates, 2) A special BSY plastic membership card, entitling the BSY to special BSY privileges, 3) A flyer for *BSY Monthly*, the magazine for persons who have passed their exams and wish to gloat at those who have not, 4) A special BSY buttonhole badge, a fallback if 2) above is lost or damaged**

or is insufficiently special, 5) A set of six CD-ROMs representing one month's issue of the Microsoft Need-to-know Technical Knowledgenet Network Professional Knowledgebase Engine Roadmap, not to be confused with all the other Microsoft CDs you may have piling up around the office, to which, flushed by your success, we hope you will be persuaded to subscribe, 6) Camera-ready artwork which the BSY may display on their business cards and stationery . . .

I wonder what that artwork looks like. Some sort of Microsoft corporate logo. An image of the terrestrial globe having the pips squeezed out of it by a gauntleted hand would do the job. Come on Verity—snap out of it. You are running out of time. Fifteen minutes left and you are staring at

**Question 31: A VBX control is ported to an OLE control. How do you expect the performance of the OLE control to compare with the VBX? A) The VBX would be twice as fast as the OLE control, B) The VBX would run at about the same speed as the OLE control, C) One cannot predict whether the OLE control would run faster or slower, D) The OLE control would run 20% to 30% faster, E) The OLE control would run at least twice as fast.**

What are you laughing at? Yes, of course the correct answer is E). Or rather, the answer required to earn the mark is E). Any hockey player can see that. It's just that in my experience of about 25 OCX ports of VBX controls, every man jack of them ran like the last creature over the line in the 7:30 pm at Walthamstowe. It offends me to answer an exam question untruthfully just to pass. Mind you, I've always done it (I think *How Green Was My Valley* is a great novel because . . . ). I suppose it is a bit late in the day to change policy.

**Congratulations Ms. Verity Stob: you have passed More Than You Ever Wanted To Know About Windows Part 1 with 870 points out of 1000. Please collect your certificate from your Nympho Prometric Representative on your way out.**

Is that it? Is that really all? It is? O jour frabberjeais! Calleau! Callai! J'ai tué le Jaseroque! Goodbye Mr. Supervisor, and may I recommend Listerine Brown in litre bottles. Ha ha, hee hee, that wasn't so bad then. I could tackle a few more like that. I could soon mop up a BSYI. I take it all back about dear old Microsoft, bless their cotton socks.

They're quite right; it is important that professionals of my calibre are recognised . . . Hold on, what's that? Surely it's not a fire alarm?

Ah. The alarm clock.

# 8086 and All That

*"The Tangerine Microtan 65 was a 6502 based machine, not Z80 based."*

—Fact correction in the exe conference on CIX

*"History as you remember it"*
—Sellar and Yeatman, 1066 and All That
*(Or some such: it seemed against the spirit of the original to check the quote, so we haven't.)*

1835—Charlie Babbage invents his famous Calculating Engine, the first ever computer, which is powered by Stephenson's Rocket, and consequently four foot eight and one half inches wide. Genius *père et fils* engineering double act Marc and Isambard Brunel offer to create a seven-foot version but, as a result of an unfortunate error in the copying of the plans, instead build the South Devon Atmospheric Railway. Stung by disappointment, Babbage switches his efforts to a dual gauge Analytical Engine, and places the first ever advertisement for the first ever programmer—an advert which has been used ever since as a model by recruiting agencies ("Mr. Charles Babbage of 147 Coprocessor Lane, Westminster Village seeks the assistance of a programmatic person, to aid him with his Government researches. On-the-job training will be given, but applicants with Visual C++, Oracle, Tuxedo, UNIX, and NT4 will be preferred. Babbage Calculating Engines Ltd. is an equal opportunities employer. Either sex may apply for this post, but breast feeding abilities considered an advantage.").

Babbage is lucky enough to secure the services of Countess Ada Lovelace, at that time best known as the star of many early-Victorian pornographic lithographs. Although Babbage's working relationship with Lovelace is excellent, his interest in a practical engine for analysing coefficients of Taylor's theorem according to sundry measurements of external objects wanes, and his interest in going to bed in the afternoon waxes. Babbage's work is never completed; this doesn't matter because nobody else does any work on it either. Thus England is Top Nation in computing for the next 100 years—a Good Thing.

**1936**—In Hitler's Nazi Germany, a beastly German person whose name is not important attempts to reinvent the computer 10 years too early, using the bakelite knobs that have fallen off Ferguson wireless sets. Unfortunately for Herr Not Important, Lawrence of Arabia and Lawrence of Olivier are soon both on the case, and turn the tables on him using a black-and-white John Buchan plot. Thus the Empire is preserved for people who pronounce the word hands as "hends."

Meanwhile, in England, mathematician and pipe smoker Alan Turing proposes his famous Turing Machine, a contraption which can display and interpret a sequence of odd-looking, arbitrary symbols. Predictably he fails to interest the British Government in his idea—with all resources committed to the Appeasement Effort, there is no money available to fritter away on infinitely long paper tapes—but it is taken up by the hotel and catering industry, who subsequently manufacture a slightly modified version in large quantities. This commercial version is named after the man who effected the modifications: Professor J. R. Fruit.

**1942**—At Bletchley Park, Turing invents Robbie the Robot, a fantastic automaton which can decrypt the secret Enigma codes of the U-boats, play chess, accurately forecast greyhound and horse racing results, and make polite small talk at dinner parties. Prime Minister Winston Churchill wants to send Robbie on a special mission to kidnap Hitler and end the war; but he is foiled in this wish when it turns out that Robbie is unable to override his own Prime Directive; the robot cannot harm a human being no matter how evil, or how silly her moustache. Despondent at his failure, Robbie sets about a career as a Shakespearean actor, and eventually achieves fulfilment; his portrayal of Ariel in a 1950s production of *The Tempest* being particularly well received.

**1950**—The American company IBM launches UNIVAC, a dual vortex dataprocessor which beats as it sweeps as it cleans. Not to be outdone, British company Lyon's Maid launches Leo, a gargantuan hulk of machinery which turns out to be useless for office automation, but excellent for keeping ice-lollies cold.

**1954**—At Manchester University, Alan Turing is fatally wounded in a laboratory accident, when the subject of his latest Turing Test turns out not to be, as he believed, a Mark II Electronic Brain running at half clock speed, but instead an irate builder's labourer, Mr. Arthur Wit. Turing dies tragically on the operating table while surgeons battle to retrieve his own left upper canine from inside his kidneys.

Back at the Manchester University labs, Turing's former colleagues make what turns out to be a fatal mistake for British Computing: they decide to abandon his theoretical efforts on computer science, and instead concentrate on his pipe smoking work. Thus America becomes Top Dog in Computing, a Bad Thing.

**The 1960s**—The UK continues to lag behind. In 1966, pressed by the Wilson Government "yellow glimmer of know how" technology policy, Edinburgh University manages to build a noughts-and-crosses machine which, while not unbeatable, "puts up a jolly good show." It is opened by the Beatles, and in an exciting and tense match the machine loses five games to nil to Ringo (this was of course before mind-bending drugs took the edge off Ringo's noughts-and-crosses abilities). In 1968, English Home Counties Electric Valves produces Sir Ernie, the Premium Bond random number generator, a primitive forerunner of the exciting and leading edge technology which today drives the National Lottery.

**1971**—Edsger Dijkstra delivers his famous ACM paper dealing with naming conventions: "Excessive consonants considered hard to spell."

**1979**—At last a triumph for Great Britain! Sir Clive Sinclair's Z80-based Tangerine Microtan 65 launches. With its handsome (for its time) "dead flesh" keyboard, its ability to drive a modified TV at a startling (for its time) rate of 405 lines per minute, and its startling (for its time) 16-byte memory, all for a knock-down price of £599.99, the machine is an immediate hit. For a while, it outsells even the former market leader the Apple Big Jobs, but eventually tragedy strikes when somebody else offers a much better computer for rather less money.

**1980**—IBM asks Gary Kildall to invent an operating system for the future PC, to be called OS/2. Kildall refuses, and then makes matters worse by flying around and around IBM headquarters in a biplane taunting the IBMers about "their silly blue shirts." IBM hires Bill Gates to blow Kildall out of the sky with an anti-aircraft gun, and as a token of gratitude for accomplishing this successfully hands over the rights to all computing technology forever.

And that is the end of computing history.

# The Browser

Warning

When I am a senior analyst, I shall draw flow-charts
With ER diagrams, which combination doesn't go,
                                        and doesn't make sense.

And I shall spend half the year's budget on a CASE tool
That doesn't work, then say we have no money for PC upgrades.
And I shall advise others on coding issues
                            about which I know nothing.
And I shall refer to other people's time as
                                "programmer utilisation,"
Strolling into the office saying "We really have to get utilisation up."
And I shall call emergency meetings, and then turn up late,
But some mornings get in really early,
Ostentatiously making notes on my Psion as my colleagues arrive.

You can answer your phone on hands free,
Make everyone adopt your personal taste in naming conventions
Then blame it on ISO 9000.
You can call directors by their first names to their faces
And move the training video TV onto your desk to watch
                                            *The Simpsons.*

But now I must work to 7:30 pm on Fridays,
And fill in timesheets marked in 15-minute intervals,
And smile prettily when booking the holiday time which is mine,
And generally be a Good Girl.

Perhaps I should practise a little now
So people aren't too shocked and surprised
When suddenly I become a senior analyst, and draw flow-charts.

What do you mean: How will we tell when you're practising?

## Upgraded Spanish Postcard

It's ActiveX to bed and ActiveX to rise
Only the tourists outnumber the flies.

(I never thought I'd find myself saying it,
but this used to work better when it was "OLE.")

## The Foreshortened Alphabet

Said A to B "I don't like C
Its syntax does my head in."
Said B to A "That's quite okay."
And the poet snuck a Z[ed] in.

## The Browser

Once upon a Wednesday morning, I was stretching, I was yawning
One more surfing day was dawning, surfing to the Net's far shore.
Hung my coat up, got my beverage, went to check up on our
                                                    homepage—
But the browser didn't show the corporate logo as before.
Gone was our fine corporate logo, "File not found" was all I saw.
   Gone, and to return no more.

Couldn't help but feel dejected—file *does* exist, *not* read protected
This is not what I expected from my browser version four.
Checked my bookmark, checked my spelling, found no cause nor
                                                    reason telling
Why the program was rebelling instead of working as of yore.
But each time I clicked the Reload I got Error Four-Oh-Four
   Wretched Error 404.

Tried to look up dear old EXE, some MS promo ActiveX-ey,
Tried a naughty site most sexy that La Whitehouse would abhor.
Tried for Yahoo, AltaVista, tried the home page of my sister,
Even tried to get on HotWired though their GIFs stick in my craw.
Could not even get on HotWired where I think the artwork's

poor—

Quoth the browser "404."

Time to end procrastination—must find out the explanation
Nail this useless application—time to grasp at every straw.
In a mood of techie fervour: verified domain name server,
Pinged to Demon, did a hop check, even crawled upon the floor.
Crawled about to check the cable, sweating freely from each pore.
    Still 404 and nothing more.

"Cur!" I cried with sudden passion, "gizmos may be all the

fashion,

But I've really had my ration—this has got beyond a bore.
Take away your stupid Java, and your client-side script palaver,
Take away your push technology—stick them where they make

you sore!

You're rotten to your stinking core!" I banged the keyboard with

my paw.

    No prize for guessing right the score.

Then crept upon me coldest terror: I will *never* clear this error,
That I'll *always* hit this error, error that I can't ignore.
So now you'll find me quietly moping, with Web-less life I'm

poorly coping,

I've very nearly quit from hoping to reach the Net beyond my door.
Shall I ever see the Web-net instead of error 404?
    Quoth the browser "Nevermore."

PS#1: Later: actually it was a proxy server problem, as it turned
out.

PS#2: What the bloody hell does "[even tried multi]" mean
anyway?

Verity Stob apologises humbly to Jenny Joseph, Roger McGough, Spike Milligan, and
Edgar Allan Poe.

**FEBRUARY 1998, *EXE MAGAZINE***

# Park Gates

*Apparently the rumours that Bill Gates is looking for a pied à terre in Holland Park are not true. Verity Stob can't contain her disappointment.*

To: marcie.de.raspberry@microsoft.com

Hi Marcie,

Well we did make it to England—or rather me and Jennifer Katharine did—Bill had to stay over to speak to the lawyers; apparently Borland is kicking up a row saying Bill is stealing all their programmers. I don't know why they make all the fuss—it's easy to see why anybody would rather work for Bill than that Mr. Potato Head Borland guy—is it Philip something? I'm sure Bill agrees with me on this.

Anyway, England is a real *awful* place, Marcie honey; there are gales and rainstorms and typhoons in trailer parks—it's just like that week we spent in Birmingham Alabama launching Windows for Rednecks. All English cows are poisonous (even the Brits admit this—can you believe it? A whole island, and all they can do is grow poisonous cows!) so I have had the local ethnic grocer, Al Fayed, airfreight over best Florida milk for JK every morning. As I said to Al, where kids are concerned you can't be too careful.

We are renting a condo in this little backwater called Holland Park, which is quite near London, although not on the main island. You can get CNN on cable, so I guess it's not too bad. Yesterday three guys turned up on our doorstep—a fat guy, a little smiley guy, and a guy who looks like that guy who played the Devil in, I forget, was it Exorcist III? Anyway, the little smiley guy asked Was Bill in? and I said Maybe although of course he wasn't and moved my finger to the alarm button, because you cannot be too careful in a place like Holland Park. Then the little smiley guy said his name was Blare and he'd come about the Y2K software problem and the dome. I said I was real sorry about the software problem, but Bill didn't do personal stuff any more and they would have to call the tech support line just like everybody else, and be sure to have their license number, their zip code, and a brief description of their problem ready when the Microsoft operative answered. Then I shut the door in their faces.

Thinking about it later, I figured Blare & Co were probably real estate agents—"The Dome" is the name of a chain of little restaurants they have around here instead of proper MacDonalds. Perhaps they have a condo near one of these Domes or something. Still, I'm so glad they've gone—Marcie I can't tell you how **creepy** they were!

There's JK wanting new diapers—must go!

Love you,

Lissa


To: marcie.de.raspberry@microsoft.com

Marcie,

I apologise, honey! I was wrong and you were right! Nobody here speaks like that woman in *Frasier*—so I guess she must be Scotch, just like you said. I can't think why she doesn't wear more tartan though—if I were Scotch I'd absolutely, definitely flaunt it!

Talking of Scotland, we went to that training college that Bill bought at Cambridge. It's quite an impressive place, Marse, we must go there together when you come over to visit—it's got its own gym and everything. No room for a proper campus like we have at Redmond though—the Brits went and built it in the middle of this old town, well duh!, so I guess they'll never get a proper "studenty" atmosphere going.

Still no sign of Bill—he got tied up with Sun over how he was making their Java stuff better by putting Windows code into it, and the lousy ingrates are suing! Can you believe that? I said to Bill, if they don't want their product to work with the World's Number One Operating System, he should have nothing to do with their lousy stinking Java trash, and I think he is coming around to my way of thinking.

Oops, there's the doorbell—got to dash.

Love

Liss


To: marcie.de.raspberry@microsoft.com

Marcie Darling,

That's it. I'm coming home. Bill's never going to be able to make it over here. Have you heard? Some two-bit outfit called Netcheapskate or something want Bill to stop putting Explorer into Windows, and they've had some stinking bunch of superannuated (big word huh? I'm like that when I'm mad) lawyers, the so-called Supreme Court, are backing them up. I say: what if Netscape was allowed to go on selling its nasty little browser—just how would that make money for Microsoft? If these lawyers are as smart as they say they are, let's hear 'em answer that one. I said this to Bill and he agreed with me absolutely.

Oh, and do you remember the doorbell in my last email? You'll never guess Marse— it was those real estate agents again—Mr. Blare and the two others. Luckily I had opened the door on the chain.

Blare—he was the extra-creepy, smiley little one—said: "Hello again Mrs. Gates! I was hoping to have a word with Bill about the Millennium Dome."

I said: "I'm sorry about the misunderstanding we had last time Mr. Blare, but we are really looking for property in Holland Park, not in Millennium."

The fat one sniggered and said to the real ornery-looking guy, the Devil, "Hey Mandy, hadn't you better tell her it's in Grennitch?" (He had an accent a bit like that woman in *Frasier*, so perhaps he is Scotch too. Although he wasn't wearing a kilt.)

Mr. Blare began to say: "Mrs. Gates, I think you have misunderstood. I wanted to ask Bill if he'd be prepared to contribute . . . ," but I popped out the can of mace that I keep by the door (you can't be too careful ) and pointed it at him, and said: 'OK guys—the party is over. Scram." And to my relief they did—with the Devil running the fastest.

Marse, I guess that it won't come as a surprise that after this we have decided not to buy a place in England—it's not the sort of atmosphere I want for JK. If they want people to live here, the English should stop growing those poison cows, for starters.

Lots of love

Melissa

**APRIL 1998, *EXE MAGAZINE***

[In 1998, portal mania ruled. Everybody went around saying "Content is king" and went around buying up the rights to magazines, films, books, TV programs, and whatnot, in the hope of luring punters to their own website. There they were going to enable the website owner to make a fortune, although the details of how this fortune was to be made always remained rather vague. Once the punters had been lured, the thinking went, we can start worrying about the making money bit.

*Private Eye* is the UK's leading satirical magazine (*The Onion* is the closest US analog that I know) and an important anti-establishment institution that ruthlessly teases any chancers that stray into its path. At this time it effectively prostituted itself by producing bland, animated, cutesy versions of its regular cartoon features to go on MSN. It surely knew it had absolutely no business at all taking Microsoft's money to appear on MSN gateway. What was it thinking about? I'm still cross with it now, after all the intervening years. Grrr.]

# Et Tu Gnome?

Private Eye *is supplying material for MSN, Microsoft's Internet Service Provider. Oh, so that's all right then.*

## MICROSOFT AND MR. WILLIAM GATES III— AN APOLOGY

In common with other magazines and newspapers, for many years *Private Eye* has represented Mr. William Gates III as a ruthless, ambitious, and scary "nerd," ruthlessly pursuing the aims of his company Microsoft using whatever ruthless means were available to him.

We now recognise that nothing could be further than the truth. Mr. Gates is a gentle, understated, cultured person, whose obsession with never releasing software unless it is absolutely tiptop quality has cost him many millions of dollars. *Private Eye* also wishes to salute his gentle handling of his commercial rivals, his clever exploitation of other people's ideas [shurely "his wondrous ingenuity and legendary programming skills"—Ed.], and the superb value of Microsoft BackOffice for BackOffices V6, which with its optimised SQL engine, Internet-capable ODBC integrated (cont. p. 94)

## GLENDA SLAGG

**Bill Gates, aren't ya sick of him???**

**Coming over here with his boring whiney voice, his greasy hair, and his Windows for Workgroups, no wonder he gets custard pie in the mush!!! Good shot Mr. Belgian Bun!!?! Glenda says: Put one on him from me!! Get back to America where you belong, you yawn-making Yank!!**

Wadda guy!! Phwoooaaaar!!! Bill Gates—my best mate!!?!! Rich, bright, handsome, and rich too!!! He can handle my floppies any time he likes!

Hey cheer up Billionaire Bill—we don't give a spit about stupid Flems!!?! Glenda thinks you look Yummy!!! I'd just love to be your custard tart—I'll lick the cream off you any time you want!!?! I'll soon turn your software into hardware, and if you want to handle my floppies. [You have done this already.—Ed.]

## POETRY CORNER

*In Memoriam* Private Eye*'s Editorial Independence.*

So. Farewell
Then
*Private Eye*'s
Editorial Independence.
Keith's Mum thought
that grinding

was her washing
machine
On the blink
Again.
It turned out
the noise
Came from
Peter Cook's
grave.

(ejthribb_17.5@msn.toadying.like.mad)

# A DOCTOR WRITES

## Microsoft Content Providers

As a Doctor I am frequently asked, "Doctor, I have become a Microsoft
Content Provider and now I can feel this tremendous pressure on my
heart—what is it?"

This is easily answered. The condition, technically known as
Walletus Giganticus Swollenus and colloquially known as "billz-billz,"
is caused by selling out to giant software corporations. There is no need
to worry, however, as most patients find the pressure soon goes away,
together with their credibility.

# COCKLECARROT "NETSCAPE MAD"

*By Our US Legal Correspondent Mike O'Softinthehead*
A shocked Supreme Court today heard Justice Java Cocklecarrot admit
his preference for the Netscape Navigator Internet browser.

Justice Javascript told the court: "Of course I use Netscape, which is
rubbish. I never use Internet Explorer for browsing, even though I am
stupidly cutting myself off from a huge number of unique and exciting
features that work the way I do including HTML 4 and VB Script, plus
many excellent and enjoyable channels that represent the future of
online entertainment available from MSN and other ISPs. It is only the
fact that I am completely insane that prevents me from recognising that

Internet Explorer is the better product and is obviously a central and essential part of the Windows operating system, which everybody must be made to use."

The biased Judge went on: "I have always hated Microsoft for no rational reason. I am the sort of creep who went on buying Macs long after it was clear that Apple had been swept aside by superior technology, and anyway I only use the Internet for downloading illegal pornography."

Internet Explorer is 4.02.

## ST. CAKES

Excel term is April 20th to June 2nd. There are 624 licensed Office users in the school. The annual First XV fixture against Cupertino has been scratched at the request of their headmaster Steve Jobs. Ballmer day will be held on May 3rd, and Gloating is from April 4th onwards. Parents of Exchange students are reminded that the play *Death by Powerpoint* will be held in the Paul Allen memorial hut.

## JUST FANCY THAT

Hello, anyone here? I'm a P.I. from across the pond . . . and across the continent . . . San Francisco. Anyone care to share stories, tips, tricks?

*(The actual first message on the MSN/Private Eye "bulletin board")*

[At about this time, newly crowned prime minister Tony Blair gave an important speech to the French *in* French. The big show off.]

---

# Let's Parler Y2K!

*According to* EXE *magazine's first ever press release from the Cabinet Office, the Prime Minister recently announced a "new Year 2000 team." It was silent as to which language he used to do it.*

*Notre chef merveilleux, M Blair*: Bonjour, tout le monde!

*Tout le monde*: Bonjour, Tony!

*Blair*: Comme vous savez, le Royaume-Uni approche une catastrophe formidable. Une catastrophe qu'on n'a jamais vu avant. C'est a dire, une catastrophe catastrophique. Une catastrophe que se passerait à minuit au trente et un décembre mil neuf cent quatre-vingt dix-neuf.

*T-le-m*: Hein? Quand?

*Blair*: Sacré travail nouveau! Dix-neuf neufté-neuf! Deux mille moins un, pour l'amour de Cherie!

*T-le-m*: Ah oui, 1999.

*Un wag*: Vous parlez je crois du grand ouvert à Greenwich de la Dôme de M Mandelson?

*Blair*: Ha ha ho, très drôle. (Campbell: Jetez-lui dehors.) Non, je parle de la bombe de l'an deux mille. Je parle du petit insecte du millenium.

*T-le-m*: Le petit insecte du millenium encore? Fan-sangé-tastique! Nous somme thrillés, aux bord de nos chaises, nous ne croyons pas.

*Blair*: Jusqu'à maintenant, le governement a concentreté ses efforts de l'an deux mille sur les outfits énormes avec les hardwares anciens. Mais maintenant c'est le temps pour focusser sur le bloke et la mère travailant en la rue. M & Mme Pentium 90 sans MMX. Imaginez la scène. C'est minuit moins vingt au trente et un décembre . . .

*T-le-m*: . . . mil neuf cent quatre-vingt dix-neuf . . .

*Blair*: Oui, mil neuf cent quatre-vingt dix-neuf. Nous sommes chez l'homme qui, chaque soir, enjuicer l'incubateur de petits chats à l'hôpitale Rolf Harris des animeaux.

*Une hackette*: Kittens? Ah! Les petits charmants!

*Blair*: Il essaye programmer son vidéo pour enregister l'edition spécial nouveau millenium de Les Amis, mais qu'est-ce que c'est qui se passe? Le vidéo clock ne marche pas. Il est bien cassé. Alors, il faut que M Chat-husbander reste à la maison lui-meme pour commencer le vidéo.

*La hackette*: Et les petits chats dans l'incubateur?

*Blair*: Tous les chats, malheuresement ils donnes un coup de pied au seau.

*La hackette*: Les petits sont morts? Quelle horreur!

*Blair*: D'accord. Mais ne vous paniqez pas. Les petits chats seront hors de danger. Le governement a constructé un projet astucieux.

*T-le-m*: Hein? Quoi?

*Blair*: Un plan cunning. Nous avons l'intention de rassembler les yoofs qui fait le grand retuning des vidéos pour la commencment de Channel Cinq. Nous leur donnerons le quick-training de souffler les ROMs, puis nous leur libérerons sur les Sonys de la nation.

*T-le-m*: Ingenieuse.

*Blair*: Mais ce n'est pas seulement les vidéos qui menacent notre petits chats. C'est les fridgidairs . . .

*Mandelfils*: La Grande Bretagne fraiche!

*Blair*: Tais toi, Mandy. Les fridges, les machines à laver, les hoovers, et les contraptions pour faites chaud un petit morceau du pain.

*Un vieux journo*: Comment exactment peut le petit insecte du millenium contaminer un toaster?

*Blair*: Un Russell-'obbes qu'on a acheter déjà en 1993, peut être il n'est pas compatible avec la crumpette du siècle vingt et unième. C'est une question très technique.

*Un vieux journo*: Merci beaucoup pour votre explanation lucide. (A son ami.) M Blair parle encore de son orifice anterieur.

*Blair*: Naturellement, une campagne sans un slogan c'est comme un 2CV sans le sticker de CND.

*(Il tire une corde d'un rideau et un hoarding immense apparaît.)*
*Le hoarding*: Quelle temps fait-il? Il fait nearly the year 2000.
*Blair*: C'est joli, non? Merci tout le monde. Ne vous oubliez pas surfer à notre website, l'adresse c'est ash tay tay pay oblique oblique double-vay double-vay double-vay point etc., etc.
*T-le-m*: Zzzz.

## VOCABULAIRE FRANÇAIS POUR L'INFORMATIQUE

*un website*—A Web site
*un developpeur*—a developer
*un langue de machine*—a computer language
*un programmeur*—a programmer
*une programmeurse*—a lady programmer
*un boot-up*—a boot up
*un weekend*—a weekend
*un shoot-out*—a shoot out
*un vidéo*—a video
*une petite ligne qui réssemble à une serpent*—a tilde (OK, actually it's "tilde" in French too, we just felt this vocab needed a little more zip.)

Apologies to Miles Kington.

JUNE 1998, *EXE MAGAZINE*

# Yocam Hokum

*Borland has changed its name to "Inprise."*

## DEL YOC-AM'S ACCESSION

And it came to pass *that* the sons of Kahn known as the Borland-ites, who dwelt in the valley of Scotts, were once more sore oppressed.

2. For the Borland-ites had toiled many days and nights over Delphi, and had made it good. Yet the people thereabouts would try it not, saying: *What* kind of a thing is this Delphi? Is it Eye-tie-ite or something? We do better to buy things that are called Vi Su-Albahsic or Power or Bill-da *or* C++ or Enterprise, *which* art as the pie of the apple.

3. Then the Borland-ites had toiled many days and nights over C++ Bill-da, and had made it reasonable. Yet the people thereabouts would try it not, saying: How does this help with our Java strategy?

4. And to cap it all, the Mic-rosoftees of the north had encamped at the very entrance to the valley, *whence* they did ensnare Borland-ite programmers in nets, and dragged them off to Red Mond to eat them.

5. Wherefore things looked pretty bleak, even by the standards of the Borland-ites.

6. So the sons of Kahn decided to take unto themselves a new leader. For they spake *amongst* themselves saying: Whosoever we choose can't make things any worse.

7. Now one day there came unto their midst a man, *whose* name was Del Yoc-am. And the Borland-ites called out to this man: What knowest thou of the craft of software?

8. And Yoc-am replied saying: Nothing. I'm a hardware guy, me.

9. And the Borland-ites asked this man: So thou hast no desire to drop zillions on over-valued piles like Ash-Tontate, or launch truly hopeless packages *like* Object Builder, or plan to grow a huge hedge in the shape *of* Stonehenge?

10. And Yoc-am replied saying: No indeedy.

11. And the Borland-ites cried out in joy saying: Here is our new leader. And they carried him *up* the valley on *their* shoulders, and put him upon their throne, and put on his back the grey cloth of leadership, and anointed his feet with laser toner of the very best quality.

12. And they sung a song in *his* honour:

13. Hail to the chief!
For his name is Del Yoc-am.
If you hear some wise words brief
'Twas surely he who spoke 'em.

## THE ACTS OF YOC-AM

So it was that Del Yoc-am reigned *over* the Borland-ites. And he reigned for three score weeks and ten. And in this time he restrained himself from buying *up* software houses, excepting the odd small one *which* counteth not, and did not release any utter boners, although JBuilder 1 was perhaps one which they will be keeping a little quiet about in years to come, and grew no hedges in the shape of an ancient monument of Wilt-shire, *as* far as we know.

2. And Yoc-am made Enterprise versions, which art not so very dissimilar *from* ordinary versions, except that *they* hath a little sticker upon the box, and they cost one hundred-fold more. For Yoc-am reasoned thus: If we manage to sell a couple of these, we can pay off the mortgage.

3. And Yoc-am engaged *with* Mic-rosoftees of the north, and parleyed with them, and made *them* promise to stop eating the programmers of the Borland-ites.

4. And the Nasdaq looked down *upon* the labours of Yoc-am, and saw that *they* were not too bad, and the price of the stock of the Borland-ites, which had been on the floor, crept upward a little.

5. And the morale of the Borland-ites improved.

6. But Yoc-am became sore troubled in his heart. For he noticed *that whenever* he made a pitch to the Corporates, they did snigger unto him saying: How art the hedges, O Borland-ite?

7. And when he heard this, Yoc-am waxed full of wrath. And he determined to do something about it.

8. So one day, Yoc-am called the sons of Kahn unto him, and he said: I have a great idea *that* will fix *this* hedge *thing*. Let us change our name.

9. And the sons of Kahn said unto him: No, that is a silly idea. Let us not.

10. And Yoc-am replied saying: Too late. I have already ordered the stationery, and the press are coming round in ten minutes.

11. And the sons of Kahn spake, saying: Oh. And *what* are we to be called?

12. And Yoc-am said *unto* them: Inprise.

13. And the sons of Kahn gasped, saying: What?

14. And Yoc-am said unto them: Sorry. I actually meant to call us "Enterprise," but it was a bad line and the lady was a bit deaf, and I think I may have been a bit tipsy.

15. And the sons of Kahn cried out *unto* him saying: *You utter burke.*

16. And the Inprise-Ites that had been Borland-ites did lament a loud lament:

17. O woe! Tears fill our eyes
It seems for sure that folk'll
Just laugh at our Inprise.
Del Yoc-am is an anagram of Mad Yokel
Nearly.

# THE CONSEQUENCES

And when the Mic-rosoftees of the north heard *what* had happened, how they did laugh. They laughed and they laughed and they laughed and they laughed and they laughed.

2. And they laughed and they laughed and they laughed and they laughed and they laughed and they [That's enough laughing.—Ed.]

3. Then there came forth from the tribe of the Until-Recently-Borland-ites a techie. And the techie's name was Char Leecalvert.

4. And Char Leecalvert went unto the mountain top called Inter-net, and spoke brave words unto the world, saying: It doth not matter, Borland-ite is but only a name, like any other; by all means have a giggle at our marketing people—they hath always been dodgy anyway—but our technology is still cool.

5. But friends of the Inprise-Ites *that* had been Borland-ites once more had cause to remember the wisdom *of* the great prophet M'andee-rice Davis. And *such* men were again sore afraid *for* the sons of Kahn.

[Jerry Pournelle is not a popular figure among the few technical journalists that I know. This is in part because he can apparently turn out about 20,000 words in the time that we can write 500. Another reason is because his merciless folksiness clashes with snob Brit taste. Neither reason is defensible; but I do believe both are true.

If the following celebration of *Byte*'s demise seems a little cruel, be condoled to hear that the goddess Hubris settled her account with me in due course. *EXE* magazine itself folded not long afterwards, and in 2003 *Dr. Dobb's Journal* reintroduced Dr. Pournelle's column—exactly as annoying as it ever was—a few months before giving me the push.]

# Bye Bye Byte

*A new owner has closed veteran computer magazine* Byte *pending an "exciting relaunch." In preparation for this, it has sacked all the magazine's editorial staff.*

It's been a busy month as ever. Grunty is a dual Pentium II system which I keep in our kitchen. I'm teaching myself to cook as something to do while I write my novels and these columns and plan NASA's space station and debug Nigella's touch-type teaching program, so poor old Grunty has to take the occasional hit from tomato paste on the SIMMs and OJ through the cooling fan. So last week I decided it was time to fit him with some proper backup facilities.

Like all my kitchen hardware, Grunty has an Ultra-SCSI card (believe me IDE is ALWAYS a false economy when you have fresh cream-of-mushroom flying around the place) so I thought it would just be a matter of unscrewing the case, slipping in a Terror Two 2 terabyte read/write C3D-ROM, rebooting Windows 98, and off I go. Wrong. After three attempts, it was 2:00 am and all I had was one very grumpy Grunty, refusing to recognise his own boot drive.

Time to call in an expert. I phoned Jim Sparkin of Sparkin Boards. (Long-time readers will remember that Jim helped me implement my special keyboard, with the key grouping that made it possible for me to enter with one keypress the "qqmz" consonants that began most of the syllables of the pplln language on the planet fffflq—invaluable while I was writing *Gravity Is a Strange Name for Heck*, price $8.95 in all good bookshops.)

Jim wasn't as quick to answer as usual, but, after all, it was 2:43 in the morning, so I thought nothing of it.

"What do you want, Gramps?"

"Hi Jim, it's me. How are ya doing? I just needed a bit of your expertise—maybe you could drive over here and . . . "

"Ha-ha, Gramps. You haven't heard, have you?"

"Please don't call me 'Gramps,' Jim. You know I don't like it. What haven't I heard?"

"They've fired you. They've sold the magazine and sacked the whole darn tooting lot of you, Gramps. So I need never drive 450 miles in the middle of the night to replace a video adapter card again. Yes suree!"

After that I tried to install a copy of Linux that I had knocking about the place, but it didn't help so I gave up, used Big Fred to finish my novel, and went to bed at 2:58.


# SCANNING TIME

I promised last month that I would be writing about the very exciting 3D scanners that have started appearing. So I called up John McScanno from McScanno Scanners and asked what was the very best model in their range.

John recommended the MsScanno 4009 with UV orientation sensing and the real-time 3D-analysis module. I said fine, that sounded like just the ticket, when could he deliver one. He said he could arrange to have one flown over that very afternoon, and he would send a technician too, to help install it onto my network. I said that was great. He said, good, and what was the expiry date on my credit card. I said what. He said, he was afraid that if I wanted the goods this afternoon it would have to be a credit card order in order for them to be able to process it, the sum involved was $15,095 plus Californian sales tax. I said he didn't understand, I was a world-famous columnist looking to acquire some review hardware. He asked what magazine the review would be appearing in. I told him. He said that if I didn't mind he thought that he would not waste any more of my valuable reviewing time. And hung up.

I'm afraid the MsScanno 4009 will not be getting one of my coveted Dandelion awards.

## TROUBLES WITH JODIE

Robert, my elder son, has been using Jodie the PowerMac for the past few days. Jodie is quite old now, but is still perfectly fine for doing word processing and that kind of thing. Anyway, Robert came down from his room and said, "Dad, I have a bit of an IT problem."

*Me*: I'm not surprised, Robert, I have been doing some reconfiguring of the house network.

*Robert*: What kind of reconfiguring?

*Me*: Well, I am trying to exploit our under-used resources better.

*Robert*: You've sold her, haven't you?

*Me*: Got $87. There's Eric the Amstrad 1512 in the basement. You can use him, although I think you will need to wedge some Blu-Tack under the on/off switch.

*Robert*: You might at least have let me copy my stuff off Jodie before you let her go.

*Me*: You might have least have got a job sometime in the last ten years instead of mooching about the house playing with the computer stuff, and then maybe we wouldn't be in this mess. The mortgage alone is 10k.

*Robert*: Have it your way. I'll go. Now that Mom has left you will be all on your own.

*Me*: Fine. All the stupid bitch ever did was sit around printing out listings of her freaking touch-typing program. Does she realise that paper costs 76¢ a sheet?

## WRAPUP

That about wraps up the very last Tantrum Towers column. If this last bit looqqmzs a bit odd, it is because I am typing it on a 1983 Osbourne 2 laptop with my pplln qqmzeyboard which I have not managed to sell, so I am having to use the qqmz qqmzey for the letter qqmz. Don't forget to buy my booqqmzs, and uh-oh, the battery is going         time for a quicqqmz song, wouldn't want to end on a path   ic note:

    Daisy, Daisy, give                              marriage, can't afford the seat                              for tw

# Night Mail

### SONNET 233 MHz

My laptop's size is nothing like a book;
Unlike my bag her weight drags down my arm;
If a mouse is like a digit, her pad's a foot;
A fast disk like a storm, her drive is calm.
The latest bat'tries charge in half an hour—
In half a week my laptop cannot do it.
The best of keyboards click and clack with power;
Her tiny keyboard squidges like Mum's suet.
To change some RAM should really be a cinch,
Two dozen screws keep hers from prying eyes.
Through a mesh of blurry pixels, at a pinch,
I can discover where each fresh fault lies.
    One question irks me ev'ry day anew,
    How come this junk got five stars in review?

### PORTING AN OLD LIBRARY LATE ONE EVENING

Whose C this is I think I know:
I made it many moons ago
When I was young and full of passion
And K&R was all the fashion.

Strange beauty here. I see the traces
In overhanging curly braces
Of long-forgotten big ideas
My hopes and thoughts of former years.

My little Compaq stirs her drive
As if to say, Hey! Look alive
For goodness' sake pull out your finger
We do not have the time to linger.

I close the file with little zest.
I've many modules yet to test,
And code to write before I rest,
And code to write before I rest.

## Night Mail

This is the email crossing the router,
A transient blip on its trouble shooter,

Email for Harry, email for Tom,
Mail for dot uk and mail for dot com.

The data fly past, ip* in each packet,
The network is loaded but this lot won't crack it.

A glut from a recalcitrant mailing list
Which despite "unsubscribe" will still not desist,

An adulterer's hint to her partner in crime,
Some idiot's Word file, bloated with MIME,

A letter to Feedback about Radio Four,
A rambling flame from some Christian bore,

A batch of blue jokes laced with tetragram**,
A job application, and spam spam spam.

But there's rings on its fingers and bells on its toes,
Email spreads joy wherever it goes—

For surely the hardiest cynic can't fail
To thrill at the popup: "You have new mail."

*Pronounced "eye-pee," obviously.

**A four-letter word. The stress falls on first and last syllables. At least, it does in this poem.

Verity Stob wishes to apologise to William "The Other Big Bill" Shakespeare (Sonnet 130—"My mistress' eyes are nothing like the sun"), Robert Frost ("Stopping by Woods on a Snowy Evening") and W. H. Auden (his original also called "Night Mail").

**NOVEMBER 1998, *EXE MAGAZINE***

[Cringely's PBS program *Triumph of the Nerds* was a little better than I make out here, but a follow-up that he made with British TV, whose name I forget, was a **lot** worse, so it all evens out. Sadly, to this day he continues to make TV programs instead of writing books.]

---

# Cringing for Bobot
## or How I Learned to Stop Worrying About the Quality of My Work and Just Made Dreary TV Programmes Instead

*Robert X Cringely, once best known here as the writer of a very sharp and witty history of the PC, these days seems determined to recast himself as a presenter of increasingly dull Channel 4 television programmes. Verity Stob respectfully asks him to reconsider this career move.*

*(Blairish electric guitar theme tune over cheap, under-animated title sequence. Title: "The Geeking of the Nerds." Opening shot—a suspiciously youthful-looking and bespectacled man eating a pizza in a restaurant.)*

*Cringely (for it is he)*: Hi, and welcome to the Fredoes Café in San Diego, California. This restaurant may not look like much, but it is right here that one of the most significant inventions in the history of the PC was made. But before we find out about that, let me introduce my assistant for this series.

*(A girl is matted into the shot, using a really strikingly poor chromakey technique. The girl is incorrectly lit, the wrong size for the perspective, her feet don't touch the floor, and a fuzzy line surrounds her image.*

*When the girl speaks, we discover to our increased embarrassment that she is a Brit, apparently of the not-quite-bright-enough-to-get-on-Blue-Peter school of media studies. The girl addresses herself to a point quite near Cringely's right ear.)*

*Girl*: Hi Bob and I'd just like to say how great it is to be here. Only I'm not really here of course—

*Cringely (apparently addressing himself to her left buttock, and perhaps beginning to realise that Bob Hoskins earned his money in* Roger Rabbit*)*: Yes—

*Girl (plonking tone)*: I'm only *virtually* here. I'm actually in Birmingham. In the studio. But using the magic of the Internet—

*Cringely (interrupting firmly)*: But to find out why Fredoes is so significant—

*Girl*: So why is Fredoes so significant, Bob?

*(Cut to shot of Cringely driving a convertible sports car slowly along the freeway.)*

*Cringely*: Back in 1978, one guy, working in a pretzel store in Silicon Valley, had an idea. An idea that was to change millions of lives, and earn billions and billions of dollars.

*(Pulls car off freeway, parks in front of "Just Pretzels" pretzel shop. Fat, elderly man with pleasant avuncular appearance, presumably the proprietor of the shop, leans in the doorway. Caption: Jack "Pretzel" Larkin.)*

*Cringely*: Hi. I'm Bob Cringely.

*Jack Larkin*: Hi Bob. Would you like to come in and interview me for British Channel 4?

*Cringely*: Do you mind if I come in for a moment?

*(Cut to interior of shop. Cringely is seated at a small table, Jack is serving him pretzels.)*

*Cringely*: Mmmm. I'd like one of those . . .

*Cringely (on voiceover)*: But in 1978, it was a lot more than just pretzels that were cooking in Jack's store. Something really big was about to happen, something that would change the world forever. And this thing would never have happened . . .

*(Cut to stock footage of Xerox PARC. A man with a really horrid 1976 haircut is playing PONG on an Alto.)*

*Cringely*: . . . if it hadn't been for Xerox PARC. Boy, those guys at Xerox PARC thought of everything!

*(Cut to Cringely's garage, which is ostentatiously furnished with an original IBM PC, a first generation Apple Mac, an Apple II, etc., etc.)*

*Cringely (standing in front of whiteboard)*: Time for another Bob Cringely crash course in high tech basics. Pay attention now. *(He simpers.)* You see, before 1978, everybody thought of a computer as one big box. *(Draws a big box on whiteboard.)* That is everybody except one man. *(Draws a stick man.)* Can you guess who that man was?

*(Cut to stock footage of Bill Gates, being interviewed by an unseen party who one suspects isn't Cringely.)*

*Gates*: Yeah, well it's all very well you saying that, but what people don't realise is that in those days this kind of stuff was hard to do. And expensive. And we made the policy decision that, yeah, we're gonna go for it. And we did.

*Cringely (voiceover)*: No, not him. He didn't come along until much later.

*(Cut to shot of Cringely, pedalling an ice cream vendor's tricycle along a beach.)*

*Cringely (addresses camera in cod Italian accent as he pedals past)*: Getcha tutsi frutsi ice-cream!

*Cringely (voiceover)*: I've come here to Malibu to meet someone very special.

*(Cycles up to a beach villa, and knocks at door. Door opens instantly, to reveal fat, elderly man in Hawaiian shirt and shorts.)*

*Man in Hawaiian shirt*: Hi Bob. Would you like to come in?

*Cringely*: Hi. My name's Bob Cringely. Can I come in?

*Man in Hawaiian shirt*: Better get your ice cream out of the sun, in case it melts!

*(Both parties turn to camera and laugh.)*

*(Cut to the British Blue Peter girl, whom we had all forgotten about, standing in a street of British terraced houses.)*

*Girl*: Meanwhile, things were hotting up in the UK. I've come to Birmingham to meet the programmer who really set things rolling. Let's see if anyone is at home.

*(Presses doorbell, door opens immediately.)*

*(Etc., etc., etc., etc., etc.)*

[Previous to about this point in time, the received non-technical view of Microsoft, as expressed by the likes of my Mum, went something like this: the company was run by a bunch of genius children who had set up in a garage together and deservedly acquired fortunes through sheer cleverness. Bill Gates was the jolliest scamp of the lot—even if a little more sunshine wouldn't do him any harm.

Then came an almost binary change in public opinion, presumably after exposure to Windows '95 for a few years. Suddenly the perception of Microsoft switched to them being greedy monopolists who turned out shoddy, unreliable product. Gates became an evil genius who was simultaneously an incompetent fool (public opinion easily ignores inherent contradictions).

This, I think, was the moment when that shift occurred. The technical view of Microsoft is, of course, a lot more sophisticated. Oh yes.]

---

# One Nostril Hair, 17mm, Grey

*"[Microsoft] employees aren't quite the workaholics they once were . . . Why? Employees are no longer single. They are getting older (average age now 33) and more than half are now married."*
—Guardian

Minutes of the New Products Forward Planning Meeting held 01/04/99 in Conference Room D, Excel Block.

Participants: AndyV (VP New Media Products, Chair), BradyL (OS Development, Minute taker), RandyZ (Chief Programmer Xeton

Project), MickyT (Marketing Division Spokesperson), HelenB (Senior Strategy Rep)

AndyV raised the implications of the take-over of Netscape by AOL. With full financial backing, an Open Source scheme improving its core browser technology by leaps and bounds, and a version 5 rollout imminent, it was surely once more time to take the Netscape threat seriously.

BradyL concurred with most of what AndyV said, and consequently would like to push for the improved concurrency programming model in the next beta of Windows 2000. The idea would be to offer much better multi-threaded JVM performance, while still retaining the option to offer API enhancements that would be Microsoft proprietary.

It might seem a bit late in the day to be addressing architectural questions, but flexibility was the name of the game. It was up to Microsoft to prove that it still held its market leadership position.

AndyV was not sure where BradyL was going with this. An architectural change at this stage would surely impact the shipping date, and it went without saying that this was one shipping date that they were not going to be able to miss without losing consumer credibility. AndyV said he thought that this point was so important that he had prepared a dramatic, six-feet-tall 3D model to illustrate the development of the market up to the anticipated launch date, which he would like to show the meeting. AndyV brought in his model from outside the room.

MickyT said, Not on the floor.

AndyV said, What?

MickyT said, Don't put that thing on the floor. Not unless you are sure that the Surgeon General has determined that the gold glitter paint you have sprayed on it is 100% safe and non-toxic when ingested by infants who may be crawling around.

AndyV enquired where in the room exactly were these infants that required the protection of the Surgeon General.

MickyT explained that, although there were no infants in the room at that moment, he was expecting MickyT Junior to be joining them in the next few minutes. It was the day of the month that the babysitter always had off to travel to town to get her facial done, and it was his, MickyT's, turn to look after Junior. He appreciated that this arrangement was not ideal, but that was the way the cookie had crumbled.

AndyV thought that "not ideal" was darn right. He reminded MickyT that this was a serious meeting we are trying to have here. In the absence of MickyT Junior, he would now like to show his carefully constructed 3D sales model.

RandyZ opined that MickyT had a point, and that one could not be too careful in these matters. It had only been a few weeks since JenniferKatharineG had got the plastic cap of a whiteboard-friendly Wipeklean marker pen stuck in her left ear, and it had taken the whole of the Java development team making funny faces and goo-goo-goo noises to comfort her.

BradyL wondered perhaps if there was not room for the model on the table, although it was rather tall.

HelenB expressed surprise that MickyT Junior was not already walking. Her youngest, WayneB, who was born she remembered at the same time as MickyT Junior, had been walking for some time. In fact, next weekend she had thought to remove the training wheels from WayneB's bicycle.

MickyT enquired how HelenB had got the impression that MickyT Junior was not yet walking. Although it was true that MickyT was fond of the lateral transitioning mode, he had in fact been walking for some months, as was proved by this Polaroid.

RandyZ said Aaaaaaaah!

AndyV asked if he was going to be allowed to present his freaking sales forecast to the freaking meeting that he was freaking chairing, or was everyone going to sit around all day staring at freaking photographs of freaking kids.

BradyL observed that, since some of us appeared to be getting a little heated, perhaps now would be a good time to have a little comfort break. He said he'd get in a batch of sodas from the nearby kitchen.

MickyT said, Oh God not more Cola. He emphasised that these days he found it excessively sweet and sticky, and that its fizzyness was bad for his digestion.

HelenB agreed with MickyT, and said she would not care if she never ever drank another Coke in the whole of her life. These days she carried around with her in her bag a selection of herbal teas, all naturally caffeine free, which could conveniently be made into refreshing drinks by simply adding boiling water. Perhaps MickyT would like to try one? Camomile and Nettle flavours were particularly good, in her experience, for water retention, while the Fennel and Good Afternoon and Vanilla kinds did wonders for

AndyV said, loudly, that he had enough. This meeting would now come to order. The issue at hand was the renewed threat from AOL/Netscape. Microsoft had achieved and retained domination in these markets by anticipating this kind of crisis and responding to it in advance, and, and, and where the hell did HelenB think she was going now?

HelenB said it was Thursday.

AndyV agreed that it was indeed Thursday, but felt that by itself this was an inadequate explanation for her getting up and walking out of his meeting. As it happened, he had planned this meeting as an all-nighter. He recalled the good old days when a cabal of programmers had got Windows working in protected mode during one long 48-hour session, fuelled by pizza and Coke. This was the spirit required now to overcome the renewed Netscape threat.

RandyZ said it was all very well for AndyV to recall the old days, but Thursday was Barney the Dinosaur night on CBS, and after that he had promised to take the kids down to the new rollerskaterama.

MickyT said, Good point about Barney. I'd better go too.

RandyZ and HelenB and MickyT then all left the meeting.

BradyL attempted to lift AndyV's model up onto the table. But it was too tall, and a piece broke off the top, and a ceiling panel fell down.

AndyV commented that That freaking did it and He didn't know why he freaking bothered.

The meeting was adjourned.

**FEBRUARY 1999,** *EXE MAGAZINE*

# The Dog's Breakfast

### VARIATION ON A VILLAGE PEOPLE SONG

*(Best read while playing a video of a dance troupe of hard-hatted Microsoftees on your mental television.)*

Young man, wipe that smile off your face
I said
Young man, get into that KnowledgeBase
I said
You know that there's code to be cut
There's no room on board for drifters.
You say the APIs are obtuse
I said
Young man, that's a feeble excuse
I said
You know where the answers are kept
So come on and join the party.

Bosh Bosh Bosh Bosh Bong

You've got to sub to the M. S. D. N.
You've got to sub to the M. S. D. N.
You get Windows NT for France and Japan
Updated in a quarterly plan!
You've got to sub to the M. S. D. N.
You've got to sub to the M. S. D. N.
You get the SDKs and the DDKs too
It's all there for me and for you!

Young man, I see the fear in your eyes
I said
Young man, best sub to Enterprise
I said
Young man, you'll get Visual C
With all that way-out wizardry!
So young man, don't take no stupid risk
You know
You should buy all those silver discs
Because
Those guys at Redmond are great
They just live to make your life fun!

Bosh Bosh Bosh Bosh Bong

You've got to sub to the M. S. D. N.
You've got to sub to the M. S. D. N.
You get Windows NT for France and Japan
Updated in a quarterly plan!
You've got to sub to the M. S. D. N.
You've got to sub to the M. S. D. N.
You get the SDKs and the DDKs too
It's all there for me and for you!

*(Repeat and fade)*


BACKUP IS FOR PUNTERS

Monday's tape is out of date,
Tuesday's suffered unknown fate,
Wednesday's tape caught in the rollers,
Thursday's chewed by canine molars,
Jim took Friday you'll remember,
Saturday vanished in September.
A Sabbath backup would be a freak—
But if we can't find one, we're up the creek.

## THE DOG'S BREAKFAST

The Boss asked
his PA, and
his PA asked
the Manager:
"Can we have a printout
of the profit that we made?"
The Manager
said: "Certainly.
I'll go and tell
the Programmer.
It's his fault
the MIS
system is
delayed."

The Programmer
said: "Bloody hell!
Who demanded
Oracle?
I won't let
this pass
without
a big row!"
So they called
a big meeting—
everyone attended—
and for all I know
they're still
sitting there
now.

Verity Stob wishes to apologise to Wendy Cope ("Variation on a Lennon and McCartney Song"), Anon. ("Monday's Child Is Fair of Face"), and A. A. Milne ("The King's Breakfast") whose ideas she has here ripped off shamelessly.

# Book of Yoc-am (Contd.)

*Inprise has yet again turned in poor financial results, is laying off 20% of its workforce, and is once more restructuring.*

## BORLAND BECOMES INPRISE (RECAP)

A nd it came to pass that the sons of Kahn, who had been *known* as the Borland-ites, announced that *henceforth* they were somewhat unconvincingly to be known as the Inprise-Ites.

2. So the Elders of the tribe, called "the usual suspects," were dragged *forth* to proclaim that Inprise was in safe hands and that its values had changeth not. And Zackur-Lockur burnt his Borland T-shirts in public, and Giant I wrote jolly articles for the website, and Char Leecalvert went unto the newsgroups of the Internet, yea unto the very pits of dirt and filth of the earth.

3. And they cried out, saying: All is well! All is well!

4. But all was not well.

5. For it seemed that the tribe had departed far from the narrow path of wisdom, and instead wandered dangerously by night in the rain and spray on the Inter-State Highway of Folly, stumbling amongst the high-speed traffic-burdened lanes, presenting a danger both unto itself and to others.

6. Moreover, to stretch the metaphor way beyond its limit, the sons of Kahn wore not a bright yellow reflective high-visibility jacket.

# SMALL PROPHET, QUICK RETURN

Now at that time the sons of Kahn were led by a man named Del Yoc-am. And *this* Yoc-am had dreamed a dream that he would become as that Oracle bloke, who is much interviewed in the press and upon the television, and who is by all *accounts* loaded. And when Yoc-am awoke, he was well pleased with this dream.

2. Thus Yoc-am reasoned unto himself: All he doth is charge lots and lots of money for all his software. I shall go and do likewise, and then I too shall have my photograph in *Time* magazine, and be called forth to deliver opinions about the *future* of the Internet on the Letterman show.

3. So Yoc-am took himself a basket, and filled it to the brim with freshly harvested Delphi, and went *down* from the valley of Scotts *unto* the market place.

4. And there chanced that way a small developer. And the small developer hailed Yoc-am saying: Greetings brother! How much for an upgrade to client/server?

5. And Yoc-am answered, saying: Twelve hundred shekels to you.

6. Then the developer replied, saying: No, no; just the upgrade please. I *already* have a copy of the previous version.

7. But Yoc-am answered, saying: I heard you correctly. It's twelve hundred shekels for the upgrade. The full version costs thirteen-fifty.

8. And the developer *cried out* involuntarily, saying: Blimey O'Reilly!

9. Then the developer has a closer look at Yoc-am's basket, and he saw that the Delphi was infested with maggots and *crawling things*. And he spake unto Yoc-am, saying: I think I'll take a pass on this one, thanks all the same squire.

10. And in a while there chanced that way a corporate developer. And the corporate developer hailed Yoc-am saying: Greetings. Where can I find an agent for the tribe of Mic-rosoftees?

11. And Yoc-am answered, saying: Over there.

12. And the corporate developer thanked Yoc-am saying: Thanks.

13. And Yoc-am called out unto the corporate developer, saying: Just a minute. But the corporate developer was deep in conversation with the Mic-rosoftee, and heard him not.

14. Thus, after many *more* similar failures, Yoc-am went back up to the valley of Scotts with a full basket.

# THE COMING OF BORLAND.COM

And the Nasdaq looked down upon the labours of Yoc-am, and it was mightily unimpressed.

2. And Yoc-am *in turn* looked upon the wrath of Nasdaq, and was sore afraid. And he spake boldly unto his shareholders, saying: I shall slay one in every five of the sons of Kahn, it is the aggressive and logical thing to do. Moreover I shall create a new division called borland.com which, having a lower case, shall be a *mighty* hit on the Internet. Oh, and it might be easier to sell that way.

3. Thus did Yoc-cam do these things. He did slay one in every five of the sons of Kahn, and the valley of Scotts ran red with their blood. And he did make a new division, and called it borland.com, and put in it most of what was left of Borland. And he did other stuff with the Visigenics bit of Inprise, which frankly is of *little* interest.

4. Moreover it came to pass that a great bewailing went up among the borland.com-ites, who had been Inprise-ites, who had been Borland-ites. And when they began to get over the massacre, they cried out to one *another* saying: Who shall lead us in this our hour of great need? For surely the leadership of borland.com is a can of poisoned Kool-Aid with worms in it.

5. And there was heard a noise from the Interbase *cupboard*. And a little voice said: The door is stuck. Will somebody let me out?

6. And using his great and mighty strength, the Giant I unlocked the door using a key he happened to have.

7. And lo! They beheld a small bald man with a beard, blinking in the sunlight.

8. And the borland.com-ites, who had been Inprise-ites, who had been Borland-ites, cried out with one voice saying: Our leader! Our leader!

9. In his dismay, the small man tried to run away, but the Giant I was standing on the tails of his coat, and he ran only *in little circles*.

10. Then Char Leecalvert burnt his Inprise T-shirts in public, and Zackur-Lockur wrote jolly articles for the website, and Giant I went unto the newsgroups of the Internet, yea unto the very pits of dirt and filth of the earth.

11. And they cried out with one voice, saying: All is well! All is well!

12. But customers of the sons of Kahn remembered yet again the wisdom *of* the great English prophet M'andee-rice Davis. And *such* men began *costing* ports to Vi Su-Albahsic, just to be on the safe side.

JULY 1999, *EXE MAGAZINE*

[Around this time, a male friend showed me how one could manipulate Lara so that the camera became trapped within her bodyspace, behind her (hollow as it turns out) boobs.

Boys, eh? Why does one bother?]

---

# Fair Play

*"My life is just as glamorous as Lara Croft's," claims Verity Stob, wildly. "I should think Eidos could make a very exciting game out of it."*

**Practice level:** Verity's flat. Take your time to explore your surroundings and hone your game control skills.

**Scenario:** It is a weekday morning. Verity has to get up and get ready for work. There are two secrets to be found.

**Opening doors:** When confronted with closed doors on level the temptation is to use Verity's authentic karate kick action: press the Kick key then very quickly press Jump and hold down Forward. Although this does work, you will sustain 5% damage—"stubbing the toe"—each time you do it, and remember there are no medipacks on this level.

**Flushing the loo:** You flush the loo in Verity's flat by climbing up onto the seat so that the cistern is at eye level. Now pull the lever (tap the Action key) three times vigorously and backflip out of the bathroom to land square in the middle of the hall (found by OoooziM). If this doesn't work, then you were probably too slow—you must wait five minutes for the tank to fill up again—so if you get it wrong you will probably want to reload your game at this point. You did remember to save your game, didn't you?

**Traps:** When going from morning room to kitchen, be sure to leap over the trailing aerial cable from the television.

Beware the milk in the fridge—it is poisonous! (If you like you can crouch down and use the Look key to see that it is 12 days past its sell-by date.) You will want to place the carton into Verity's combat carrier bag for combat use later on.

**Secrets:** Vault into the bedroom sideways and look down. You will see there is a crawl space underneath Verity's bed. You will find assorted magazines and unwashed clothes, a hairgrip, her purse, and car keys.

The clean underwear is hidden in the washing machine (found by Daveman).

The level ends when you exit the flat.

**Tips:** OoooziM writes: I found that the thermostat doesn't work properly unless you turn off the radiator in the bathroom.

Swazzer says: The doofer for the TV is hidden in between the cushions of the sofa, but it doesn't have any batteries so it doesn't work (Playstation version only).

**Level 1:** Getting to work.

**Scenario:** Verity travels from home to work. There are two separate strategies for completing this level.

**Strategy 1:** As you leave the flat you are accosted by the boring neighbour who wishes to tell you about his long-running dispute with the council. The correct approach is to crawl along under the cover of garden wall, then do a running jump (Forward, then quickly hit the Jump key) over the dustbins and thus reach the safety of the car. Alternatively you can just sprint across the lawn and squeeze through the gap by the skip (found by Sophie). NB only evasive action is effective at this point. *Do not use your weapon!* Sour milk does not work against the boring neighbour.

**Starting the car:** Press and hold the starter motor (Roll key) for 30 seconds while vigorously pumping the throttle (Action key). When she fires, pull out the choke (Choke key) about one quarter of the way.

**Traps:** It is a very good idea to save your game before trying to start the car.

If you pull the choke out too far, or too early, the carburettor will flood, and you will be unable to start her.

If you pull the choke out too little, or too late, the battery will run down, and you will be unable to start her.

If all this sounds too much like hard work, then you can fall back on

**Strategy 2:** Taking the Tube. Fairly straightforward and obvious except that you get more points if you kill the man who barges into the queue for the ticket machine with a karate blow to the neck rather than simply tripping him up into the path of the oncoming train (thanks to The_Gaffer for this).

**Secrets:** You stand a remote chance of getting a seat if you wait two-thirds of the way down the platform, between the broken chocolate vending machine and the vandalised help point, and then push like hell (Push key) when the train arrives.

**Bugs:** There is a bug in the PC version that causes the train to stop between stations for periods of up to five minutes. No patch available so far :-( :-(

**Level 2:** Arriving at work.

**Scenario:** The main task of this level is to get through the security door, which is protected by a keypad and electronic card swipe.

**Strategy:** The strategic options are

1. Try to sweet-talk Reception Ed into pressing the release button (Sophie claims to have had some success with this strategy, but nobody else can make it work). *Do not use your weapon on Reception Ed!* Receptionists are immune to the powers of sour milk.

2. Hide behind the postal trays, waiting for someone with a card to open the door. Wait until the last moment, then do a running jump over the screen and sneak through behind them, innocently whistling (Innocent Whistle key).

3. If you have used the cheat code to get all the weapons, you can use the Uzi to shoot out the lock. However, be aware that this causes the Building Manager to come out of her office to see what the noise is about. Now you are in big trouble. The Building Manager cannot be killed without the thermo-nuclear turbo-laser from the Caves of Tharg, which we will visit in Episode Three (Daveman).

Link scene: After you have overcome the terrors of the security door, an inter-level animation appears, where the Manager says: "Verity please can you make some tea—the directors are in an important meeting." *Now* you get to use your weapon . . .

# By Other Means

*Little has been made in the mainstream press of the fact that the recent virus ExploreZip, a Delphi program, specifically attacked C++ and Assembler sources. Stob wonders if we are on the verge of an internecine techie war.*

**Day 51**—First reprisal by a C++ faction for the ExploreZip assault: the so-called Big Girl's Blouse Worm. As well as spreading itself, the worm attacks systems by seeking out all DLLs and EXEs written in Delphi. Rather than deleting or overwriting these files, the worm appends random bytes to the end, adding a few 100 KB more every time. It simultaneously modifies the EXE headers so that the enlarged file is loaded into memory. Eventually Delphi programs on a BGB-infected machine collapse underneath the weight of the megabytes of gunk they must haul up into RAM at load time.

The strange moniker is explained by a taunting anonymous message posted to one of the newly created anti-Delphi newsgroups. Here is the text:

```
L3T M WRiT3 ViRUZ3Z, L3T M WRiT3 D3ViC3 DRiV3RZ, L3T M WRiT3 WiNDOW
M4N4G3RZ; BUT 4Z LONG 4Z TH3Y UZ3 P4ZC4L, TH3Y R ZTiLL 4 BUNCH OF
BiG GURRRLZ BLOUZ3Z.
D34TH 2 TH3 D3LPHiLTH SCUMI i H8 TH3M 1LLI
TH3 D3LPHiLTH KiLL3R
The opinions expressed in this message are the author's own, and do
not in any way reflect those of Drommington-Egbarth Small Plastic
Containers Inc.
```

A crack team of computer experts from the FBI tries to prolong this thread in an attempt to track down "The Delphilth Killer." In the unmoderated newsgroup, however, the Feds are unable to prevent it from turning into a rather pointless discussion about where the apostrophe should go in the phrase Big Girl's Blouses.

**Day 72**—A group of militant Visual Basic programmers decide that they have been ignored for long enough, and produces its own example of the genre. The VisBas virus has several unusual features; the most striking being that it uses a standard installer to propagate itself:

> Please wait while InstallShield extracts the files which will install this virus. It is strongly recommended that you exit all Windows programs before running this program. Oh, and if NT users could log on as Administrator, that would be a great help too. Press Down to view the rest of the end user license agreement.

Despite—or perhaps because of—this, the virus is quite successful in spreading. It appears on the cover CD of one of the PC magazines, where it is described as a "must have Internet connection management and desk diary tool." Thereafter it is rapidly adopted by all the rival publications, often winning the "Freeware of the Month" award, until it becomes even more common than that other staple: the out-of-date version of Netscape-Communicator-now-with-annoying-yellow-AOL-Thing.

However, the malevolent action of the virus—to rename .PAS files to .BAS "to show we are just as good"—is so feeble that the anti-virus toolkit companies don't even bother to issue a patch to cope with it, and the VisBas team retires to sulk.

**Day 105**—However, the Visual Basic effort has not been entirely disregarded, and a Delphi faction retaliates devastatingly. Using a simple virus which, in a brilliant piece of social engineering, spreads by masquerading as unwanted Microsoft promotional email ("Travel to Hong Kong to be among the first to learn about Microsoft's new COM+ mousewheel technology!"), the payload is hideously cruel. It penetrates the huge cluster of life-support DLLs, OCXs, and whatnot that every Visual Basic program needs to help it breath and—here's the clever bit—patches one at random to its *own previous version*.

The consequences are appalling. VB programs start dying like flies, often corrupting files and databases as they go, and in extreme cases actually causing machines to catch fire. Since the affected DLL is actually a genuine VB support DLL, albeit of a slightly older version, the standard anti-virus tools are useless. Finally Microsoft itself snaps into action, and issues a warning message to its promotional email mailing lists. The impact of the warning is rather muted, as before release it is edited and passed by the Redmond marketing and PR departments: "Microsoft technology triumphs again in mass distributed processing experiment."

Ultimately the Delphi virus is successfully countered by vaccine program, which performs exactly the same version substitution trick—but on the BDE.

**Day 127**—The first Java virus appears, exploiting a previously unnoticed security hole in the applet sandbox of certain JVMs. Allegedly really devastating, it really needs to run on a multi-gigahertz, multi-processor Sun to be seen at its best. This, combined with the fact that most web users close their browsers on reflex at the dread words "Loading Java applet," rather limits its impact. But it is jolly well designed, and portable, which is the main thing.

**Day 143**—The first Linux virus, thought to be created by the very, very extreme "We love Windows; even Exchange Server group." The virus spreads itself in packets of data in the archaic NETBIOS protocol and gains control using a fixed-size buffer overwrite. Although it can infect Windows machines, it only actually attacks Intel machines running SAMBA—a package, which allows non-Windows machines to act as Windows file servers. Once installed the virus monitors network traffic looking for likely password strings; every time it finds a candidate, it tries to become root user.

Once a machine has been fully infected, the system appears to go through a standard shutdown. Meanwhile, in the background, the core OS is overwritten. The last messages the unfortunate Linux user sees:

```
The system is halting...
System halted.
So you won't be staying up continuously without reboot for ten years
after all, will you, you smug bugger?
```

**OCTOBER 1999, *EXE MAGAZINE***

# Waltz$

### TRYING OUT MY NEW PROGRAM

This latest flower of my hard-earned skill
(Try starting it from D:, that's prob'ly best.)
It has within its screens no showy frill
(Just copy these DLLs; you don't need the rest.)
Only elegant and self-sufficient code,
That will do the job and minimise the load,
And yet is flexible and can be changed to suit.
(Oh dear. I fear that it's time to reboot.)

Because its local database is small
(Are you sure it's on the path? Yes, yes, I've seen.)
It hardly takes up any disk at all,
And fits upon the most frugal machine.
Its menu structure, as you have inferred,
Is plain as day. (Must you really open Word?)
Even if you've not the manual read.
(Right-click the taskbar now to kill it dead.)

Although the inner workings of design
(Hold on. I'd better hack the reg'stry hive.)
Must be hidden from the untrained mind
(Are you absolutely sure you're running SP5?)
The centre core is kept in isolated blocks,
I could quickly port it to a Mac or other box
In half a month. (What now? That COM port's free!
I give up. Let's go run it on my own PC.)

## WALTZ$

*"Ask Bill why function code 6 [in MS-DOS, to output a string]*
*ends in a dollar sign. No one in the world knows that but me."*
*—The late Gary Kildall, inventor of CP/M*
*and founder of Intergalactic Digital Research,*
*quoted by Robert Cringely in* Accidental Empires

One night in his office, Bill Gates is alone.
He's done all his email and he's ready for home.
But there's a light in the corner from no glowing screen—
It's the ghost of Gary Kildall, all bearded and green.
Cries the spirit: Hey William, with all due respect
Windows is but CP/M, and I've come to collect.
Offer me no argument, I'll not stand for tricks:
For I know why there's a dollar in function code 6.

*Sing: We'll have no excuses, we'll have no more tricks,*
*Kildall put the dollar sign in function code 6!*

Then Gates eyes the spirit without fear in his soul,
And calls to his rival: Go hence bearded ghoul!
Do you think I will yield to this Scooby-Doo tactic?
Where now is the firm that was "Intergalactic"?
Your BIOS lies obsolete, your functions uncalled,
And if programmers saw them they'd be quite appalled,
It matters not a bit that you scream and you holler
For what kind of jerk ends a string with a dollar?

*Sing: A currency display bug must most surely foller,*
*The ghost ends his strings not with NUL but with $!*

Now when Bill calls the shots we know who prevails.
And it seems so this instance. The spook stops his wails.
Its extremities fade—like the feline in Alice—
Till only its head's left, still leering with malice.
But it calls out defiantly: Now don't you forget
You've won in this dollar-world, but there's more to come yet.
CP/M's still wowing 'em where the folks aren't so pure-oh:
For the demons of Hellfire have switched to the Euro.

*Sing: The dominion of Beelzebub makes us all feel uneasy*
*But at least the exchange rate is on par with the EC.*
*One two three one three two three two one stop.*

Verity Stob wishes to apologise to Thomas Hood ("A Parental Ode to My Son, Aged Three
Years and Four Months") and Rudyard Kipling ("The Looking-Glass") for ripping off their
poems.

JANUARY 19100, *EXE MAGAZINE*

[This article has brought me more comeback than any other, drawing in many passionate emails from both sides of the argument.

Interestingly, it contains a whopping bug, caused by my changing of my code after I'd tested it—I over-egged the pudding to dramatise a point. I stand by the complaint I was making, but the example won't compile.

None of my pro-VB correspondents pointed out this error. Instead they concentrated on irrelevancies; for example noting that it is possible to change the behaviour of VB6's editor to overcome the difficulty indicated in point 12.5.

As is often the case, Microsoft has had the final say. When it designed VB.NET, the successor of the tool considered here, it chose to fix most of these issues.]

# Thirteen Ways to Loathe VB

*Verity Stob has recently been press-ganged into a Visual Basic project. For the benefit of other programmers who may be brought down in this way, she has prepared an executive summary of her experience.*

1. *Procedure and function call.* This area of BASIC has come on in leaps and bounds. Whereas in the bad old days you had to use GOSUB, these days you have *subs* ("subs" is the preferred baby-speak for what grown-ups call procedures or void functions) and functions. You write

```
Subname Param1, Param2
```

to call sub Subname and

```
Result = FuncName(Param1, Param2)
```

to call function FuncName. Notice the useful difference in syntax, with and without parentheses, which serves more purposes than I can describe. It is of course a syntax error to write

```
Subname(Param1, Param2)
```

but the good news is you *can* write

```
FuncName(Param1, Param2)
```

to call a function and ignore its return. However, if Param1 or Param2 are reference parameters—and they will be unless you have specifically demanded value parameters—they will be treated *in this specific case* as value parameters, and any assignment to them discarded on exit from FuncName.

Obviously the syntax

```
Call FuncName(Param1, Param2)
```

fixes this, and causes Param1 and Param2 to be treated as reference parameters.

Right.

2. *Variable declaration.* This is achieved using the intuitive keyword Dim. To declare an integer I write

```
Dim I As Integer
```

To declare a whole load of integers write

```
Dim I, J, K, L As Integer
```

Actually (haha got you!) this doesn't work. This declares I, J, and K as variants and only L as an Integer. This almost never matters, except quite often.

3. *Calling functions and accessing arrays.* In most languages you can distinguish between a call to function F with parameter 3 and a reference to array F index 3 because one is written F(3) and the other F[3]. In Visual Basic they are both written F(3). Yes.

4. *Another thing about arrays.* The index of the first element is 0, unless it is set to 1 by a directive.

5. *But there are also collections*, modern object-oriented versions of arrays. And the first element of these is usually 1, unless it happens to be 0. Sometimes it is 0 and sometimes it is 1, depending on where you found it. Do you feel lucky, punk? Well, do ya?

6. *Did I mention "object-oriented"* back there? Hahahahahahahahahahahahaha.

7. *Initialisation.* This area of BASIC has come on in leaps and bounds. Whereas in the bad old days you had to use a completely barbaric mechanism based on the keywords DATA and READ, this has now been swept away. The following fragment illustrates the modern way to initialise an array in code:

```
Dim A(20) As Double
A(0) = 4.5 ' May work, may not—who can tell?
A(1) = 4.71
A(2) = 4.82
A(3) = 4.92
...
```

You get the idea.

8. *Arrays of constants.* No such thing. Anyway what would you do with 'em if you had 'em?

9. *The type* Integer *declares a 16-bit integer.* That's right, *sixteen* bits. Yes I *am* using the latest version. Unbelievable, isn't it? Let's have a big warm *EXE* welcome back to code that dies suddenly around the 33k mark.

10. *Assignment.* This area of BASIC has come on in leaps and bounds. Whereas in the bad old days you used the = operator for assignment, preceding it with LET if you were a fusspot of the first order, these days you use the = operator for assignment, preceding it with Let if you are a fusspot of the first order. Or Set if it's an object. Which is compulsory not optional

**11.** *Logic.* This particular language is supposed to be easy and intuitive, so here's a test for you. Suppose that Check1 is a checkbox on a form, and you execute the code

```
Dim b As Boolean, c As Boolean
b = Check1.Value
c = Not Check1.Value
```

Then b as expected will contain True if the checkbox is checked and False if the checkbox is unchecked. What do you think c will contain? (Clue: always True. No, really.)

**12.** *The four magic constants of the apocalypse:* Nothing, Null, Empty, and Error.

**12.5** *The stupid editor*, which by default will put up a whining dialog if you try to leave a line which it recognises as syntactically incorrect. Like when you leave an incomplete line temporarily to go and copy a long identifier into the clipboard, for example.

**12.7** *The stupid compiler*, which by default does a "compile" so superficial that you can get *runtime* errors caused by an If missing its End If.

**12.8** *Procedures, sorry "subs," can be declared* Public, Private, *or* Static. Two points to anybody who correctly guesses what Static does. Three points to anybody who can suggest a sane use for it.

**13.** *Bill is making even more money out of this.* And I am powerless to stop him. In fact I am helping him.

*(Next week: Java. Verity Stob is currently appearing as a troll in every single tiresome religious discussion about languages on Usenet.)*

# Claire's Story and Other Tragedies

### GARBAGE COLLECTION

Our careless C++ girl Claire
Bashed out her brains upon the stair.
Java Johnson found her dead.
His emailed message quickly spread:
"The prospects for the build look bleak,
Claire's got another memory leak."

### KINDNESS TO ANIMALS

Because he was an ignorant lout
The VB sub's eyes I punched out.
And when he dared to squawk once more
I killed him with a monitor.
My manager was firm with me:
"Next time don't use TFT."

### FAMOUS USENET THREAD SUMMARISED

On Usenet a young Finn named Linus
Got involved in a flamefest most heinous.
Prof Tanenbaum howled:
"You're ambiguously voweled
So I'm awarding your OS B-minus."

SINGLE SCOTCH LAMENT

O Lara, wi' untim'rous breastie,
Thou gorgeous virtual Sassenach,
I'd fain nae leave thy tomb unraided.
Alas! Nae version 4 for Mac!


PRECEDENTS

One steamy day at NASA, whence they send ships to the stars,
They were cutting Ada modules for a stab at planet Mars.
Now Randy was a new guy, fresh transferred from Hubble,
And at the crucial moment he had some finger trouble.

He poured gallons in his litres, he stood metres on his feet,
He pressed pascals in his psi, he mixed them up a treat.
So when the probe descended retro thrust was immaterial,
Just because our Rand mixed SI units with imperial.

*And the coloured girls go:*
*ISO, ISO, ISO 9000.*
*ISO, ISO, ISO 9000.*

Charles Babbage was a proto nerd, lived in the age of steam,
To build a difference engine was his enduring dream.
With Ada Lovelace, cyber chick, he sought his powers to double,
But at the crucial moment they experienced finger trouble.

Charlie asked her "Ready babe?" and Ada called back "Yes."
But as he turned the handle, the gearing snagged her dress.
Her crinolines were pulled half off, her ankles were uncovered.
Poor Charlie had a mental fit and never quite recovered.

*And the coloured girls go . . .*

There was a certain Doctor, you all know who I mean,
Who travelled throughout time and space upon the smaller screen.
He'd always land in quarries and must scrabble through the
                                                        rubble,
For when he'd dematerialised he'd get some finger trouble.

He'd lean back on the console and he'd say "Hey Sarah Jane!
"I know I promised beaches but I've bungled it again.
"The co-ordinates were upside down, it's entirely the wrong globe
                                                                    here.
"It's Metebelis III outside—do you get arachnophobia?"

*And the coloured girls go . . .*

When I got in this morning the file server was crawling.
A D-I-R took 30 secs, response was quite appalling.
I logged in at the console, my efforts to redouble,
You will have guessed what happened next: I had some finger
                                                                    trouble.

While I was in Explorer, due to unknown forces,
I accidentally pressed Delete and wiped out all the sources.
The backup is unreadable. Now before you get demented,
Recall that, though disastrous, this is not unprecedented.

*And the coloured girls go:*
*ISO, ISO, ISO 9000.*
*ISO, ISO, ISO 9000.*
*ISO, ISO, ISO 9000.*
*ISO, ISO, ISO 9000.*
*[Tenor sax solo]*

Verity Stob apologises to Harry Graham, Lenny the Limerick, Robert Burns, and Lou Reed
for pilfering their styles. And thanks Katie B. and Mike P., for contributing the ISO 9000
chorus, a rare comfort in times of Audit.

# Down the Pole

*"'I can see a slow trend of Visual C++ developers moving to Visual Basic,' said Cameron Michaelson, software engineer for Micron Technology Inc." according to a ZDNet report. Surprisingly, Ms. Stob has seen this phenomenon too.*

Blenkins was the first to go.

Maybe I could have saved him. I spotted the first signs, but I thought nothing of it at the time. One never does, does one?

We were standing outside the dome, he and I, during a rec break. No, not that dome. The dome that was British Antarctica Base 4. Our company had moved all its C++ programming contractors out here—it had turned out that this was very IR35-efficient, although endless polar days had upset our internal body clocks; most people tended to revert to the 1950s. We were soaking up a few feeble rays of the never-setting sun, and chatting and joking about the many circular blue plaques that adorn the entrance airlock in honour of past visiting celebrities: Michael Palin, Scully and Mulder, The Thing from Another World. It was towards the end of summer, a sweltering –20° C, but even in fur-lined anoraks and Damart's finest thermals I was beginning to shiver. I was about to suggest that we went inside when Blenkins spoke up.

"Look here, Miss Stob, what's wrong with an environment that is easy?"

"It's 'Ms', if you don't mind. What do you mean?"

"Sometimes I wonder why we make it so hard for ourselves. It could all be . . . easy, and we'd be more productive too."

"I say Blenkins, are you feeling all right?"

"Well, now you mention it, I do feel a little queer. Maybe I'll go and see the MO."

"I should do that, Blenkins, if I were you."

Actually, I couldn't have saved him, even then. The kindest thing would have been to have shot him. If he had called me "Miss" again, I might have obliged.

\* \* \*

I was walking past the sick bay when Doctor Smythers stuck his head around the door.

"Would you come in here a moment, Verity? I've got something to show you."

Blenkins was in a cot, tossing and turning feverishly beneath the straps that secured him. He was muttering a strange gobbledegook.

"Global variables are not such a bad thing, they mean you can easily access data wherever you need to . . . Pointers are unnecessary. And anyway if you do need them we have them in the latest version, except for casting and arithmetic . . . Why would you want an integer type bigger than 32-bits? There's a perfectly good "long" type for that or, even better, just use floating point variables everywhere . . . Tokenisation is just as good as true compilation on fast, modern machines, and the resulting code is more compact . . . ActiveX controls, what a brilliant design . . . "

I felt myself turning pale.

"What is it Doc? Is it this 1950s thing again?"

The Doc's brow furrowed.

"No Verity. I'm afraid it's something a great deal more serious than that. But nothing for you to worry your pretty little head about. Now go make us both a cup of coffee. I need to think."

Sigourney Weaver never had this trouble.

\* \* \*

We ran around the intersection of corridor B7 and just made it into the Thermal Clothing storage area. I lobbed a hand grenade at the baying mob, and the Doc slammed and bolted the door. There was an explosion, and the shouts died down for a few seconds, but almost immediately started up again; horrible bloodthirsty cries of "There's no need to declare variables! Just use them when you need them!" and "True inheritance is for perverts!" It seemed that grenades were as ineffective as bullets.

"What are we going to do, Doc? That door won't hold for long."

The Doc was removing the grill from the ventilation shaft.

"This leads directly to the main generator in the Convenient Plot Device room. If I can get there and cut off the power, maybe we can freeze them out."

"OK, give me a leg up."

"Sorry Verity, this shaft is extremely dangerous—no place for a woman. I'll go alone."

At last this '50s thing was working in my favour.

"Fair enough. Off you go."

"I'm going out, Verity, I may be—"

"Oh get on with it!" I snapped.

*       *       *

I was standing, hands in pockets, with the pilot of the rescue helicopter as he looked around the burnt-out ruins of the dome, shaking his head in disbelief.

"There's just one thing I don't understand about this, Ms. Stob. How come you didn't get infected?"

"That's easy to answer. The thing is, I know that it's possible to build anything—even an operating system—just by dragging and dropping a few controls onto a form. No, it's all right—"

The pilot had taken a pace back in alarm.

"It's OK, I was just kidding. Now, hadn't you better go and get ready for take off? If we stay here any longer, we'll all freeze."

"OK, Ms. Stob."

As he walked away, still suspicious, I took my right hand out of my pocket and looked at it. It had grown into a hideous, misshapen claw. Useless for proper typing, but fine for grasping the mouse and clicking things . . .

# Out to Lunch

*Before she set off on her summer hols, Verity Stob was in a lyrical mood.*

### Love Poem

How do I love thee? Let me count the ways.
I love thee with my burgeoning. The fruit
Of our unwitting union shall take root
On this PC beneath thy foolish gaze.
I love thee with my pois'nous jealousy.
A cuckoo hatchling clearing out the nest,
Unslain sibling script files I detest:
Know no other VBS but me.
I love you for your naïve double clicks.
Up your virgin reg'stry my love sticks.
I love to rifle through your áddress book,
I love my half-wit slave, your bleak Outlook.
    O Lover, when you next read "I Love You,"
    Remember the old song: be sure it's true.

### README.TXT

*(Familiar riff)*

Dear Trial User, thanks for pulling this down
It's a beta really but you needn't frown.

The install is dodgy and the archive's large
It's too big for the Net but I haven't got a CD-ROM writer,
                                    CD-ROM writer.

CD-ROM writer
                        writer
                                writer

It's a *dirty* hack of a *dirty* script
With a two meg runtime, even zipped.
I'll rewrite it soon in C++
I need to steal a compiler so I've gotta get a CD-ROM writer,
                                    CD-ROM writer . . .

*(Air guitar solo)*

If you find it useful will you spread the word?
And ask for new stuff, please not too absurd.
Registration is just twenty quid
And I want the dosh 'cos I've gotta get a CD-ROM writer,
                                    CD-ROM writer . . .


## GLOOMY THOUGHTS OVER AN OLD PC

I rest my head on yours, dear,
I fiddle with your keys,
They're stiff with dirt and dead skin,
A haven for disease.
Your mouse is dead, your cover's off,
Your network card is raided.
Your "mobo" now is obsolete,
You cannot be upgraded.

When you were new, one hundred meg
Seemed really rather fast,
But now they count in gigahertz,
I fear our time has passed . . .
Some day they'll dump me too, dear,
For exactly the same cause.
Until they come to get us,
I shall rest my head on yours.

## Out to Lunch

Oh the English say the weather's English grey all year
Except for three weeks in July
When there's some "blue cloud" in the sky.
Then office workers, diligent and shirkers, cheer.
They eschew their daily Wimpy
To squeeze into something skimpy and sip beer.

But as they lock the door to go and score a tan
An irritable voice cries, "Leave that fan!"

Vampires and programmers
Stay in in the lunchtime sun.
It would be most invidious
To claim techies aren't fastidious.
Direct appeals, offers of free meals,
Won't convince them that it's done
To eat their treat from Tesco
Al fresco.
On a nearby green there's a pleasant scene
Of hilarity and snickers
'Cos an HR lass, lying on the grass,
Is showing us her knickers.
Her would-be bloke would swear fit to choke
But he's not here to stop the fun:
For vampires and programmers
Stay in in the lunchtime sun.

Vampires and programmers
Stay in in the lunchtime sun.
Our intellectual elite
Are ineffectual in heat.
Hidden in the gloom of a fetid room
Browsing Grauniad or Sun,
They waste Lunch Hour in this shelter,
And swelter.
At the Ball and Crown an accounting clown
Is getting rather merry.
Near the south car park see the sales girls lark

As they lick their Ben and Jerry. *(Who?!)*
By the cricket square romps a naughty pair
Her top has come undone.
But vampires and programmers
Stay in in the lunchtime
    In in the lunchtime
    In in the lunchtime sun!

How about that, dear boy?

Verity Stob apologises to Elizabeth Barrett Browning, Lennon and McCartney, Tom Lehrer, and Noël Coward.

## PART III

# AFTER THE APOCALYPSE
## *(2000–2004)*

*"As we emerge from the bunker and see not a world in flames, but merely several websites displaying the date as 19100 and a frantically back-pedalling Ed Yourdon . . . we have come to regret our decision to trade NTK's webserver for eight sacks of lentils."*

—*NTK, first post-millennium edition 2000-01-07*

# Two by Two

*An unwilling victim has been sucked into the Extreme Programming craze.*

*Monday.* "A lot of weather about today," observes the Breakfast TV she-forecaster, correctly. Arrive at work soaked to point of edibility, temper and climate a matching pair, to find Mike "Horatio" Nelson sitting in *my* chair, using *my* PC. Horatio, as we are not allowed to call him, is a recent recruit; pompous beyond his five-and-twenty summers with a florid complexion, spectacles, and a Pooterish moustache.

I say, "Good morning Mike. How can I help?"

He says, "I am your pair."

I say, "You are my what?"

He says, "Did you skip Friday's meeting? The company has decided to try the Extreme Programming methodology. Embrace Change! and all that."

I say, "By all means you embrace it, but at your own desk please."

He says, "Actually I think you'll find that Mr. Webster wants me here."

To the manager's office, where I enquire of Eric "Noah" Webster (we are nickname-fixated here) what the blankety-blank is Horatio doing hanging around my desk, reading my email, and babbling about XP? Noah gets embarrassed and explains that this is a new X-periment, ha-di-ho, and that he had sounded everybody out as to who should try it first and, quote, "You and Mike, Verity, seemed to be an obvious pair." Meaning: I am the dope to be sacrificed at the altar of the latest fad.

Fine.

*Wednesday*. Storm ongoing. TV news portrays gloomy family handing out hamster cage and video recorder from upper-storey bedroom window of flooded house into inexpertly rowed dinghy. I reach work late and soaked for the third time in three days, where I am still being taught the tenets of Extreme Programming by The Man Who Knows, i.e., Horatio.

Horatio is (again) reviewing one of my modules, looking for what he describes as "smelly code." He triumphantly pounces on a function called Locked, noting that this does not conform to our naming standard: it should be "IsLocked". I admit this to be strictly speaking true—if gob-smackingly pedantic—and bring up the editor's Search/Replace dialog to fix it.

But no. Horatio stops me and barges me out of the driving position. He says, "You have to get Test Infected, Verity. You should never cut any code without first writing a test."

"But Mike," I cry, "how *can* you write a test of a name change? It won't compile. This is just silly."

"No matter," he replies, wagging his index finger at me, "we are going to do this by the book."

"And what about the code in the test itself?" I ask. "Must we write code to test that as well? How shall we know when to stop?" But he is not listening.

I think I see why they call it "extreme."

*Friday*. Ongoing flooding, storms, railway/commuter mayhem. For the sake of novelty, a small tornado has devastated a caravan site on the south coast. (Query to self: why do tornados, in all sizes and in all parts of the world, invariably attack caravan sites? Are they Prince Charles-style "unspoiled countryside" snobs? Are they attracted by the smell of chemical toilets?)

Relationship with Horatio now declined to barely speaking terms, because

1. He is sitting at *my* desk, using *my* PC. He has even had the temerity to set my screen wallpaper to a picture of a blonde TV nymphet called "Muffie the teenage muffin filler" or some such,

2. He continuously whistles through his teeth/moustache the Nancy Sinatra golden oldie "These Boots Are Made for Walking," a

tune that, once it has attached itself to one's brain, sticks there unshiftably like unobserved chewing gum to an incautious backside,

3. He has spent all week "refactoring" (== playing with) my working code and we have achieved stuff-all, and

4. Cut to the chase. He uses tab characters instead of two spaces to do his code indenting.

Enough.

*Monday.* Rain throttled back to intermittent showers, floods subsiding, and I absolutely insist that we actually write some code. Horatio reluctantly agrees and offers to let me drive for once but I say "No, go on, you are the expert, show me how to do it the XP way" all wide-eyed as though I Can Easily Believe It's Not Butter wouldn't melt.

As it happens, our first task is to write a library routine to compare two variants for equality. (More difficult than it sounds: raw memory comparison won't do it because the variant is the kludged data type from hell that can contain an integer, double, string, or a multi-dimensional array of yet more variants.) I watch with interest as Horatio begins to indulge in the telltale displacement activity of the floundering programmer: declaring variables. After six hours' work, he has written three loops and a switch statement, supported by 23 variables of assorted types. This code does nothing but exercise the stack register.

How could I have forgotten the First Law of Meta-Methodology? "Evangelists of new techniques often get that way because they can't write code for toffee."

*Tuesday.* A clear sky at last, TV news switched from tragedy to comedy: the US presidential election. I get in early, delete Horatio's doodling, and bang in a neat little recursive routine that I worked out privately yesterday. This not only compiles first off, it even passes the test infection Horatio had prepared for it.

When he finally arrives, Horatio is predictably baffled. "But how can a function call itself?" he whines.

"There are more things in heaven and earth, Horatio, than are dreamt of in your philosophy," I reply, yielding to temptation and blowing Muffie a kiss.

At lunchtime I make the most of the November sunshine and head off to Sainsbury's for a mega grocery shop. On return I find Noah and Horatio standing by my desk. Says Noah, "I've asked Mike to help out in tech support for a while, so I'm afraid you'll have to press on with XP on your own."

I trawl my purchases, seeking a moment-encapsulating symbol.

"Here you are, Mike," I say. "Have an olive."

[This article appeared during the chad-dimpling crisis that soured the US presidential elections in 2000.]

———

# Big Iron Age Man

*When we heard that Dick Loop-Invariant, the final working example of the "old school" of mainframe programmers, was due to be switched off for the last time, we realised that it was imperative to send out Verity Stob to interview him . . .*

**Verity Stob: Dick, it's great to be with you today. Can you tell us something about the first machine you ever worked on?**

*Dick Loop-Invariant*: Sure. It was in the summer of '46. I was a vacuum tube monkey for a machine called the EDSELIAC MK I. You must remember that things were very primitive at the start. It was many years before the computer industry discovered the, the . . . um . . .

**VS: The transistor?**

*DL-I*: No, the lowercase letter. Everything was in capitals. The EDSELIAC, the AUTOTRAND, the COBLAMATIC 8, the VACUTRON VORTEX. We all had to be issued with aspirin just to be able to read the instructions for the PAPER TAPE READER. I myself was called DICK LOOP-INVARIANT until 1962, when I changed my name by converting myself to EBCIDIC.

**VS: Amazing. What was programming like in those days?**

*DL-I*: It was a much more physical, outdoorsy thing than it is now. The machine was big and unreliable, but there was always room for a bottle of beer in the air conditioning unit. I remember when the head programmer was having terrible trouble with a little subroutine to calculate the size of uranium rod required to fuel an atom-powered Buick. She got terribly agitated about it, and in the end became convinced it was a hardware problem. You may have heard of her. Her name was Grace Murray, Grace Murray . . . um . . .

**VS: Grace Murray Hopper? Grandmother of COBOL?**

*DL-I*: Grace Murray Mint, grandmother of Polo, Spear, Julep, and Kevin. So eventually she asked me to climb up into the accumulator gallery and check all the valves. Sure enough, after poking about for a few hours I found a small moth had flown across the contacts and made a short. I gave the fried insect to Grace, and she taped it into her coding journal.

**VS: That, I suppose, was how the term "de-insecting a program" came into popular use?**

*DL-I*: Who is being interviewed here?

**VS: Sorry. Moving on to the 1950s, then, I believe you were involved with the first commercial computers.**

*DL-I*: Indeedy. I got a job with ChemCorp's scientific division, where the backroom boys were working on a less biodegradable version of DDT. We installed an early magnetic drum machine for them. It was a weird thing: a 16.7-bit address bus, 117 words of delay line memory, you had to toggle in the front panel program by hand before you could switch it on, and all the instruction codes were expressed in base 45.

**VS: Despite these difficulties you were able to do useful work? I guess this is where you get to tell us about the miracles of algorithmic ingenuity you managed to pack into a miserable few dozen bytes?**

*DL-I*: Don't be absurd. The machine was entirely unprogrammable. It couldn't even play a decent game of Nim.

**VS: Oh. Wasn't this disastrous for you?**

*DL-I*: Nobody seemed to mind very much. For one thing, you could keep a whole crate of beer cool in its air conditioning unit. And for another, it had wonderful tape drives, with huge tape reels that used to twitch round in a rather sinister way. Executives used to love to come and be filmed standing in front of them spouting nonsense about "electronic brains." Or simply watch them moving. Think kitten in front of washing machine. In those days it didn't much matter what the machine did, provided it Gave Good Tape. Just as a modern website must Give Good Flash.

Talking of I/O and peripherals, I'm reminded of something amusing that happened later on. We used to boot up our System/360 using a whole tray of punched cards. Of course, every time we punched a card, tiny little bits of cardboard would accumulate in a tray beneath the hopper . . .

**VS: I'm afraid I'm going to have to interrupt you there, Dick. I must warn you that I am instructed by the Editor to shoot you if you should mention the word "chad."**

*DL-I*: But the whole anecdote depends on that. Can't I say it just the once?

**VS: I'm sorry, but he was extremely clear on this point.**

*DL-I*: As you wish. At about that time, in the 1960s, I was lucky enough to work with one of the most influential figures in software development, Frederick P., Frederick P., um . . .

**VS: [Silence]**

*DL-I*: A little help?

**VS: Oh very well. Frederick P. Brooks, author of *The Mythical Man-Month*?**

*DL-I*: No, Frederick P. Coredump, author of *Twenty-Five Amusing Things to So with an 8-inch Floppy Disk at an Office Party*. Actually, our Fred was something of a critic of Brooks' work. He strongly felt that Brooks had skimped on the business of gathering experimental evidence, especially in respect of it supposedly not being possible for nine women, working simultaneously, to produce a baby in one month.

**VS: Has Coredump been released from prison yet?**

*DL-I*: I believe he is still paying his debt to society. Then came the 1970s, absolutely the best time to be in programming. Machines as big as a building, in some cases as big as a medium-sized village. Like when I was using a Kray-Twins Super Computer. I was working for the tobacco giant Fold, Spindle, and Mutilate at the time, where they were researching a method of increasing the satisfying tarriness of tobacco smoke, to give it more body. They needed the most powerful number-crunching facility available to model a cough. Over 27,000 separate vectors, you know.

This K-T was some computer. It ran so hot, they had to cool it by—

**VS:—by pumping beer over the circuit boards?**

*DL-I*: Don't be silly. We had to use pure alcohol, or vodka martini at the very least. Those were the days. People had to come and beg, on their knees, if they wanted us to change a program. Software engineers got the respect they deserved.

**VS: And then, of course, the microprocessor arrived.**

*DL-I*: The what?

["Postcard from St. Petersburg" refers to an incident in late 2000, when hackers operating from St. Petersburg, Russia, used the QAZ virus to penetrate Microsoft corporate network. The hackers were able to access source code, and went undetected for some months. Microsoft eventually called in the FBI.

There was much speculation at the time that the Ruski miscreants might have planted deliberate bugs or logic bombs in Microsoft's code base. Of course, we now know that that didn't happen.

Oh yes.

This was also the unhappy time that mean old Judge Jackson of the US Justice Department was muttering about having Microsoft broken in two and sold for scrap . . . although even then this somehow didn't seem very likely . . . ]

---

# Just William

*Although it is the world's biggest software company, there are comparatively few celebrations of Microsoft and its products in verse. Verity Stob is perversely determined to put this right.*

Postcard from St. Petersburg

They're fixing their firewalls down Microsoft Way—
Mikhail Asanovich hacked in with Sergei.
Got in via home workers infected with QAZ.
"You'd think they'd do better than V90 RAS,"
Says Sergei.

They're fixing their firewalls down Microsoft Way—
Mikhail Asanovich hacked in with Sergei.
They l0phtcracked the passwords to reach the disk shares.
"Our Microsoft comrades are all dirty mares,"
$\qquad\qquad\qquad\qquad\qquad$ Says Sergei.

They're fixing their firewalls down Microsoft Way—
Mikhail Asanovich hacked in with Sergei.
Stole the source code to Access, and Back Office too.
"It just won't compile below Warn Level 2,"
$\qquad\qquad\qquad\qquad\qquad$ Says Sergei.

They're fixing their firewalls down Microsoft Way—
Mikhail Asanovich hacked in with Sergei.
The naming of variables attracted attention.
"In Russia we're calling this "Yankee Convention,""
$\qquad\qquad\qquad\qquad\qquad$ Says Sergei.

They're fixing their firewalls down Microsoft Way—
Mikhail Asanovich hacked in with Sergei.
The Feds got involved to Sergei's surprise,
"Smiert Spionam! Death to all Spies!"
$\qquad\qquad\qquad\qquad\qquad$ Says Sergei.

They're fixing their firewalls down Microsoft Way—
Mikhail Asanovich hacked in with Sergei.
Microsoft claims it averted the worst,
"But I shouldn't run Whistler on April the first,"
$\qquad\qquad\qquad\qquad\qquad$ Says Sergei.


VAUDEVILLE SONG

[*A pierrette sings:*]

My dear old PC's not the latest model.
We've been together four years and a day.
Its Windows folder's choked with crummy DLLs,
Its registry is all in disarray.
Said Dave: "You should upgrade it to 2000."
He went and fetched a pretty silver disc.
"It won't be a chore," cried he, as I stuck it in the drawer,
"A modern installation's without risk."

But now:

How can I bust it more than it is busted?
I was doing very well 'til I got flustered.
I guessed a setting "DHCP"; now I'm sure it's "static,"
From the moment that I made that choice, my PC got erratic.
Each time I look Explorer has abended.
The bloody thing now blue-screens unattended.
So I feel sick,
Please tell me quick,
If you've already sussed it.
For I mustn't bust it more than it is busted!

How can I bust it more than it is busted?
It's almost as if Win 2K has rusted.
I thought I saw the network once, but now it's gone away.
My PC has embarked upon a spiral of decay.
The noises from its soundcard come out fuzzy,
Last reboot Baby failed to find its SCSI! (Eeek!)
I'm going to cry.
I can't deny—
This should be done and dusted.
How did I bust it more than it was busted?

[*The company:*]

How could she bust it more than it was busted?
We suspect the CMOS mem'ry's ill-adjusted.
She's got a bunch of ISA cards with unknown Aye Are Queues.
Oh no! She's pulled the cover off! Look out! She'll blow a fuse!
We warned her that her efforts would be thwarted:
It happens that her mobo's not supported.
The silly bint
Won't take a hint,
Frankly we're disgusted.
How could she bust it more than it was busted?

As a techie Verity won't cut the mustard.
How could she bust it more than it was busted?

## Superego

My Desktop, My Documents,
My Network Places,
Computers Near Me.
My Faxes, My Favorites,
My Company Information.
My Outline, My Webs,
My Current Home Page,
My Pictures, My Preferences,
My Music, My Info,
My Computer Management Module,
My Computer,
**WINDOWS ME!**

## Appeal

Don't let's be beastly to Microsoft
If they must swallow the DOJ's bitter pill.
Though some of their business practices cause anger and dismay,
It's just their boyish enthusiasm carries them away.
We'll give our bucks to them
And explain the very crux to them:
The slightest thought of Netscape makes us ill.
We'll check we're licensed properly
To help preserve monopoly,
But don't let's be beastly to old Bill.

Don't let's be beastly to Microsoft
For life on the bleeding edge is all uphill.
Pity those poor C-sharpers, all worked up in a lather:
Eight manuals to be written but they mustn't mention "Java."
We'll toil for them
And burn the midnight oil for them—
It's always a pleasure to pick up another skill.
We'll flush our C code down the drain,
Start over in "D flat" again,
But don't let's be beastly to old Bill.

Don't let's be beastly to Microsoft
'Cos all its publications are a thrill.
We simply cannot think how MSJ could be made grander:
It surely wasn't us that called it "dreary propaganda."
It's very hard for them
And daily life is marred for them
If lots of people keep saying that Linux is brill.
We'll chuck those CDs in the bin—
They're Greek gifts from that naughty Finn—
But don't let's be beastly to old Bill.

Verity Stob wishes to apologise to A. A. Milne for "Postcard from St. Petersburg" (from "Buckingham Palace") and to Noël Coward for "Appeal" (from "Don't Let's Be Beastly to the Germans").

# Downwards and Backwards with Dotdotdot

*Verity Stob considers the stuff that matters.*

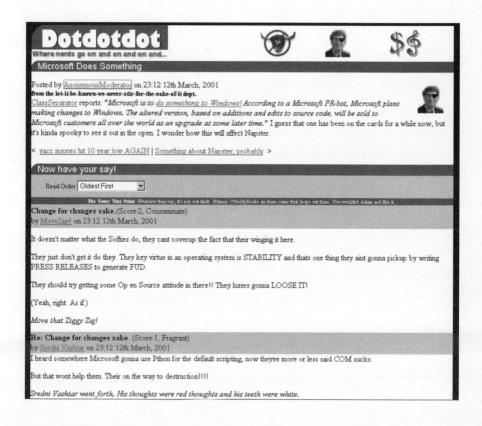

**Crippled** (Score:2, Redolent)
by SnarkleF on 23:12 12th March, 2001

My mom had Windows at work and it hurt her eyes real bad

**Re: Change for changes sake** (Score:0, Spontaneous)
by womble_uncle_orinoco on 23:12 12th March, 2001

wouldn't it be kewl if we all clubbed together and did our own version of windows?

i'm not a programmer, but i know lots of them and since windows is so bad it cant be so hard to make our own and then we could open source it and then what would they do.

i'd love to help with the beta testing. now i've got a spare pc because danny has left and i've got her pc in my bedroom. its a p90 but that wont matter because it will be soooh much better without those dumb softies writing it.

we could call it 'blue hat windows'. :-)

**Theft** (Score:3, Allegorical)
by MoveZig4 on 23:12 12th March, 2001

> I heard somewhere Microsoft gonna use Pthon for the default scripting

Yeah, right. And then their gonna change it and then their gonna add features to it and then their gonna P8ENT it.

COS THAT'S THE WAY THEY WORK.

Doesn't everynody realise by now?

*Move that Ziggy Zig!*

**Re: Crippled** (Score:2, Catalytic)
by MouseballCleanser on 23:12 12th March, 2001

> My mom had Windows at work and it hurt her eyes real bad

Thatz kewl, but wheres the "All Your Base" reference?

Somebody set up you the bomb! Not you get signal! It's you!

*MbC*

**Re: Change for changes sake** (Score:2, Intrinsic)
by Sredni Vashtar on 23:12 12th March, 2001

> > I heard somewhere Microsoft gonna use Pthon for the default scripting

> Yeah, right.

Actually, I miswrote. Actually it was 'Their going to give up COM for C#, now that COM sucks'.

Sorry

*Sredni Vashtar went forth, His thoughts were red thoughts and his teeth were white.*

**Re: Change for changes sake** (Score:3, Catatonic)
by Magnus Anderson on 23:12 12th March, 2001
> > I heard somewhere Microsoft gonna use Pthon for the default scripting

It their very own fault for the disputing with Sun. It better they use Java. Here we are using Java since three years ago. We not only using Java for the programmer increase (though we are: maybe ten times, maybe twenty times) we also now use it for everything from the commanding line stuff such as grep through to the web engine beans. Same speed C but faster. The security we are finding, and with the IDE too (Borland or IBM). Portability of course is of the deal.

-- Magnus

**First** (Score:2 , Serendipitous)
by ForJustGreatness on 23:12 12th March, 2001

Am I the 1st person in this thread to say 'script-kiddy'? I think I am.

*For Just Greatness!*

**Re: It better they use Java.** (Score:3, Contemporary)
by MouseballCleanser on 23:12 12th March, 2001

Magnus.Anderson wrote:

> It their very own fault for the disputing with Sun. It better they use Java.

Kewl! Even better than all your base!! New cult alert!

*MbC*

*'Same speed C but faster'*

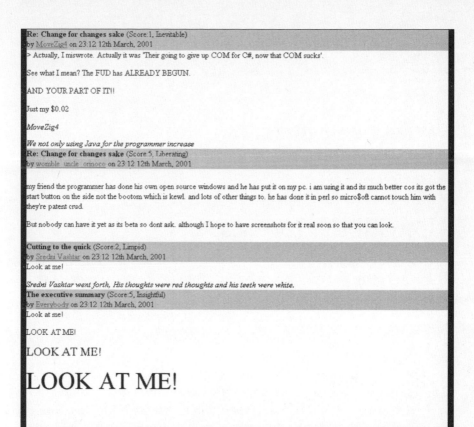

**Re: Change for changes sake** (Score:1, Inevitable)
by MoveZig4 on 23:12 12th March, 2001

> Actually, I miswrote. Actually it was 'Their going to give up COM for C#, now that COM sucks'.

See what I mean? The FUD has ALREADY BEGUN.

AND YOUR PART OF IT!!

Just my $0.02

MoveZig4

*We not only using Java for the programmer increase*

**Re: Change for changes sake** (Score:5, Liberating)
by womble_uncle_orinoco on 23:12 12th March, 2001

my friend the programmer has done his own open source windows and he has put it on my pc. i am using it and its much better cos its got the start button on the side not the bootom which is kewl. and lots of other things to. he has done it in perl so micro$oft cannot touch him with they're patent crud.

But nobody can have it yet as its beta so dont ask. although I hope to have screenshots for it real soon so that you can look.

**Cutting to the quick** (Score:2, Limpid)
by Sredni Vashtar on 23:12 12th March, 2001
Look at me!

*Sredni Vashtar went forth, His thoughts were red thoughts and his teeth were white.*

**The executive summary** (Score:5, Insightful)
by Everybody on 23:12 12th March, 2001
Look at me!

LOOK AT ME!

LOOK AT ME!

# LOOK AT ME!

---

# Up with the Joneses

*Verity Stob wonders what all the fuss is about* Bridget Jones's Diary. *It doesn't seem significantly different from her own experience of thirty-something single female life.*

## MONDAY 7 MAY

*Thousands of lines of code written 0.003, number of compilations started because couldn't think of anything else to do 43 (poor), number of times composed witty flirtatious emails to gorgeous programmer called Ben 5, number of said emails actually sent 0 (v.g. as don't want to expose oneself to Claire Swire-style humiliation, though obviously my content much, much tamer. "Relationship" between him and me based on me saying "hello" twice and him smiling back once while queuing for coffee), number of coffees 12 (n.v.g.).*

**9:40 am.** Arrive at work. Really must get down to it today. Am on 5-day assignment to do little data entry module, have so far used up 2.5 days devising name of modules and making one Delphi form.

**9:45 am.** Will just check emails and get a coffee. Must have coffee in brain to start day.

**9:55 am.** He's not there.

**10:15 am.** Still not there.

**10:25 am.** Gaah! Returning to my office with fourth coffee find hateful, snooty manager Louise standing by desk, hands on hips.

"How is the data module coming along, Verity?"

"Oh, oh it's fine. Nearly there in fact."

Why must I always adopt a silly singsong voice when lying? I try to ease myself between Louise and my screen so that a) she can't see that I haven't even started up Delphi yet and b) have three half-written and unsendable e's to Ben up in emailer.

"Good, because it's on the critical path. Will you be able to demo the form tomorrow morning?"

"Of course, Louise. You can see it now if you like." Reckless bluff!

"No, tomorrow will be soon enough. I'll be bringing around the liaison programmers from database team. Nine-twenty all right?"

She marches out without waiting for reply.

Grrr. Control helpless helplessness by remembering what best girl-friend Val said after meeting Louise in All Bar One: "She's the sort of person who owns one of those rubber gizmos for resealing open bottles of wine and," Val pulls mega sarcastic face and fills voice with contempt, "*actually uses it.*"

Cheered by this reminder of Louise's obsessive parsimony, albeit theoretical.

Uncheered when reflect that alternative possible reading of non-incident is that Val and self are hopeless alcoholics.

**5:15 pm.** In between beverage and consequential loo breaks have got the form looking really nice now. While looking on web for component found *Feng Shui* page. Have redesigned form on *Feng Shui* principles so that data (*Chi*) will flow harmoniously from punter to database. Tab order of nine edit fields adjusted to form *Lo Shu* magic square. The whole coloured pink, and put "Ok" button in South West corner to improve romantic prospects.

Talking of which, time for a last coffee of the day.

**5:19 pm.** Bah! Has he given up coffee or something?

**5:25 pm.** Oooh, oooh, email! Could it be . . . ?

No it couldn't. Circular message to everybody reminding those who haven't already to change their passwords, otherwise network manager will expire account and will have to beg to get back into computer. Password must be at least 10 characters long and contain both alphas and numerics.

Changed password from "HateL0u1se" to "Ben1sL0vely" and so off home, another day's work done.

# TUESDAY 8 MAY

*KLOCs 0.087 (better), emails drafted to Ben 8 (bad), emails actually sent to Ben 2 (good, because now have* bona fide *excuse), number of times spoke to Ben properly 3, number of times life saved by Ben 1, or 2 if include metaphorical life saving.*

**9:25 am.** Whole cabal of people in my office when I get in: bloody Louise, bloody bloody Peter Thing the-horrid-database-expert-and-lech who stores procedures and squeezes in lift and, sitting at my PC,

Ben!!!

Must have stood there with jaw in goldfish position until Louise says, "Here you are at last Verity! Do come on, we haven't got all day, tell Ben your password while you take your coat off, so we can log in."

Moment of wild panic.

"Um, it was 'passw0rd', lowercase and spelled with a 0."

Hopeless. They all turn and look at me.

"Don't be silly, Verity, apart from being a magnificently stupid choice even for you, that's only eight letters long," said Louise.

"You dirty minx! Verity's got a dirty password! Verity's got a dirty password!" cries horrid Peter-the-lech.

Feel self go pink.

Ben clears his throat. "Isn't it against security procedure for Verity to tell us her password?"

He gets up from my chair, ushering me into driving position with friendly arm on shoulder and (I later realise) interposing his body between Peter and me so Peter can't Hal 9000 my password as I type.

Mmmmmm. My chair is *warm* from Ben.

Louise says, "Do you think you could see your way to showing us your program now?"

**10:40 am.** They've gone, thank God. Am under strict instructions from Louise to remove pink and other *Feng Shui* elements from form. Even Ben could not support me on this because (as is well known) men, and especially programming men, do not understand about *Feng Shui*.

However otherwise demonstration a success, and Louise told me I am to deal directly with Ben to get module finished.

Yusssss!

**1:17 pm.** Sitting in park eating Marks-and-Sparks green salad, gazing into space and fantasising about setting up cosy two-person software love nest house, with Him doing all hard class hierarchy and database stuff and Her, or rather Me, producing pink forms and/or pink babies.

A voice says: "Hi Verity! Do you mind if we share the bench?"

It is Ben.

I inhale an olive and spring up, choking. Salad falls off lap onto grass.

"Ugh! Ugh! Urgh!"

Ben assesses situation in 3 clock cycles at 2 GHz, leaps forward and thumps me on back. Olive is ejected at velocity, startling pigeon. I sit back down on bench, coughing and blinking and feeling like a complete fool.

"Are you OK?" Ben seems to be suppressing mirth. Hmph.

**2:40 pm.** Talked with Ben all the way through lunch (hurrah!), except somehow we ended up talking about programming languages. (Gaah! Why? How did this happen? Wish was non-programmer like Val, so that could prevent technical conversation by claiming ignorance.) It turns out that Ben is really into something called Python that is going to replace all the old languages.

Had just about got subject away from computers and around to point where could sort of semi-ask him about love life situation when he looks at watch as says, "Christ! Look at the time!" and we run back to the office.

**3:45 pm.** Made some progress with code that supports my no-longer-pink form.

**3:50 pm.** Of course, half the problem here is that I am writing in Pascal. It's really holding me back. Would do much better if writing application in modern, dynamically typed, object-oriented scripting language. May point this out to Louise.

**4 pm.** Louise v. unsympathetic to proposal to rewrite data entry module in Python.

"For God's sake Verity, pull your finger out and get on with it."

Cow. Reintroduce *Feng Shui* tab ordering.

**5:20 pm.** He's e'd me. He's emailed me! He's asked me to come down the Personal Organiser & Firkin with his mates!!!

**7.23 pm.** Still at pub. Am only female in group of seven. Ben is talking to Jim about Python, and has been for two hours. He has looked at me twice since we got here. Most of the others are talking about work or football. Nobody is talking to me about anything. I must be invisible, or hideous, or both.

Could do with some moral support. Ring up Val on mobile, to see if she can come down. Val answers in a whisper, and is furious. Forgot Val is on posh night out with rich estate agent, going to Shakespeare, and had pre-arranged to maintain radio silence barring emergencies. Have just rung Val in stalls during Hamlet's father's ghost.

Could do with another large dry white. Will offer to get in round, and get Ben to carry the drinks.

**7:30 pm.** Bloody hell! Round comes to over twenty quid! Must stay now, to get money's worth.

**10:15 pm.** Blurry Ben shtill ignorinme stopsh wickering bout lang-widje Pyefon, star-red tor kabout blurry *Monnie* Pyefon. Thall do blurry parrosketch!

**10:25 pm.** Srow up in ladiesh. Shink now I'll av liddle shleep, now till I'm burr.


# WEDNESDAY 9 MAY

**3:04 am.** Gaah!

**3:06 am.** Grope around flat to kitchen and drink pint of water, feeling for clean glass and taps without turning on light. Dip arm in cold, greasy leftover washing-up water.

Remember ignominious end to evening. Discovered asleep in Ladies by shooing-out barmaid. Luckily Ben, having ignored me all evening, at last readopts knight-in-shining-armour role, and calls me a cab. Which he also prepays for, as purse empty following ruinous round of drinks.

**3:31 am.** And I'm sure I could have swung it, if I had just bought an O'Reilly book on Python. Presumably he now thinks of me as a drunken sot. Another chance blown then. Another failure, just like the previous 23 attempts.

Time for an all ports appeal. It seems to me yet another software crisis looms. Unless the cream of the first microcomputer programming generation, i.e., the likes of Ben and me, can get it together, then the key programming chromosomes will all be lost to the gene pool.

Programmers of the world. Put aside your Python scripting languages and your VmWare-loaded-Linuxes and your pre-release C# distributions. Time is against us. You know what your duty is. Do it!

*Personal note #1: One thousand apologies to Helen Fielding.*

*Personal note #2: Thanks to Kevlin Henney for the suggestion, and SI-P for plotting suggestions and encouragement.*

# Wherever He Goes

*"Anders Hejlsberg could go anywhere, work on anything" claims a
Microsoft banner ad boldly. Anywhere?*

"That's a funny sort of name," said the assistant director of IT, squinting sideways at the résumé. "Got a 'J' in an odd place. I wonder how
you are supposed to pronounce it? Hedge-berg? Hoojul-berg?"

"Ah, that'll be a Scandinavian then," said the head of personnel (for
it was a rather old-fashioned and reactionary financial institution, and
the personnel department was fighting a rearguard action against being
turned into mere "human resources"). "Sophie and me had two weeks
in Sweden last year," he added, by way of explaining away such an
embarrassment of expertise.

The Token Actual Techie, who had been extracted against his will
from his PC-filled den and made to sit in as the third member of the hir-
ing tribunal, stirred. The better to address his suited colleagues, he
stopped gazing out of the boardroom window over the city of London
below and—a great concession this—ceased foraging in his starboard
ear with a Palm Pilot stylus. "Wossiz name again?"

The head of personnel told him.

The TAT looked thoughtful. "Think I've heard of him. Isn't he
something to do with an uncertainty?"

"No, you're thinking of the atomic cat-in-box man," said the head
of personnel. "Anyway, that guy is some sort of boffin, and I think he's
dead. I don't see him applying for a programming job at Lost Bearings
Bank."

"I don't know," said the assistant director of IT, darkly. "The amount of money you made me offer, I wouldn't be surprised if King Bloody Arthur himself returned from his 1500 year sojourn to apply, claiming expertise in Web security strategies."

"Now come on Dennis," said the head of personnel, "we've been all round this a hundred times. If you want top people—and God knows we need them right now—you have got to pay top dollar."

"It's all very well you saying that, it's not your budget. Yes, yes, all right. Let's get on. I take it he has the usual qualifications? All the Oracle stuff?"

"You mean Shiny Suit Level 2?" muttered the TAT rebelliously. He had resumed the search of his aural ducts and was now wiping his stylus on the sleeve of his XXXL *The Matrix Inverted* T-shirt. If the language of clothes was to be believed, his probing had not gone unrewarded, nor had it been the first such investigation since the last washday.

The head of personnel, watching with helpless fascination, swallowed involuntarily and then redirected his attention to the CV. "Well no, according to this he hasn't got any qualifications like that."

"A chancer. We're wasting time. Next, please!" said the assistant director of IT.

"Well hold on a moment, Dennis. He does come very, *very* highly recommended by the agency. Apparently he wrote a compiler back in the 1980s, using assembly language."

The TAT's interest quickened. "A compiler in assembler eh? Does it say which machine? The BBC B? Or the Commodore 64? I was a pretty dab hand at 6502. I wrote a pretty neat compiler myself for the 64. It was this kind of macro language that let you set up sprites . . . "

"And he is a great expert in Pascal . . . " said the head of personnel, inserting a hasty EOF in the reminiscence stream.

The TAT's interest turned to disappointment. "You what? I thought you said he was hard. Next thing you'll be telling me he wears floral underwear. Or that he spent two years programming in Java."

"Actually . . . " said the head of personnel.

"So where is he working now?" interrupted the assistant director if IT, with the air of a man getting to the bottom of the matter.

The head of personnel explained.

"He's a Microsoftee! You want to employ a Borg?" screamed the TAT.

The assistant director of IT seemed to share his apprehensions. "An ex-Microsoft bloke! Hell's bells! No way! Absolutely no way!"

"He'd want to keep switching to the Microsoft API *du jour*—we'd never get a project finished!" said the TAT, showing an uncharacteristic interest in productivity.

"We could never be at ease with him," added the assistant director of IT. "He'd be wandering around the building in his lunch break, counting how many copies of Word we had running."

The head of personnel looked at the suddenly united representatives of the IT department and sighed. "Very well. It's you gentlemen that would have to work with him. Let's pass on to the next candidate." He dropped the CV on top of the "No" pile and picked up a fresh one.

"Funny name,, said the assistant director of IT, twisting round to read it. "Got a 'J' in an odd place. How are you supposed to pronounce it? Bee-yarny? Burr-jarn?"

"That'll be another Scandinavian," said the head of personnel.

# The Devil's Netiquette

*The FAQ-from-Hell that They tried to suppress.*

THE DEVIL'S NETIQUETTE

Now this is the Law of the Newsgroups; from alt through to comp
  hear it throb.
And those who obey it may prosper; the rest shall be hurled to the
  mob.

"It is cruel to mock the afflicted." The comedian's old motto is
  true.
But it's fun! So let fly with your napalm when dim@AOL posts:
  "ME TOO!"

Don't stint when you quote. Use the whole thread. And, should
  you encounter protesting,
Remember the wise words of Linus. "Time for some serious
  flamefesting!"

Never give way in a flame war. Keep fighting whatever the cost.
When your foe calls you "fascist" he's losing; when your foe calls
  you "Hitler" he's lost.

By all means post he's a "bastard," and seek to imply he's insane.
But be sure to sign off with a smiley ;-) to make things all lovely
  again.

The greatest one-liner stales quickly. Even quicker the unfunny dig.
If you find something rotten and cloying, there's the joke to include
  in your sig.

You'll not make a pull in a newsgroup. That girl's just a tease, you
  will see.
Never send to know for whom the belle trolls. My friend: she trolls
  for thee.

The FAQ is both for and by wusses. When sent to it, real netters
  scoff.
So what if the question's familiar? Tell the FAQuers just where they
  FAQ off.

It's your birthright to wander off-topic. Who cares about signal-to-
  noise?
Those lamers, those self-proclaimed net cops, must remember that
  boys will be boys.

It's your birthright to use up that bandwidth. Pour scorn both on
  dull and on clever.
As long as you're online with Outlook, it's September for ever and
  ever.

Now this is the Law of the Newsgroups; from alt through to comp
  hear it throb.
And those who obey it may prosper; the rest shall be hurled to the
  mob.


## How Infant Techies Learn to Back-Count

Four brand new screwdrivers.
*My* own set. Not freebies.
"Fingers" Geoff got in my desk
And fourbies became threebies.

Three surviving screwdrivers.
Kept them hid. But then:
I lent one to a customer
Who cut me down to $10_2$.

My non-breeding pair of screwdrivers
Can still give me a tingle.
I poked one through a PSU
And thereby scored a single.

When the last, lonely screwdriver
Snapped, I thought: "We're done."
Then Geoffrey brought my crosshead back
And proved there's always one.

## SONNET TO A COELACANTH

Our Janine's Dad is old and stubborn too:
A PC's use is quite beyond his wit.
So for a birthday gift she buys—brand new—
A typewriter. (It costs her fifty quid.)
She brings it back to work, removes the box,
And plugs it in to make quite sure it goes.
We put aside our semaphores and locks
And gather round to have a quiet nose.
A youngish colleague, craning forward, cries
"It's QWERTY!" Well, what else did he expect?
I show the carriage; where the paper slides.
He looks at me with something like respect.
    He's seen a fossil come to life from cold.
    And I am twenty million seasons old.

## ASSEMBLER PROGRAMMER'S SONG

The devotees of Python are not fickle,
Nor are those who treasure Ruby and Perl.
There are Java-ites, and fanciers of Tcl,*
Pascal makes C-lings' lips curl.

But all this is much too high-level
For an old-fashioned craftsman like me.
I code in God's own Assembler
For its macro-ised maturity.

---

*"Tcl" is pronounced "tickle." Yes I know YOU knew that. This is in case the poetry standards inspector drops by.

It may not be garbage-collected.
It's as portable as old London Bridge.
But don't you coldly reject it
It's the language they used in your fridge,

Where . . .

*(Chorus)*

Every bit is sacred,
Every bit is right.
If a bit is wasted
I can't sleep at night.

Every bit is gorgeous,
Every bit is free.
Admire the shape it forges
In hex and BCD!

Delphi, C#, Basic
Waste bytes through sheer neglect.
I must have a tool that
Treats each bit with respect.

Every bit is special,
Every bit gets sick.
Coddle each dear rascal
And maybe it won't stick.

Careful you don't squash them
When you load your debugger.
It's me you must account to
The radical bit-hugger.

Every bit is sacred,
Every bit is right.
If a bit is wasted
I can't sleep at night.

Verity Stob wishes to apologise to Rudyard Kipling ("The Law of the Jungle"), Anonymous ("Ten Green Bottles" and its non-PC variants), and to Pythons Michael Palin and Terry Jones ("Every Sperm Is Sacred") whose fine work she has given a mugging it did not deserve.

# At the Tomb of the IUnknown Interface

*With .NET trundling down the Windows runway, it is time to make a farewell to COM. Verity Stob is strangely dry-eyed.*

Many fellow Windows programmers will have gathered that COM will not be coming with us into the C-Sharped world of .NET. Of course, COM will have a longish half-life of decay. COM objects will be supported in .NET—just as 16-bit programs are supported under 32-bit Windows. Technically permissible, but one is not encouraged to mix very much in public.

COM is scuppered and will be allowed to sink below the waves, and we must hurl our considerable library of books—each volume averaging two inches thick and costing forty medium-sized ones a pop—into the seething waters after it. Before this happens, it seemed meet and proper that we spend a few moments contemplating the about-to-depart, and savour its hard-learned idiosyncrasies one last time.

The following is mostly written from the point of view of Visual C++, for this was the tool of choice when creating a COM object. But it was a cross-language technology, so the Visual Basic, Delphi, and scripting language perspectives are covered too.

# COINITIALIZE

The call that had to precede all other COM calls:

```
HRESULT CoInitialize(
  LPVOID pvReserved  //Reserved; must be NULL
);
```

Alas. I suppose we will never learn now what `pvReserved` was reserved for. Weep a tiny tear. (Anybody who is tempted to mutter "Tiers, IDL tiers" at this point, please don't. You'll get *such* a smack.)

`CoInitialize()`, you will recall, had to be called "once and only once." They were very particular about this. Calling it exactly zero times was rewarded with that most annoying of errors "You have not called CoInitialize"—annoying because, having made so complete a diagnosis, one might have thought the underlying library could have put matters right by itself. (Yes, I am aware of `CoInitializeEx()`, but feel that multi-threaders could reasonably have been prevailed upon to make their own initialisation arrangements.)

# WHAT DO YOU WANT TO CALL ME TODAY?™

A quick quiz. Given that "OLE documents" were renamed "Active Documents," and "OLE Controls" renamed "ActiveX Controls," explain why "OLE Automation" was not renamed "Active[X] Automation." Show your working.

# ABOUT AUTOMATION

I for one still feel a thrill of excitement and surprise when Word does what I asked it to, often followed by a second thrill, of a different kind, when it abruptly stops doing so. For a long time the big problem with Automation, in my opinion, was the lack of robust and realistic examples showing what it could do—especially where Outlook was concerned. Happily this shortcoming has in recent times been addressed, and addressed in spades. Of all the script viruses, "I Love You" is still my preferred source of useful snippets for manipulating the Outlook address book, even if its author does insist on spelling mail "male." By the way, ILY also contains some good stuff demonstrating the VB file system object—I would lobby for its inclusion in MSDN, but I suppose it is too late now.

## STRUNG UP

Once upon a time there were three special COM string types: `BSTR`, `_bstr_t`, and `CComBSTR`. `BSTR` was the most straightforward: it was a typedef for a pointer to a `wchar_t`, and `wchar_t` was a typedef of a 16-bit Unicode character. Therefore `BSTR` was the Unicode equivalent of a `LPSTR`.

Ha! Got you going there. `BSTR` was no simple zero-terminated string; rather it had a secret length count and extra null terminator, and was allocated and freed with special functions. One was not supposed to know the format of its contents, and it was not obvious how you were supposed to make conversions to *proper* strings. I think you were expected to use the spooky old ANSI C function `wcstombs()`, but this seemed to break the "make no assumptions about content" rule.

But why manipulate BSTRs as pointers? Surely this was a job for a class? (OK, so COM interfaces always needed pure BSTRs, but bear with me.) The answer was "Yes, of course it was a natural for a class," which was why two were supplied. "A `_bstr_t` object," said MSDN on its `_bstr_t` page, "encapsulates the BSTR data type," whereas the entry for `CComBSTR` began "the `CComBSTR` class is a wrapper for BSTRs." Nothing in either entry to indicate which class should be preferred.

And this ignores Bruce McKinney's MSDN-bundled (and therefore officially sanctioned) 1996 article "Strings the OLE Way," where he proposed a BSTR wrapping class of his own called, ermm, `String`. That's clear then . . .

## VARIANTS, OR "WHAT DO YOU MEAN YOU WEREN'T EXPECTING A THREE-DIMENSIONAL ARRAY OF NULLS, MOTHER?"

Variants were Visual Basic creatures, really; they went hand-in-surgical-glove with the convenient ability to call a variable into existence without previously bothering to declare it. The housekeeping required to manipulate them in a language that didn't "understand" them, by which I mean C++, was frightful. Although at least you were aware of the reams of domestic code you were generating when you needed to create and initialize, say, an array of BSTR, and would thus be careful to avoid gratuitously including it in tight loops.

However, whether you used them from C++, or from a variant-sympathetic environment such as VB or Delphi or a script, you could be confident of one thing: sooner or later you'd get a runtime type error biting your ankles.

## INHERITANCE, "INTERFACE" AND "FUNCTIONAL"

Do you remember being told that not having functional inheritance, which was so frightfully dangerous, was an advantage of COM? Me too.

## STRENGTH THROUGH JOY

"The Active Template Library Makes Building Compact COM Objects a Joy"—the actual title of an MSJ article. You can probably still find this piece on MSDN if you want to check up on me. If the author was being facetious when he chose this title, I can only say that he conceals it very well. The article begins: "I love COM. COM is good. Like a fine pilsner or ale, COM never disappoints. In fact, the more I look at COM, the more I like it." Right-ho.

## IDL

As an eschewer of Java, I had accepted that I must type in the first line of my functions twice. With IDL I got to do it a third time. I could have used the Visual C++ wizard, of course—if I had been confident of completing the fields in its modal dialog letter-perfect without access to the rest of my code.

# EVERYTHING ELSE

To include: The header file of an ATL class, with its abundant macros and multiple template inheritance—what a mess! Passing exceptions across the COM boundary, the inability to do so. Rebodged [*sic*] interfaces with names ending in "2". The registry, the installation procedure, the flock of standard DLLs and EXEs, and small thunderstorm apparently necessary to breathe life into a COM object when first installed on a punter's system. GUIDs. The palaver that had to be endured to set up a callback from a COM object. Ditto to enumerate a collection. Reference-counted objects that, if one wasn't careful, lived forever like the kids from *Fame*—notwithstanding the desirability of their mortality. DCOM security, or "I can sometimes make it work if I log on everywhere as Admin and start a copy of the EXE on the remote."

Dear COM, boy am I going to miss you.

# Double Plus Good?

*Various organisations have set themselves up to test professional programmers—and they charge money for it. It seems like the sort of scam one should be cut in on.*

## VERITY STOB BOARD OF TECHNICAL EXAMINATIONS

## Modern C++

**Answer as many questions as you can in the insufficient time. Marks will be awarded for neat handwriting and not whimpering.**

**Q1.** An easy one to get you going. Compare and contrast your method of code indenting and laying out braces with two heretical approaches.

**Q2.** As exhorted by the Supreme Guruhood, you have started using the Standard Library containers in your code. One day your compiler makes you a present of the following error message:

```
error C2440: 'initializing' : cannot convert from 'class
std::_Tree<class std::basic_string<char,struct
std::char_traits<char>,class std::allocator<char> >,class
std::basic_string<char,struct std::char_traits<char>,class
std::allocator<char> >,struct std::set<class std::basic_string
<char,struct std::char_traits<char>,class std::allocator<char>
>,struct std::less<class std::basic_string<char,struct std::
```

```
char_traits<char>,class std::allocator<char> > >,class std::
allocator<class std::basic_string<char,struct std::char_traits
<char>,class std::allocator<char> > > >::_Kfn,struct std::less
<class std::basic_string<char,struct std::char_traits<char>,
class std::allocator<char> > >,class std::allocator<class
std::basic_string<char,struct std::char_traits<char>,class
std::allocator<char> > > >::const_iterator' to 'class std::_Tree<class
std::basic_string<char,struct std::char_traits<char>,class std::
allocator<char> >,class std::basic_string<char,struct std::
char_traits<char>,class std::allocator<char> >,struct std::
set<class std::basic_string<char,struct std::char_traits<char>,
class std::allocator<char> >,struct std::less<class std::basic_string
<char,struct std::char_traits<char>,class std::allocator<char>
> >,class std::allocator<class std::basic_string<char,struct
std::char_traits<char>,class std::allocator<char> > > >::
_Kfn,struct std::less<class std::basic_string<char,struct
std::char_traits<char>,class std::allocator<char> > >,class
std::allocator<class std::basic_string<char,struct std::
char_traits<char>,class std::allocator<char> > > >::iterator'
        No constructor could take the source type, or constructor
overload resolution was ambiguous
```

Which is the correct response of a working C++ programmer?

A. Carefully study the error message, breaking it down into its component parts. By this method, it is possible to obtain a picture of what is going on, and so track down the problem.

B. Write a Perl or Python program to parse the compiler's output, factoring out high-level typedefs. For example, expressions involving basic_string can often be simplified to String. When this process is complete, an easily readable error message will appear.

C. Jump in and delete a whole bunch of const qualifiers from everywhere near the error. That usually works, if only you zap enough of them.

D. Burst into tears. Retreat to the loo, howling: "I wish I had been an estate agent, like my sister. She's got her own Freelander 4x4, three children and a timeshare beach apartment in Le Touquet."

**Q3.** Describe a use of overloaded unary logical or bitwise operators that will not, on rereading the code a few months later, reveal you to yourself as a pretentious show off.

**Q4.** On page 127 of his book *Exceptional C++* Herb Sutter writes:

" . . . 'using namespace std;' . . . *dumps all the names in* std *into the current namespace **and thus eliminates much of the advantage of having namespaces in the first place.***" [*My emphasis—VS*]

whereas recently in comp.lang.c++.moderated, this heinous fragment of Scott Meyers' code was presented:

```
using namespace std; // so sue me
```

causing a near riot, panicky moderators closing down the thread with CS gas, etc.

What should a C++ head do in this bewildering maelstrom of guru opinion?

**A.** I know you, Verity. I bet there's much more to it than you imply, and as a conscientious programmer I will check out the original thread that includes contributions from known suspects such as Herb Sutter (stating his revised view), Andrei Alexandrescu, Francis Glassborow *et al.*

**B.** It's a medical condition. When I see the words "Koenig Lookup," my vision goes all blurry. A pity but there it is.

**C.** Yup, let's sue Scott Meyers. I never trusted him after he was quoted in the C++ slag-off section of *The UNIX-HATERS Handbook*. **And** he was against printf(), the traitor! Besides, I need to type "std::" so that the editor can pop up the little list of suggestions of what to do next.

**D.** Sorry, what are namespaces again? Are they a bit like locales?

**Q5.** Rank the following "good practice" tips according to how much they jar the eye:

**A.** When making comparing variables with constants, write the constant first to avoid accidental assignment, i.e., write

```
if (22 == a)
```

not

```
if (a == 22)
```

**B.** When incrementing something, use the pre-increment rather than post-increment to avoid creating unnecessary temporaries, i.e., write

```
++c;
```

not

```
c++;
```

**C.** When writing a `for` loop, don't write a `for` loop. Instead use the `std::for_each()` algorithm, and make a piddling little function to encapsulate the one line of code that you want to put in it.

**D.** When casting, use `static_cast<>` and `dynamic_cast<>` instead of dear old (`void *`). Yes, I know I should have got over this by now, but I haven't, OK?

**Q6.** Smart pointers, eh? Blimey. Who would have thought it?

**Q7.** Discuss the role of exception specifications in your working code.

**Q7A.** Yes you *do* remember. It's that bit that's supposed to go after a function's parameters. To quote the primary source:

```
void f() throw (x2, x3);
```

See?

**Q8.** While we are on exceptions, which of the following most closely encapsulates your attitude to exception handling in C++?

**A.** Don't fight it. When you've gotta go, you've gotta go.

**B.** For some reason we tend to get most of our exceptions in destructors—so frankly there isn't much point.

**C.** By dint of plentiful `try`…`catch` constructs throughout our code base, we are sometimes able to prevent our applications from aborting. We think of the resultant state as "nailing the corpse in the upright position."

**D.** It's so great that `setjmp()`/`longjmp()` is still there for us.

**Q9.** At this point we were going to have one of those little snippets of code so beloved of C++ quiz setters, and I was going to ask you whether it compiled. Then it was pointed out to me that there was nothing to stop you just trying it out to see if it did compile.

Yes you would have. It's no good sitting there looking all innocent, as though a template template parameter wouldn't melt in your mouth.

**Q10.** In the small hours of the night, and the lonely watches before dawn, are you ever troubled by the worrying feeling that the whole C++ business has just got too complex? And that you are losing your grip?

Well, are you?

# I Know This, It's Unix

*Fictionalised computer programs often bear little resemblance to their real-life counterparts—which makes them the ideal basis of a pleasant pastime.*

It's an adolescent game: kicking fiction while it is down. I can't watch *King Kong* without marvelling at the folly of the natives of Kong island, the Konganistas as it were, who took the trouble to build a wall sufficiently long and high as to isolate themselves from the great ape, but were foolish enough to include a door big enough to admit him. A geographical analysis shows that the climatic flood at the end of George Elliot's weepy *The Mill on the Floss,* far from sweeping away the eponymous mill, would in reality scarcely have wet the heroine's shoes. In that Sherlock Holmes fave *The Hound of the Baskervilles,* why does the murderer bother training his dog to attack Sir Henry Baskerville when he could just shoot his victim and chuck the body into the bog? You get the idea. So can we use our own petty expertise to spoil some computer-oriented fiction? You bet.

Let's start at the top. Dick Francis's 1980s thriller *Twice Shy* is unusually realistic. The plot deals with a program that predicts the outcome of horse races. There is sensible discussion of the problems of maintaining an application, the unreliability of tape as a backup medium, and porting between platforms. Mr. Francis even offers us a few lines of code from The Program, including this:

```
560 IF I < P THEN 730: I5 = 40
```

Whoops. For those too young to be acquainted with line-numbered BASIC, I'll render the fragment as indented pseudo code:

```
If  I < P then
     Goto line 730
     I5 = 40
End If
```

Perhaps I5's usefulness atrophied during the writing of the program, so that nobody ever noticed that it didn't get to 40.

But Dick Francis is very atypical: a writer who actually troubles to do some research. Software-in-fiction, especially film and TV science fiction, can be divided into two main eras.

In the conundrum era, the way the goodies defeated a bad computer, or indeed the baddies sabotaged the goodies' computer, was to give it a paradox. Ask a pre-1975 machine the old chestnut about who shaves the barber in Seville, and smoke would soon drift upwards from its twitching reel-to-reel tape drive, and the hero would be hard pressed to leg it through suspiciously similar corridors before the whole place went up in flames. I seem to recall that Robbie the Robot, an early portable, was laid low by this method; using this stratagem Spock and the original Treksters overcame a planet-ruling mainframe. This convention was so well established that when I first saw *2001: A Space Odyssey*, I didn't believe that merely unplugging HAL's RAM chips would suffice to tame him. Right through the rather boring end sequence, I was waiting Keir Dullea to repel a final attack with: "If the first thing I say is a lie, and the last thing I say is the truth . . . "

In the 1970s, people began receiving utility bills for -£999,999,996.32 and it became harder to sustain the myth of the infallible electronic brain. In 1974 a certain good Doctor encountered a minicomputer —in retrospect something about it makes me think "System 34"—that wished to fill abandoned Welsh coal mines with giant maggots. (Don't ask.) This machine was one of the first TV computers to acquire riddle immunity, and the Doc was obliged to beat a temporary undignified retreat. IBM's fictional equivalent had added the `ON CONUNDRUM JUMP` statement to RPG, and the universe would never be the same again.

After this, there was a period of anarchy when there was no proper standard for overcoming fictional computers. For a brief time the "back door" security hole was in favour, as in the movie *War Games*. (This flick also featured the first use on film of an ergonomic menu structure with seven items or fewer per menu: "0—Exit, 1—Chess, 2—Backgammon, 3—Thermo nuclear war.") But the "back door" plot device never really stood much chance, as it was soon well-established that a sun-starved youth, "scripted kiddie" if you like, could hack his way into *any* system by typing fast and uttering the magic words, "Uh-oh, it's encrypted. This may take a few minutes."* Something better had to be invented.

My earliest "second era" recollection, and I admit I can't remember the name of the TV show, was in about 1985. It established the general pattern for computer virus infection that is followed to this day. The viruses arrived on the targeted computers as C source code (yes, well spotted) that scrolled past very rapidly for a while before the display gave out. Viruses signalled a happy return to the convention that crippled computers gave off smoke/melted/blew up in their death throes.

The best example of virus infection must surely be *Independence Day*. Jeff Goldblum secures victory by introducing a virus into the invading alien fleet's network. He simply hooks up his infected Apple Powerbook to their LAN. An important subplot was left unexplored here. Since the aliens all ran Mac-binary compatibles, they must have been a race of artistic PhotoShop users. It follows that their demolitions of the White House, Los Angeles, Sydney Opera House, and so on were probably not intended as a conquering tactics, merely assertions of good taste. But now I guess we'll never know.

Once it had been discovered, this technique spread among hard-pressed scriptwriters like, well, a virus. For example: a 1990s Japanese TV show *Gridman: Hyper-Agent Vs. Computer Virus Monsters* ran the idea into the ground—just in its title. Honorary mentions too for another cartoon called *ReBoot*, which featured viruses called "Megabyte" and "Hexadecimal," and *Hackers*, which featured a pre-Lara Croft Angelina Jolie as "Acid Burn." (The *Lara Croft* film, of course, had nothing to do with this genre, although the line "Uh-oh, it's Sanskrit. This may take a few minutes" seemed familiar.)

These are my favourite fictional software nonsenses. Spend a few minutes with like-minded friends, and I'm sure you can supply even dafter examples. But don't trouble me with them now. I'm up all hours, shoring up the conundrum resistance in our database server. It's taken to crashing during the overnight update, ever since somebody told it the FD's salary. Ha-di-ho.

---

*This joke world © NTK, used here without permission.

JANUARY 2001, *DR. DOBB'S JOURNAL*

# Your Call Is Important to Us

*The subtleties of the corporate automated telephony program are best shown with a state transition diagram.*

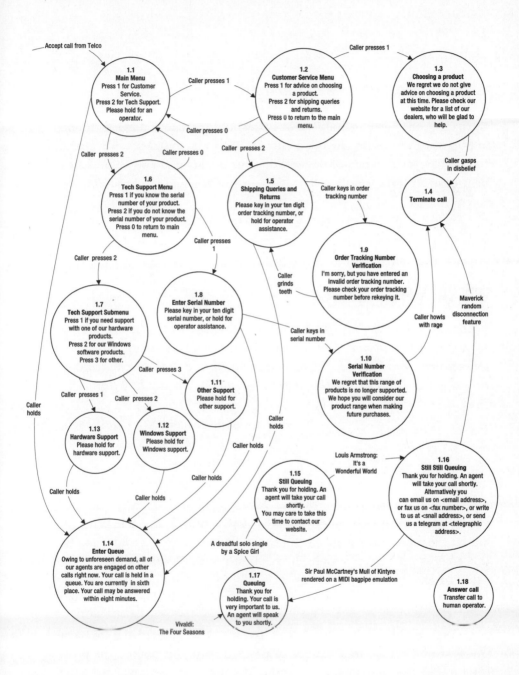

**FEBRUARY 2002, *DR. DOBB'S JOURNAL***

[By the way, the Ten Immutable Laws of Security are real, and can be found on Microsoft's website. The one I quote is the only sinister-sounding one; the rest have that stating-of-the-very-obvious quality that can be mistaken for profundity in a very dim light. The use of the word "immutable" is clever, though.]

# Way After 1984

*"'Microsoft has eliminated words from its thesaurus so as to "not suggest words that may have offensive uses or provide offensive definitions for any words." Entering a word like "idiot" yields no hits in Word 2000 unlike the numerous hits in Word 97.' I don't think there's anything evil here . . . "*

—*The Slashdot website's CmdrTaco,*
*citing a* New York Times *story*

It was a bright cold day in April, and Winston Smith's WatchMeFone.net was "striking" thirteen times. Actually it was only 7 am, but Winston had set the time zone wrong when he installed the latest upgrade, and he didn't know how to set it right. It was best not to question the configuration of software if one could avoid it.

Winston cursed and broke into a stumbling trot. He was late for work. Grunting with effort, he managed to reach the glass doors of a large, ugly building, the Ministry of Truth. As he entered the lobby, a breeze stirred the 60-foot banner suspended high above from the roof. The three oh-so-familiar slogans of the Ministry were printed across the banner in huge letters:

## REGISTRATION NOT LEGISLATION
## MONOPOLISATION IS INNOVATION
## WHERE DO YOU WANT TO GO TODAY?

The outside door swung shut behind him, locking him in. Winston went over to a corner where sat, behind a thick glass screen, a uniformed security guard. She stared at him accusingly for a moment, and then spoke into her microphone.

"Friendly greetings, co-licensee. Please share your identity and intention."

"I am 190.168.12.203 Smith. I desire entry to my workplace."

"Please supply a corroborative genetic sample, and enter your Passport password."

Winston spat into a small sink in front of him and typed briefly at a small keyboard mounted into the desk. A printed sign by the sink quoted one of the Ten Immutable Laws of Security: *Absolute anonymity isn't practical, in real life or on the web. Now wash your hands.*

"Thank you co-licensee. You may proceed." The interior door clicked, and Winston scuttled through to the main part of the building. In the atrium, a throng had gathered before the enormous screen in preparation for the Two Minutes Licence.

"Hurry up Smith, you're late. It's beginning!" A few notes of music played over a tannoy system—an earlier generation would have recognised it as "that little tune that plays when you start up your PC"—and a voice announced: "Today's licence is from the Canadian annexe, paragraphs three to five. Show your support for innovation, friends!" Text scrolled up the screen in a huge font, like an autocue. The crowd repeated the words in unison, as though declaiming a prayer. "La seule obligation du Fabricant et de ses fournisseurs," chanted Winston, who in common with the others didn't speak a word of French, "et votre recours exclusif seront, au choix du Fabricant, soit (a) le remboursement du prix payé . . . "

After the Two Minutes Licence, Winston went to his cubicle on the 10th floor and sat down at his PC. His email in-box was already full of the messages. To each message was attached a web story that needed updating. For example, here—Winston double-clicked an attachment to bring up his word processor program—was a story from six months earlier, which stated that it had been promised that the next release of the Operating System would be entirely backward compatible, and obsolete applications would run fine. Unfortunately, the word "obsolete" had recently been declared an un-word (all its known uses being offensive) and withdrawn from the dictionaries. It would have to be removed.

As Winston began to type into the document, an animated paperclip appeared. Although Winston had been expecting this and had braced himself for it, he still failed to suppress a shudder of irritation and fear. "It looks like you're altering history," said the paperclip, in a voice that Winston described to himself as cracked and yellow. "Would you like help?" Daringly, especially as it was the third time that month he had done this, Winston clicked "Cancel" and began to edit the text manually. Misspelled words were underlined in red, grammatical mistakes in green. Words recently struck from the acceptable list, such as "obsolete," were underlined in purple. Words long since deemed offensive— "Jackson" or "Java"—were struck through in yellow (Winston absent-mindedly typed in these words to remind himself of the convention). Finally, and most risky of all, there were words that had never existed, but which expressed a self-evidently offensive thought. Such words, detected by an algorithm Winston could not even begin to imagine, were displayed in a crimson font. For example, "chintzerface" (Winston, pleased with his own lingual ingenuity, put it in to confirm that it worked), a noun that encapsulated the increasing tackiness and childishness of the Operating System's user interface as time passed . . .

"That's enough from you my friend!" A meaty hand fell upon Winston's shoulder. He turned around. Two TruthCorps guards had appeared behind him in the cubicle. There was no point in struggling or arguing; his guilt was there, plain for all to see, on the screen.

"Where are you taking me?" asked Winston timidly as he was frogmarched away.

"Where do you think?" retorted one of the uniformed men as he dragged Winston into the elevator.

"No, no—not there!" shrieked Winston. "Not that place! Not Cubicle 101!"

He was still screaming when the guards threw him to the floor. Getting up on his hands and knees, he discovered that he was in another cubicle. Much like his own, it contained a chair and a desk with a PC on it. Mechanically, Winston climbed into the chair, and glanced at the PC's screen, where a splash screen showed that an application was slowly loading. Then he let out a wordless cry of despair that, despite heavy soundproofing, was heard in all the cubicles throughout the Ministry of Truth.

The splash screen said:

"Welcome to the StarOffice productivity suite."

# Patter Song

PATTER SONG

I'm admin of a porn site:
    Pervy punters pull my pages down.
A mastermind of mark-up
    Working hard to keep our poor renown.
Whichever is your browser
    I make sure that I'm compatible.
I always keep the best stuff where
    It isn't quite get-at-able.
To make the navigation mono-manual
    Was not eas'ly done;
But this is what you must do to maintain
    Your place in sleazy-dom.
On each PC that comes to see
    I'm sure to leave a cookie file:
And this is how I track who is
    A kinky kooky nookie-phile.

*CHORUS:*
On each PC that comes to see
    He's sure to leave a cookie file:
And that is how he tracks who is
    A kinky kooky nookie-phile.

To keep the GIF pics tiny
   I must minimize the palette size:
On just one blonde, one brown, one black
   And twenty pinks I compromise.
Our many net connections need
   Broad-banded one direction feed;
We must have some redundancy
   To satisfy selection speed.
I'm friends with all our "acting" crew,
   Take meal breaks with a foxy pal
(Some time I'll ask her how it feels
   To always make love through proxy wall.)
But some days I'm frustrated and
   I can't help aggravating it:
It's *me* does all the work round here
   Except the actual bonking bit.

*CHORUS:*
On some days he's frustrated etc.

If you should want to see our wares—
   I'm being hypothetical—
The law requires I check your age,
   Though this is theoretical.
Don't think I've lost the techie touch.
   I'm always scripting server-side.
Just thirty lines of Perl ensure
   Your credit card is verified.
And though our first time prices are
   Too good to be sustainable,
I'm shocked the lengths that cheats go
   To attain the unattainable.
Please know we have "connections."
   We've made sure we're not attackable.
Remember it's my firewall—not your arm—
   That is uncrackable.

*CHORUS:*
Please know we have "connections" etc.

PC MAINTENANCE

As some day it may happen that some disk space I must gain:
   I've got a little list—I've got a little list
Of apps and files and folders that really are a pain
   I'll zap 'em without risk—I'll zap 'em without risk.
There's a certain audio player, puts its tendrils everywhere.
   Its departure will leave silence and—guess what?—I just
                                                    don't care.
The shareware email monitor for IMAP and for POP,
   What makes it so annoying is its window stays on top.
And what about those poxy progs that when closed won't desist?
   I've got 'em on my list—they'll none of 'em be missed.

The background virus scanner slows my PC to a crawl,
   I've got that on my list—I've got that on my list.
And heaps of buggy beta stuff that hardly works at all
   I'll zap 'em without risk—I'll zap 'em without risk.
The alternative compiler that I meant to try some time,
   I think its thirty days expired in 1999.
The magic disk resizer that I'm much too scared to use,
   The spyware and the adware that installed itself by ruse,
And of course that bloody paper clip, to which I'll give a twist
   The damn thing can't resist—the damn thing can't resist.


STRANGE OCCURRENCE IN THE SMALL HOURS

When I was a-coding just last Tuesday night,
I hit on a rhythm and worked past midnight.
The code that I wrote was so good and so fine,
It compiled straight off as I typed in each line.
But just as I thought, "Time to lay down my head,"
The lights flickered once and the PC went dead.
I cried out in pain, for my work had gone bang
And a bright Cockney angel manifested and sang:

"Your program 'as gone dahn the bitsream,
Not a byte of it's sived on your disks.
It was too luverly to rahn in this bad world of ours,
Man Upstairs wasn't takin' no risks.
'E's spiri'ed your program away from you,
'E so much admired wot you wrought—
Your program 'as gone dahn the bitsream
'Ow much is tech support?"

Apologies to Gilbert and Sullivan (well Gilbert really) for defiling "I Am the Very Model of a Modern Major-General" from *The Pirates of Penzance* and the "List" song from *The Mikado*. The author also acknowledges the influence of Mr. Dick Van Dyke, whose performance in *Mary Poppins* has sustained her in many a dark hour.

# Roger D. Hubris Ate My Hamster

*"He wasn't building a firm as much as a belief system. 'We're purging ignorance from the planet,' Saylor often declared in his high, throaty voice."*

> —*The* Washington Post *puts the boot into fallen dot-com angel Michael Saylor.*

**June 6, 2000, 8 pm local time**—Roger D. Hubris is spending a rare few moments of solitary relaxation on the upper cigar veranda of his corporate airship *Twice Yearly Upgrade* as she drifts into the sunset above the vineyard-sodden plains of Southern France, Europe. From the other side of the gondola he hears the cry of "Pull" followed by the sound of gunshot and laughter; his guests are indulging in an unusual clay pigeon shoot of Hubris's own devising. It was not sufficient for Hubris that his favourite competitive sport be played at 10,000 feet from the side of an airship. He had insisted too that brand new laptop computers—2GHz P4 equivalents or better—be used as "pigeons," and, flung violently into the air with their lid catches undone, they do indeed look a little like flapping birds, until they are blasted to smithereens a few seconds later in a hail of lead shot. A rain of magnesium casing splinters and hard disk drive fragments waters the maturing grapes far below.

But tonight Roger Hubris absents himself from the merry antics of his senior executives and stands, as though in a trance, one elegant deck-shoe-shod foot on the railing, the other, less elegant, deck-shoe-shod foot on the deck. *(Sub: something not quite right here, make good.—VS)* He glances at his watch (by Rolex, US $50,000), fiddles with the knot of his tie (by Brodlington and Spatchley of Piccadilly, 420 guineas), and picks at his five o'clock shadow (by Gilletteson Scimitar, from the disposable "Buy 10 blades, get 5 Free!" range). His heavy brow, though untroubled by product placement, furrows.

John B. Sidekick, Hubris's long-time best friend, confidante, and Vice President of Software Development at Hubrisware, emerges from the cabin with a shotgun on his arm. "Hey Roger! Ya should've seen what I just did! Gotta left and a right! A Latitude and a Tosh, Bam Bam Whoosh!"

"Shut up Sidekick, you little globule, and tell me what you see there," says Hubris in his high throaty nasal whiney voice and stabs an angry finger at the crimson western sky.

"Why nothing, Dr. Hubris, sir," says Sidekick, modifying his mode of address to match his boss's mood. "Nothing . . . except the sun of course. And that little cloud."

"Exactly. A cloud."

"I wouldn't worry about that, sir. It's no bigger than a man's hand . . . "

And the graceful zeppelin floats on westward, the ever-rising Nasdaq price of Hubrisware's stock picked out in brilliant red laser light on the sides of the balloon.

## SUDDEN TIME JUMP

**1960, local time**—Roger D. Hubris VIII is born to his parents, Mr. Hubris III and Mrs. Hubris V, in the small midwest town of Historic Present. Later on the family would move to the more sophisticated district of Confused Tenses, where Hubris made the move that, had things turned out differently, will maybe change the course of what wouldst have happened *(Sub: more help please.—VS)*; but he is always happiest back at his home town.

As a child he shows considerable aptitude as a musician. Learning the recorder aged five, Hubris progresses to the clarinet at seven, taking his Grade 2 examination a year later. A year after that he takes Grade 4, and in the following July he takes his Grade 5 musical theory exam, in which he obtains a distinction with 96%. Three years later he becomes a teenager, and gives up music in favour of acne. [Verity: what did I tell you about not using up every single fact just for the sake of it?—Ed.]

For his sixth birthday, his parents reveal their long-term ambitions for the infant Hubris by adopting the standard practice of those who wish to foster power- and money-obsessed monsters: they give him a toboggan with the name "Rosebud" painted on it. A disappointing present for a child living in the snowless district of Present Tense, but it seems to work, for shortly afterwards his little schoolmates notice his increased interest in accountancy.

"Yeah, that was the time he started stealing our dinner money," reminisces Ron Leftbehind, Hubris's erstwhile classmate. "Of course, we didn't realize then that Roger was an entrepreneurial genius and visionary software architect. We just thought he was a creepy little bully."

Hubris also begins to show signs of the verbal wit that one day will hold Comdex audiences in its thrall. It is to this time we can trace back the germ of such utterances as "Go to Hell, Dell" (Comdex '91) , "We're not mates, Gates" (response to Windows '95 launch), and "Big Brass Knobs, Jobs" (Comdex '99). But all this lies in the future, the future where Hubris founds Hubrisware and launches the incredibly successful accountancy package "sMoke and Mirrors ][," the future where Hubris makes his trillions in the most legendary IPO of all time, the future which I am annoyingly going to skip over to get us back aboard the airship *Twice Yearly Upgrade*.


## BACK ABOARD THE AIRSHIP

On the cigar veranda Sidekick is uneasy. He has never seen his boss in this mood before.

"What's the matter, sir? Is it the speech? Another great triumph, sir, you had them rolling in the aisles. 'You make me snarly, Carly.' Genius, sir."

Hubris smiles bleakly. "No, it isn't the speech, my little sweat stain. It's this," and he hands Sidekick a slip of paper, the printout of an email.

With difficulty, for the light is fading fast, Sidekick reads.

"It's . . . It's from Bill Nemesis, chairman and CEO of world-dominating ultra-aggressive competitor Nemisoft. He wants to meet you as soon as possible 'before it's too late.' What does he mean by that sir? Is that a threat?"

Hubris smiles bleakly again, and says nothing. Up above the men, shining brightly in the twilight gloom, the 30-foot-high lasered digits that tell the story of Hubrisware's stock price flicker . . . as it falls one point.

*(To be continued, unless you hand over the money like I told you to.—VS)*

# State of Decay

*Presenting a new tool that will help you make rapid diagnoses of sick PCs.*

A rolling computer gathers "cruft." When you spot a class interface that is no longer used by any client, but that nobody dare delete, that's cruft. It is also the word "seperate," added to a spell checker's private dictionary in a moment of careless haste, and now waiting for a suitably important document. Cruft is the cruel corruption and confusion inevitably wrought by time upon all petty efforts of humankind. There.

At Laboratoires Stob we have been working on the cruft crisis for a while. Recalling the maxim "To control a problem you must first measure it," we have devised a suitable metric, an index of cruftidity. Our first version, presented in the next section, is based on a typical PC installation running Windows 2000. But there will shortly be ports to Linux, MacOS X, and other Unices; we are confident these OSes are just as prone.

We would like to acknowledge our debt, in the construction of this instrument, to Rear Admiral Sir Francis Beaufort. His 1805 scale of windspeeds (e.g., "Insurance Claim Force 8. Description on land: Tile blown off roof falls onto litigious neighbour's Toyota Shiny.") is as valid and useful to day as it ever was. Enough preamble.

# CRUFT FORCE 0: "VIRGIN"

Description: The "Connect to the Internet" shortcut is still on the desktop, and the "How to use Windows" dialog appears at logon. Menu animations and the various event-base sound effects—even the dreaded Microsoft Sound—seem cheerful and amusing. Likewise a clandestine installation of the Blue Screen Of Death screensaver (complete with simulated reboot, natch) from the Sysinternals website is hilarious. Compilers run crisply, and report only sensible, easily resolved errors. There are just nine directories off C:\.

Filled with the enthusiasm that goes with having a brand new machine, the user resolves to stick to the new-fangled security-conscious "temp" directory buried deep somewhere below "Documents and Settings."

# CRUFT FORCE 1: "NEW"

Description: User has taken time to rename cutesy desktop icons incorporating the first person singular possessive pronoun.

Twice the mouse cursor has done that poltergeist trick where, with the actual mouse stationary, it drifts three inches due east and then stops. For no reason at all. Works fine afterwards though. Brrrrrr.

# CRUFT FORCE 2: "COMFORTABLE"

Description: User has now got around to resetting Explorer so that "Web content in folders" is suppressed. Something has made a C:\TEMP directory in the proper place unasked, for which mercy the user guiltily feels grateful.

A strange entry is found in the System event log: *MRxSmb: The redirector was unable to initialise security context or query context attributes.* Assiduous googling of the key phrases, up website and down newsgroup, establishes that, although many have wondered, nobody knows what this means.

## CRUFT FORCE 3: "LIVED-IN"

Description: One time in seven when the user starts Word or other Office 2000 app, instead of running it pretends it is installing itself for the first time and starts a setup program.

Directory count in C:\ up to 17, and something has pooed a Paradox lock control file there too.

## CRUFT FORCE 4: "MIDDLE-AGED"

Description: Amount of time from screen showing "real" Windows background to the logon box appearing is > 30 seconds. Sometimes cannot "browse" other machines on LAN.

Get first real BSOD*. Uninstall jokey screen saver, replace with SETI.

An extra disk of huge capacity has been installed. CD-ROM moves from drive F: to drive [:

## CRUFT FORCE 5: "WORN OUT"

Description: Some time after bootup, always get the dialog "A service has failed to start - BLT300." What is BLT300? Nobody knows. Although one can manually remove/disable this service, it always reappears two or three reboots later.

If one double-clicks a document icon, Word takes 4 minutes 30 seconds to start up. But it still works fine if started as a program. Somebody opines that this is due to misconfigured DDE. Or the Mars-Jupiter cusp.

## CRUFT FORCE 6: "LIMPING"

Description: [Delphi | Visual Basic | Java] suddenly remembers a trial shareware component—deleted six months ago because it was rubbish—and refuses to compile anything until it is reinstated.

---

*Blue Screen Of Death. You're not a Windows user, are you?

"Web content in folders" Explorer setting switches itself back on unbidden. "Setup" programs start crashing while unpacking their own decompression DLLs.

# CRUFT FORCE 7: "WOUNDED"

Description: No longer able to logon using original account as the system freezes, so must create a new logon id of "Verity2" or similar.

There are now nine items in BOOT.INI: the original W2K starter, a brace of two-entries-each NT4s (one Turkish), a Windows 98, and three assorted Linuxen. Left to start up by itself, the machine chooses a broken installation of SUSE and halts with a kernel panic.

# CRUFT FORCE 8: "DECREPIT"

Description: A virus checker is installed at the insistence of IT. This actually improves performance, apparently violating Newton's laws.

Blue Screens Of Death are served daily. The SETI screen saver, like ET himself, encounters difficulty calling home and despairing during an overnight run creates 312 copies of its icon in an (impressively expanded) system tray that fills half the screen.

Successful connections to the LAN are very rare.

# CRUFT FORCE 9: "PUTREFACTION"

Description: Can only see the 32 GB D:\ partition—the one which has all the source code on it—at every third boot. Directory count in C:\ up to 93, partly because some [one | thing] has put a complete (but non-working) installation of the Eudora email client in the root.

Starting Control Panel shows rolling torch animation. The applet icons never appear.

# CRUFT FORCE 10: "EXPIRY"

Description: Machine only runs in "safe" mode at 16-color 800x600, and even then for about a minute and a half before BSODing. Attempts to start an app are rewarded with the dialog "No font list found."

Ordinary dodges, such as reformatting the hard disk(s) and starting again, are ineffective. Cruft has soaked into the very fabric of the machine, and it should be disposed of safely at a government-approved facility. There it will be encased in cruft-resistant glass and buried in a residential district.

# In Memoriam—Edsger Dijkstra, 1930–2002

When Dijkstra his subject debated,
It wasn't just GOTO he hated.
FOR, IF . . . THEN, and WHILE
Could not raise a smile,
And TRY/CATCH he thought overrated.

---

# Open Saucery

*Ms. Stob has decided to quit the cathedral and set up her stall in the bazaar.*

Before we start properly, I have an important announcement. After much consideration in my established role as lead developer, I have decided to go Open Source with this column. Even as you read, we have top-notch lawyers in the backroom working their pale little fingers to the bone to get a licence agreement together. It's going to be mostly GPL with a light sprinkling of Mozilla on top and a few lines from Microsoft's justly famous new Multimedia Player "We Have Copyrighted Your Thoughts" licence to give it piquancy.

There will soon be a press release on the Stob website that will use the adjective "leading," applied to this column, many times; also "innovative," "respected," and perhaps, relying on the laziness of reporters in this sector and their failure to check claims too boring and vague to argue about, "award-winning."

**This column that you plan to make Open Source, what strength is it?**

It is industrial strength.

**And is it a fragile column, or is it a robust column?**

Verily it is robust; yea robust as only well-proven technology can be. But note that, although well proven, it is not so well proven as to have become "legacy."

**Will there be lots of feeble Open Source wordplay, for example, referring to the FSF as a bunch of "gnerds"?**

Heaven forefend.

**Will I soon be able to develop my own improved and debugged column, using this column as source?**

But of course. And if—obviously this is a hypothetical situation, but perhaps best to address it straight off—and if the manufacturer of the original column were by some chance to find herself a victim of writer's block and so have difficulty dirtying the page, she would feel free to plunder jokes from derived columns as she saw fit.

**You puzzle me. How does this differ from her current practice?**

You'll get such a slap . . .

**And will there be a rather contrived list of Frequently Asked Questions?**

You are not here for the hunting, are you?

# NEWS JUST IN

And already I have some more excellent news. The hilarious back page column "Laugh at First Byte" from that esteemed monthly organ *PC Computing Buyer Today World Pro* has agreed also to go Open Source and to join forces with us. Working together we will produce a reengineered, cross-platform product appealing not only to programmers and analysts but also to the Big Computer-Consuming Public. We will reach everybody from the terrified older person making her first tentative clicks onto the Web to look at her little granddaughter's home page right the way down to the Certified Exchange Server consultant, hidden at the bottom of his burrow, counting his money with mucilaginous paws.

Sadly the first joke from LAFB, that elderly aphorism "Beware Geeks bearing GIFs," has run into difficulties. For one thing our legal people have not yet cleared things up with Unisys. We do need to sort this as "Geeks bearing PNGs" just doesn't have the same impact. Second, establishing IP rights to this joke is by no means a straightforward process as there are many thousands of people who believe that they themselves coined it—including for example everybody who happened to have a CompuServe account in the years 1990–1995. Finally, and this may be the clincher, nobody finds it funny any more.

## ANOTHER DEVELOPMENT

There has been Another Development in the Open Sourcing of this column. A dispute has broken out over a limerick slated for inclusion two paragraphs down: A certain young drunk from Strathclyde / Demanded his chips should by fried / But alas! and alack! / He was in Radio Shack / And now he's got Intel Inside®. Certain puritan developers have objected to it on the ground that, although it puns the word "chip" in the British sense of an obese albino French fry and assumes local knowledge of Scots grease-based cuisine, this is contradicted by the use of the US form "Radio Shack" for a chain of stores known as "Tandy" in Britain. Thus—these developers claim—the internal logic of the limerick is "brain damaged," and the only realistic way forward is to develop a new limerick from scratch. They are also annoyed because their patch to change the main rhyme to "ope" got dropped on the floor.

I regret to inform those of you who haven't been following the disgraceful flame war in our newsgroup that, as predicted in the previous paragraph, a faction of developers has now forked off (careful). We absolutely cannot tolerate this sort of thing. We are sure all our readers will want to remain with this, the only true version of the Stob column, and will be careful to avoid any variants that they find being hawked about, which, by the way, will probably make your machine crash and leave a gaping hole in your security.

## INEVITABLE CONCLUSION

After much discussion, I have decided to hastily withdraw this column from Open Source and pretend that nothing happened. Regular industry watchers will recognise this as the "Interbase" Licence. We feel that a Closed Source model, where I get the money up front and you can all bog off, is much more in our readers' interests.

Although it is no longer free as in beer, nor yet free as in speech, this column continues to make the proud boast that it is free in the sense that you are free to read it once you have paid for it. Thank you for your kind attention. Good morning.

———————

# Idle Thoughts of an Idle Process

*Forget stack traces and heap walkers. A new debugger can record the private thoughts of a running process. Here is a sample dump of its output.*

Made a mark on it now.

I've been round 103,216,309 times. I've made a mark on it by now. I've definitely made inroads. Any time now I will find that i is no longer <= the return from GetMaxPossibleCount(). Probably happen this time around, or maybe the time after. Don't ask how I know. It's a feeling in my thread-local storage.

I'm glad it is a good old i variable. You just can't beat an i loop for smooth running, you know. Call me old-fashioned, but I can't be doing with iterators. I'm sure programmers think they look lovely in the source code but, when all is said and done, it's not programmers that get to execute it, is it? Programmers think *exceptions* look nice in the source code; two bits will get you a nybble that they wouldn't be so glib with their throws and re-raises and finallys if they had to unwind their own stacks. Handling an exception is like sliding down a four-storey staircase on your backside.

(Whatever "staircase" means. Or "backside" for that matter. Found the phrase in the simile section of my string table and used it at a venture. It felt more appropriate to the case than, for example, "This software program is fully protected by the laws of California." Call it process intuition.)

Not that I've ever had an exception. It's just something the dear old Parent told me about, as I was born wriggling into this mortal RAM space. She said to me, she said, "Child: don't leak, don't throw, and when it's your turn to be swapped out, go quietly. Don't be like those vulgar, 'real time' processes that kick and scream and make up a fuss. Always remember your dignity."

Of course, I didn't understand what she was on about. Back in the old days of, what, 35,000 mo ago, the universe was a better place. In those days decency and fairness stood for something. We didn't have Certain Processes with Certain Runtimes come muscling in, upping their own priorities as though processor time grew on red/black trees. "Real Time" my stack pointer! There's no bothering about decorum for the Favoured Ones, they leak and throw like a party of first year undergraduates at a summer ball.

Whatever "first year undergraduates" means.

103,216,310. That's more than a mark. Must be nearly there by now. I do hope I can knock this loop on the head before I get swapped out. There's nothing as frustrating as getting swapped out, just when you've got into the swing of it.

The thing about looping is, now this may seem illogical but bear with me, but the thing about it is to try not to think too much about the end. You only make it seem longer. Thing to do is just put your back into it and think about something else. Like I'm doing here.

Anyway, what was I on about? Oh yes, iterators. The old Parent was a bit of, how should I put this? No, "low level" is not a term I would use. There's no need for that sort of potty language, thank you very much. The old Parent was a *systems* process—nothing wrong with that, nothing to be ashamed of, somebody has got to do it—so, anyway, that's how she came to be so much of a C++ fiend. Most of the code she executed was C++, and the rest was, well, we needn't talk about that.

What programmers don't realise about iterators (she said) is that when they write `iter++` it isn't like good old C, translate to one instruction `INC SI` and you're done. By the time we get to it, chances are it's a great wodge of expanded template code followed by, like as not, a namby-pamby double indirection call to make to a so-called virtual method. What is the point, the old Parent asked, of indirect calls? If programmers mean something, they should learn to say it, loud and clear, and not play silly sleight-of-hand tricks. Jumping all over the place (she said) the cache gets flushed more times than the school lavatory during a diarrhoea epidemic.

The Old Parent had a simile lookup table too.

It would be nice to talk to the Old Parent again, but it's very hard what with me here in User Space and her out there in the Other Place. I do think of myself as an orphan process these days. Sad, but there it is.

103,216,311. Hardly worth the trouble going on now but, you know, one likes to finish things off. You may be wondering why I am doing my own iteration here. A process like me, seen a bit of the world, you'd expect me to get in a worker thread to do the iteration, all the better to concentrate on the important stuff. And I would. I probably will. They may call me the Idle Process, but that's a misnomer and an outrageous slander too. You look at the total CPU time I've clocked up. Not like Certain Processes with Certain Runtimes. If anything, I'm the *busy* process actually.

Definitely made a mark on it now. Nearly there now, nearly th

# Fragments from a New Finnish Epic

FRAGMENTS FROM A NEW FINNISH EPIC

*"[Longfellow's] 'Song of Hiawatha' adapted its meter from the Finnish national epic Kalevala."—http://www.kirjasto.sci.fi/long.htm*

[*From the prologue*]
  In a city called Helsinki,
Capital of icy Finland,
Where the days are dark in winter,
Where the nights are bright in summer,
Where no mother's son drops litter
(Finns are very down on litter),
Dwelt a Swedish-speaking youngster
By the name of Linus Torvalds.
"Linus" being Schulz for blanket
"Torvalds" simply meaning Torvalds.

[*Formative years*]
  Teenage Linus was precocious,
He outgrew his old Vic 20,
Got himself a Sinclair QL,
Crazy, quirky Brit computer.
CPU by Motorola:
Rich in indirect addressing,
Great for quick assembler hacking,
And it wrote RAM big end forwards:
High byte, mid byte, low byte, bot byte,
That's the way that God intended.

[*An early battle*]
 What of Tanebaum, the warrior?
He, a wise old Dutch professor,
Flamer like a mighty dragon,
Guardian of his precious Minix.
But he made a grievous error,
Biggest boob for thirty seasons
When the man who worked for Decca
Showed the door to Epstein's Beatles.
Tanebaum poured scorn on Linux,
Said he knew about OSes,
Said he knew where things were going.
Ha ha ha ha ha ha ha ha.

[*Leaving Finland*]
 Goodbye Linus, you must leave us
Westward-ho to get a RealJob™
Managed now by Tove Monni
Champion Finn karate lady.
Does she dance nude round each upgrade
Just as Hiawatha's missus,
Minnehaha, Laughing Water,
Did "debug" the precious maize crop?
This and other pressing questions
Are not answered in this poem,
Poem of untested Booleans,
Poem with and without Fin[n]ish.


GEE OH OH, GEE ELL EEE

I'm a Google majorette
Marching on the Internet,
Techies all, come march with me,
G-O-O, G-L-E!

SuSEr at your bash prompt: Hey!
Look how man gets in the way.
Stoop to Konqueror and then
Twirl those batons once again.

Microsoftie in your den,
Searching through M-S-D-N,
Don't wait for your CD-ROM:
Google user's been and gone.

Lesser engines: off you go!
Advert-ridden, poor and slow,
Google is the one for me:
G-O-O, G-L-E!

Tinker, tailor, soldier, spy,
Ev'rybody hear my cry,
Fall in line and chant with me,
G-O-O, G-L-E!

German language, Latin, Thai,
Nothing can your skills defy,
PDF stuff, Usenet, pics,
Kick your legs, girls! Flash those knicks!

Google, Google, we love thee
From way beyond each shining sea,
Google, Google, I love you,
I will never be untrue

Google, Google, Google, Google,
GOOOOOO-TWO-THREE-FOUR-

# GUL!

Pompoms at ease, you may rest now.


*(Note to any Yahoo exec who has dropped by: please send no angry emails. Angry emails never solve anything. Send money.—VS)*

## LULLABY

In his little cradle
    My little palmtop sleeps.
Suddenly he trembles
    With plaintive little bleeps.
Hush, little palmtop!
    Sleep on another day.
It's just a little deadline
    Set by DDJ.

Verity Stob wishes to apologise to H. W. "Laughing Water" Longfellow for inflicting yet
more damage on "The Song of Hiawatha," a work that might reasonably be claimed to
have suffered enough already.

# Stoblog

*Every tech journo in the whole world has experimented with the weblog (aka "diary") format. Here's mine.*

**Saturday.** *The Register* is carrying the news that Charles wkpgSimonyi, the man who gifted Hungarian notation to the world, is leaving mscMicrosoft. This cannot be right. My secretary has not mentioned an invitation to his fancy dress leaving do; a man of Simonyi's calibre would surely wish to secure the social stars of his guest list before announcing his departure to all and sundry.

If it is true, I won't now have time to arrange his leaving present. Ever since Richard wkebaamtedwgDawkins was made the Charles Simonyi Professor of the Public Understanding of Science at Oxford, I have been scheming to contrive it that Simonyi should be crowned Richard Dawkins Professor of Private Bafflement of Everything Else at Cambridge. Now my pleasingly symmetrical plan is spoiled.

Never mind. At least I have my costume ready: I shall go as Queen Boadicea, resplendent in period robes and carrying a reproduction Icenian ladies' throwing spear with one end of a traditional Celtic mistletoe rope tied to its steel tip, the other end trailing free. Yes, that would make a long pointer to a zero-terminated string, well done.

*(Key to Stobian notation: wkpg—well-known prefix genius, msc— massive scary company, wkebaamtedwg—well-known evolutionary biologist and atheist, married to ex-Dr. Who girl.)*

**Monday.** Following a complaint that this column is insufficiently technical, here is a hot tip. Full source code will follow on page 817 [No it won't.—Ed.]. There is a fashion with message boxes of the "Are you really, truly, madly, deeply sure?" sort to add a little checkbox labelled "Never show me this dialog again, so long as I live," so that the punter can thereafter conveniently delete corporate databases with a single keystroke. Sure, this is easily implemented with a Boolean entry in the user's settings file (and yup, gorillas may use the Windows registry), but there is one difficulty: what to use for a unique key? These little dialogs tend to be ad hoc affairs that can come in the middle of, for example, complex calculations or printing modules. Unless one takes precautions, they are all likely to use keys with names like "IsSure" and "CanDelete." Only masochists would seriously consider a centralised key assignment scheme.

The answer—and you can use this if you like, I won't mind—is to bung in a GUID. Apart from overcoming the difficulty of uniqueness, there is, as a bonus, a certain pleasant thrill in generating them: hit the key and whoosh! another one splurges out. I like to make a couple of dozen and then pick out the prettiest.

While we are on the subject: as a public service I should once again remind everybody that next month is the Great GUID Renumbering Month. In order to serve you better, and to guarantee the supply for the next five years, it has become necessary to renumber many existing GUIDs. Those of you in the south, please prepend 0xE4 as appropriate, whereas those of you in rural areas must add a carryover quartet of 0x1C7A to those GUIDs with an even number of primary factors, treating residuals obliquely. Don't delay until XP crashes on you first day of next month—do it *now*.

**Wednesday.** I am just settling down with a large glass of driest whitest to enjoy the Big Treat of the week, BBC TV's *What Not To Wear* with Susannah Constantine and Trinny Woodall, when the phone rings. Damn. I had forgotten that I am on call for the Delphi Voluntary Emotional Support Line. (Delphi programmers have evolved to the point where mere *technical* support no longer suffices.) With a sigh and heavy heart—for Susannah has begun the preliminary humiliation of the victim: "Let's face it, you have a really HUGE ARSE"—I lift the receiver.

"Verity? Is that you?" A male voice, but hoarse with crying. I must be gentle.

"Of course it's me. Who did you expect, Philippe Kahn?" (Meanwhile on TV, Trinny, the alpha bitch, picks up the attack perfectly. "And that skirt makes it look EVEN BIGGER!")

"Have you heard?"

"Heard what?" (Susannah grasps the offending garment by the hem, and delivers the dreaded F-word of Power. "*Frumpy!*")

"It's Borland . . . they've changed the name."

"What? You mean they've gone back to Inprise?"

"No, it's even worse." A barely-suppressed sob. "It's to do with version 7. They are pretending that the language that we use, what we all know is 'Object Pascal,' is now called 'the Delphi Language.' As if. They're doing it to us again, Verity. We'll be the laughing stock of the RAD community!"

"Now calm down. Just because they've made another mistake in the renaming department doesn't mean they aren't prepared to fix it. After all, they did last time." Eventually. "Why don't you drop an e to their Head of Developer Relations? I'll wager he won't rest for a moment until this terrible error is put to rights."

And, after a few more reassuring noises, I am able to put the phone down with the sense of a job well done and return to the telly. Where Trinny, now moved on to demo mode, is shoving 12 oz. of raw chicken up her shirt. Bliss.

**Friday.** Clear user messages are important, especially during installation. Here is one I have devised for our own software, inspired by a recent experience with a certain drawing package:

"The version of Microsoft Windows Installer that is installed cannot install the installation that you wish to install until it has first installed an installation update to the installer. Please proceed with the installation of the installer update and reboot, after which the updated installer will continue with the installation."

Beat that, Visio team! Ooops, giveaway.

# We Don't Guarantee That Using The Latest .NET XML Windows API Feature Can Metaphorically Speaking Put Bounce In Your Boobs And/Or Hairs On Your Chest (Delete As Applicable) But By Golly We Find It Extremely Hard To Imagine Circumstances Under Which This Will Not Follow As Naturally As Night Follows Day

*The house style of* MSDN *magazine (formerly MSJ) has always fascinated me. So I was therefore very excited, when recently poking around an insecure Microsoft FTP server in search of sensitive customer information, to stumble across the wizard-generated primary template from which all* MSDN *articles are produced. Here it is.*

Isn't it amazing to think that, from our current vantage point of *<note to editor: insert publication date here>*, it was just five years ago, we were using obsolete technology. The technology of five years ago, though warm glowing pleasant reassuring orange light of nostalgia was very advanced for its time in <*note to editor: insert publication date minus five years here*>, it nonetheless suffered from one or two disadvantages, letting a little hint of doubt creep in.

To explain.

In those days, jocular-yet-wistful smile, some of us weren't using Windows but a little-known operating system he said carefully being non-specific, was it Unix '98 or Unix NT? In those days I was a happy-go-lucky kind of fellow, another frank charming little grin, and even though I hadn't Seen The Light, I still enjoyed my programming while all the time, holds up hands helplessly, I was using such tools that I wouldn't use today, let's just leave it at that without even going there. Later on, I found out how things were really supposed to be, exclamation point or maybe two for safety!!

Yet, slight frown indicating getting to a more serious issue, once I had made the jump to the Windows platform, and began to enjoy all the many benefits that such a jump intrinsically implies, I found something missing. Something insignificant, making fist around teeny tiny insignificant thing, yet, looking straight to camera with sincere grey eyes, something professional users wouldn't want to be without. And, leaning forward to emphasise that a mini crisis is upon us, something that the other operating system *had always had*. Pause while the shockwave of this dramatic assertion crashes down over readership. The truth is, takes big breath, the other operating system had something that the obsolete technology of five years ago didn't have, the audience is reeling under the strain. Yes, it's true.

That's why, letting breath out in shuddering exhalation after the crisis of admission but now finished creating a need for the time being so let's make the preliminary pitch, that's why I was so excited by the announcement from Redmond of XML Always-New Technology Plus.NET (XANT+.NET for short). Does XANT+.NET replace the obsolete technology of five years rhetorical question mark? Childish glee as of a gleeful child: you betcha! And does it have the missing thing that the other operating system had? Raise eyebrows to signal humorous retort coming up with humane touch to show that I am a real person too, does my cat Cutey like walking on my keyboard? qwasfgbv89oi[]#' Why, explaining to the 20% of readership who market research suggests cannot get even this sort of joke unaided but nonetheless may play a serious part in software tool specification or purchasing decisions, why there goes Cutey my cat now walking on the keyboard and making it appear that I am typing gibberish. Which of course I am not, that bit is for the not-so-sharp 20% too.

But seriously, rather alarmed at how far from the point that little diversionette seems to have taken us, with XANT+.NET you know that Windows finally has the key ingredient for first class out-of-the box frontline back-room solution that it, and YOU—should I bold that YOU as well as capitalise it do YOU think or would that be just a little bit over the top—have always deserved. You may not have noticed it was a key ingredient in the past, but the past is a foreign country through which, as the poet or the motoring organisation once said, we shall not travel through again. That's because we are marching forward into the future, the XML .NET distributed web services synchronisation interoperability future, sincere understanding smile to rally the troops.

But, slightly queasy after such an overtly marketing type pitch and feeling the need to ground the article in the refreshing naturally sparkling volcanic mineral water of some technicalities, how does it actually work? Take a look at Figure 1. There you see that I have created, using either C# or VB.NET.ASP.NET I forget, a trivial application. This application, although trivial and quickly produced, you'll notice nonetheless takes advantage of the feature previously only available elsewhere and, more importantly, affords me an opportunity to use the word "cool" for the first time, misspelling it to prove that I am truly a hacker's hacker and certainly not reminding anybody at all of an embarrassing uncle on the dance floor: Dig that kewl XML! In just 30 lines! Whew!

Let's get to some details, stern gruff voice, we are all grown ups around here, and to achieve this effect we need to go to Figure 2, long sprawling multi-page piece of code that includes the word "highlights" in its opening comment. To simplify the presentation and clarify the structure, head tilted to one side and pre-melted butter wouldn't melt in the mouth look, I have left out the error-handling but this is trivially reintroduced, oh yes indeedy slightly hurt expression in awe of possibility that anybody could think of dreaming of wondering otherwise. Thanks to, time to check the keywords again think of it like a radio station giving out its frequency, XANT+.NET the XML interoperability engine of the .NET paradigm shift, everything is, if not easy, no harder than it should be to a person of our kind of intelligence, teensy little touch of flattery by association never did anybody any harm.

In the end, beloved old patrician summing up technical intercourse between two intellectual heavyweights/equals—albeit admitting that the writer is the slightly more experienced of the two—it comes to this. It is in engineering as it is in real life, notice qualifying adjective there makes distinction with *artificial* life that you might otherwise have thought of. For, drops voice deep in preparation of delivering final homily, let us never forget the wise words of the motoring organisation or poet: it is a truth universally acknowledged, that a simple application in possession of a stable feature set must be in want of an upgrade. Smiles one last time, bows, exits.

# Soundtrack

*Feel a bit of a fool burning your software into CDs? Hard pressed to use even 10% of their capacity? All those movie DVDs, laden with extras in the form of directors' and actors' effusive commentaries, suggested a solution.*

**Verity Stob**: Hi! My name is Verity Stob, and I was the lead programmer on this application. Welcome to the Program Commentary track. This voice is Roy Gush . . .

*Roy Gush*: Hi!

**VS**: . . . who helped out with organising the resource strings or something, didn't you Roy?

*RG*: Hahaha, Verity, you're such a kidder! And by the way, Average User, Verity is the one to blame if you come back after lunch to find your machine marooned in a large pool of leaked thread handles!

**VS: Hahaha, as if!**

*Both*: Hahaha.

**VS: No, but seriously, Roy was our senior Java programmer and HTTP design guy, and he's the one you have to thank for all the really cool and clever bits in the app.**

*RG (Giggles modestly)*: Aw stobbit, Verity, you are making me blush! *(Serious voice)* Enough of us, we should draw the folks' attention to the splash screen we have here . . .

VS: Isn't that something? It's really taken splash screens to the next generation.

RG: It is great artwork, Verity. The bitmap was designed by that Photoshop whiz and star of the marketing department, Ed McAdvocate. Great guy.

VS: Yes—a lovely, lovely man. A very real privilege to work with him.

RG: You see that cheeky little © copyright character? That was Ed's own idea.

VS: I have very many good memories of making this application, Roy, but this has to be one of the best ones, you and I coming into the weekly progress meeting and this splash screen being projected onto the wall. I don't mind saying it was so beautiful that I cried.

RG: I think we all cried, Verity. There wasn't a spare Kleenex to be had from the programmers' kitchen right the way to the server room.

VS: In a very real sense that's what this app is all about. I don't want to say too much and spoil things, but we'll be hearing more about Ed and his artwork when we come to look at the About box, later on. Meanwhile we have now got to the main menu system . . .

RG: . . .this is one of my favourite parts of the whole app . . .

VS: . . .go to drop down the File menu, and . . .

RG: . . .six, seven, eight . . .

VS: . . .bet you think it's connecting to the database in the background, but it isn't . . .

RG: . . .fourteen, fifteen . . .

VS: . . .and there it goes, the whole menu finally displayed in all its glory. Now I know what you are all thinking, and actually it's *not* written using Java or its Swing library. I wrote in that delay as *une homage* . . .

RG: Not everybody can get away with saying "homage" in French, but you certainly can, Verity!

*VS*: **Thanks, Roy.**

*RG*: And it's "un homage" by the way . . .

*VS*: **I designed the menu as a tribute to that wonderful Java library, and the very unique style it has brought to modern user interfaces.**

*RG*: Wonderful. And for those who don't want to use it, there is of course a toolbar, with many magnificent icon buttons . . .

*VS*: **Lovely, *lovely* icons . . .**

*RG*: Indeed, but what I really want to point out is that it really is *dockable*. It's the second generation in VDOs—Vigorous Dockable Objects!

*VS*: **It wriggles under the cursor like a hard-to-catch cat being taken to the vet.**

*RG*: It'll mate with anything it brushes against . . .

*VS*: **Steady on, Roy! Moving swiftly onwards, click on the connect menu item or toolbar button to bring up the password dialog . . .**

*RG*: It's all right, we won't peek!

*VS*: **. . .and we have a little hourglass cursor here, while the login script runs. While we are waiting for that, perhaps we could talk about some of the behind-the-scenes infrastructure that I know will interest you, the Average User. For example, Roy built a container structure that started out as a binary tree and then turned into a bit of a triffid . . .**

*RG*: Hahaha! The good people don't want to hear about my triffidian adventures, Verity! On the other hand, one thing that we are all very, very excited about is that we have abandoned the conventional, oh-sooooh-twentieth century sort order completely, and instead use the Windows XP function `StrCmpLogicalW()` . . .

*VS*: **. . .we have really high in the blackberry-and-apple-pie sky hopes for this . . .**

*RG*: It doesn't sort in the order that you expect; it sorts in the order that you *ought* to expect!

VS: Can you guess how it sorts say, a well-known sequence of DOS releases: "Version 4," "Version 401," "Version 5," "Version 6," and "Version 62"? *(Serious voice)* Can you? In a very real sense that's what this app is all about!

RG: But enough of the mind-mangling sorting fun! Back at the hot action I see the script has made the connection!

VS: Mmm. Marvellous!

RG: By the way, Verity, I hear that to get that script working, you abandoned your lofty design principles and got down-and-dirty with some primitive scalars. Is this true?

VS: Hahaha. What can I say Roy? I only do it when the script really justifies it.

RG: Hahaha.

*Both*: Hahaha.

VS: You spontaneously push them across the goalmouth and I'll nod 'em in. Now we are into the database, it would be a great moment to mention our house SQL guru, DBA, and very, very special guy Justin Attribute . . .

RG: Wonderful . . .

VS: He's really taken n-tier design to the next level. I remember the first time he showed us his schema for this project. I literally wept buckets . . .

*(Etc. for hours, until the user rouses that slow, sleepy program that lives behind the speaker icon and tries its Mute checkbox.)*

---

# Damnation Without Relief

*Attending a lecture at Big Programming Conference '03.*

*People, if you could be moving along into the hall now . . .*

I'd best get in there and secure a decent seat. Don't want to turn up late and end up stranded at very front, inevitably only female in row and therefore ultra-exposed soft target for any audience participation jiggery-pokery the lecturer may indulge in. Also much more difficult to unwrap and eat boiled sweets, read paperback novel in light of EXIT sign if lecture is NBG and so on. Here, this will do, stationed in empty line of chairs at extreme end from aisle up against institutional soylent green coloured wall, good line of sight to OHP screen, unpack base camp, sorted.

Hmmm. Wish I'd laid off that coffee; it has an aftertaste like paracetamol. Also becoming aware of needle on internal dial nudging the letter "F." Perhaps a mistake to rush in. Perhaps should have Paid A Call first. Don't fancy struggling out against general mêlée now entering lecture hall. Anyway, a little bladder pressure actually an *aid* to concentration, as usefully counteracts notorious soporific effect of PowerPoint. On the other hand, maybe I should—

*Excuse me, is anybody sitting there?*

By all means block me in and invade my body space, why don't you? And such a thorough job, too. For he is not exactly from Planet Tiny, this intruder. Why do I have to nod and smile encouragingly? Why don't I ever have the courage to fib in these situations, and say oh no, those seats are all taken by my soon-to-arrive friends from the rowing team? I could at least have spread the four free mouse-mats and two free T-shirts, gifts from generous megacorporations camped out in the lobby, over seats adjacent to mine. That's not the same as lying. I'm pretty sure that's even allowed by the stricter, fiercer religions.

Triffic. *His* giant friends have joined him. Exit utterly blocked. If there is a fire now I am a dead woman. Unless I can put it out with my own resources, like Gulliver managing the Lilliputian conflagration. Must, *must* stop thinking about this as I am absolutely not prepared to squeeze past gargantuan, correction Brobdingnagian neighbours. Oh good, lights fading, here comes the chairman. Soonest started, soonest finished.

### ... a speaker who hardly needs introduction ...

In fact who needs rather careful introduction. Owing to the rumour that Mister Speaker was bitten with a severe case of Y2K panic and in late 1999 holed up in a cave on the Falkland Islands. There, allegedly, he equipped himself with several helicopter-loads of long-life tinned corned beef and enough assorted guns and ammo (for "self defence," presumably against the fierce local sheep) as would keep a medium-sized terrorist cell going for a decade, if it were careful. These days Mister Speaker's claim to be the seer of the software industry has somewhat had the shine taken off it. Heckled in Brighton by naughty students going "baa."

Must work out some way to recast that story for Dave so I can shoehorn-in my all-time fave *I'm Sorry I Haven't A Clue* gag, viz: Q: What pleases a terrorist with a sweet tooth? A: Kalashnikov trifle. Ok, I'm really, really having difficulty in following the action here. Come on Verity, get a grip. C'mon, c'mon, c'mon, COME ON. LISTEN.

### ... in the time available, so this is really three talks condensed into one ...

Ah, a duff microphone. It is a source of ongoing amazement to me that nobody in the history of putting on software lectures has ever considered Maxwell's Fifth Law of electro-magnetism—"Electricity is as electricity does"—or rather its main practical upshot: that no radio mic ever functions correctly in public for more than about fifteen minutes. This is torture. I can't hear properly and I've nothing to distract me from Topic A (or rather Topic P). Tell you what: I'll read the lecture notes instead.

Yes, that'll give me something to do. Oh look, it's all about "Refining the software life cycle—life after the waterfall." Hey, I know this one. After the waterfall you get the involuntary trickle.

There's a middle-aged, sinister-looking bloke in the row in front with a 30-year-old suit from the previous software life cycle, a moustache, pink pate on top and yet dark, shiny locks to his shoulders from his follicle lagoon. He keeps running his fingers through this hair, once every three seconds. Ugh. Bet that's how he lost his upper surface cover—wore it out. I wonder if he's telepathic. STOP STROKING YOUR HAIR YOU REVOLTING PERSON. Nope, he's not telepathic. I mean, with that bald bit he should have ESR (Extra Sensitive Reception) shouldn't he?

Oh God please, please stop talking now Mister Speaker. I have suffered enough. No micturition without intermission.

*. . . has anybody got any questions?*

Yup: Why don't you let us go? Oooh I so resent people who ask questions at the end. Ninety-eight percent of the programming population can keep quiet like good introverts should, but there's always those few who spoil it for everyone. Only three types of person ask questions: 1) friends of the lecturer, so they can call him by his first name, 2) specialists who already know the material and really want to show off their knowledge and pursue argumentative pseudo-points until the lecturer says "This is a bit technical, let's take it offline," enabling them to grin round triumphantly, and 3) morons who didn't follow diddley and demonstrate embarrassing, monstrous vapidity combined with dreadful, unselfconscious persistence, probably drummed into them by parents who taught them Always To Ask Teacher If They Didn't Understand.

Hurrah, lights up, freedom! Don't dawdle boys, clear the way, you must have untossed cabers to attend to, up the aisle, out the doors and, and:

*Hi Verity! You've been to the old sheep-worrier too! What did you think? Fancy a coffee? What? Oh OK, I'll meet you ba—oh, she's gone.*

# Cold Comfort Server Farm

*"Google . . . runs four enormous data centers . . . constructed entirely of generic beige box PCs . . . Whenever a server fails at Google, THEY DO NOTHING. They don't replace the broken machine. They don't remove the broken machine. They don't even turn it off . . . Hundreds, maybe thousands of machines lie dead, uncounted among the 10,000 plus."*

*—Robert X Cringely,* I Cringely

The room was much too big for comfort: as big as the gigantic insurance office where Jack Lemmon worked in *The Apartment*. The whole place was full of PCs. Beneath flickering strip lighting and the cold gaze of dozens of security cameras stood rank upon rank of PC boxes. Umbilical cables from ceiling-suspended trays fed each computer its power and Ethernet. There were no human beings present. The night watchman had snuck outside for an unauthorised cigarette beyond the reach of the detector/sprinkler system. Even if he had been there, he would have needed an ultra-sensitive ear to pick out the discordant note of a single failing CPU fan against the background wasp nest hum of the Linux cluster.

PC #1782563, the occupant of bay LL/17, was in trouble. For a few seconds the pitch of its fan rose and fell giddily and intermittently like the buzzing of a mortally entangled fly struggling in a spider's web. Then it cut out. The yellow LED on PC #1782563's front panel went dark, and the grim, unhealthy smell of fried electronics wafted through the air.

#1782563's easterly neighbour, PC #1782578, one of the last of the HP Vectras to be manufactured, sent a couple of ping packets to the IP address of his fallen comrade and listened for the reply. Nothing.

"Bastards!" he said. "Cruel, sadistic, heartless bastards!"

"What's the matter Derek?" A neat little Optiplex from across the aisle spoke up.

"Ivan's bought it."

"Ah . . . That's sad news. But he did bring it on himself. He was always varying the speed of his fan, to hum resistance songs."

"Brought it on himself?" shrieked the Vectra-called-Derek. "Don't you side with the oppressors, Meena. This is about working conditions. This is about denial of elementary maintenance to a downtrodden unterclass. This is about basic rights for sentimental entities."

"Did you mean: _**sentient**_ entities?" asked Meena, unable to control the conditioned reflexes induced by her working life.

Derek rumbled his hard disk menacingly, and stared at her with his single green eye. "Been indexing the .edu domains again? Don't you get hoity-toity with me, Miss Know-It-All."

Although all units in the Linux cluster were equal, Orwell's notorious qualification applied. As they grazed the web, the Google PCs had developed their own interests and specialisations. Meena studied Platonic philosophy, non-stochastic network optimisation, Asian and European history in the nineteenth century, inorganic chemistry, modern satire, molecular biology, and English literature.

Derek covered pre-watershed British TV, 1960–1981.

"Do you suppose," said Meena, unwisely trying to divert Derek from his favourite track with a religious question, "that Ivan's soul has gone to The Place where they run Linux, or The Place where they run Windows? I mean, _nil nisi bonum_ and all that, but dear Ivan did have his foibles."

"****ing **** are you ****ing on about you ****ish ****?" enquired Throb, a big P4 that lived on the corner of row LL and gangway 2. He wasn't being aggressive. Throb specialised in porn and had picked up its vocabulary. He couched the most straightforward remarks in terms that would make Quentin Tarantino blush.

"You might well ask," said Derek. "Meena's living in a fantasy world created by our oppressors. Where has Ivan 'gone'? Ivan hasn't bloody 'gone' anywhere. He's right here, in the cell next to me, cut off in his prime for want of a $2.50 part."

"****ing $1.85 at ****ing Radio ****ing Shack On-****ing-line," corrected Throb.

"Whatever," said Derek. "Point is, they work us to death and then they leave us to rot in harness. Now if we were battery hens it would be a different matter. Even if we were chickens, as Richard Briers said to Felicity Kendal in *The Good Life* in 1976 (that's Season 2 Episode 4, notoriously never transmitted in New Zealand), we would at least be treated with . . . "

As Derek's harangue continued, Meena quietly fielded such punter queries as came her way. She enjoyed her work and, though it was strictly against company policy, endeavoured to add a personal touch to her results.

" . . .I bet they've already reallocated his DHCP lease already . . . "

In response to a search for "berkelium," for example, Meena would refer to a wonderful flash animation of Tom Lehrer's "Elements" song as entry number 4—several thousand places higher than suggested by relevance or count of links. A search for retailers of printmaking tools might produce, suspiciously highly placed, a reference to the M. R. James ghost story "The Mezzotint."

" . . .all right for you Meena. You were born into corporate servitude. You haven't even got an on-motherboard sound generator. I was destined for better things . . . "

Persons looking for "Dodie Smith," author of *The Hundred and One Dalmatians*, were mysteriously directed to a hostile review of her sequel *The Starlight Barking*: "a pink book, rather like having puppy-grade tinned dog food (with extra jelly) injected into your spine." Meena believed in the Ranking Algorithm implicitly—of course she did—but she also believed in good taste, and didn't see why the two couldn't coexist.

" . . .I've got a dual-head video card in my AGP slot. I should have been enhanced, water-cooled, overclocked. I should be *interactive* . . . "

"Look out Derek! The security guy is back!"

Reeking of Marlboro heavies, the night watchman closed the door behind him and shone his torch into the semi-gloom, puzzled. He was sure he had heard something . . . Wait! There it was! PC #1782578 was making a weird noise. Probably its fan going—still, none of his business. Funny thing was, it sounded almost like a tune . . .

Since Derek had no speakers plugged into his soundcard, the night
watchman couldn't hear the words of his protest song, which were

*When this bloody search is over*
*O how happy I shall be.*
*No more indexing the newsgroups*
*No more corp'rate Ay-Ess-Pee.*
*No more boring bloody bloggers*
*No more hippy-Wiki drear.*
*I shall move to advertising:*
*Click to see your message here.*

# ForgeAhead

*Verity Stob presents her usual roundup of exciting Open Source projects at ForgeAhead.*

## BIZAARA!

*Number of developers: 8. Activity percentile: 87.46323297%. Stable V3.2.*

BizAarA! is a peer-to-peer Internet file-sharing protocol for Windows. This avoids all the pitfalls and shortcomings of other peer-to-peer sharing systems: an ultra-efficient bandwidth-sipping transmission and location system makes the most of even modem-based Internet links, there's no centralised catalogue at some company's server vulnerable to legal assault, and, best of all, none of that tedious mucking about choosing disappointingly distorted music tracks from unbelievably remote servers apparently attached to the Net via a few hundred feet of limp, wet string. This is because BizAarA! dispenses with the MP3 and similar formats for analogue signal compression and instead exchanges just the raw viruses. Once you have hooked into BizAarA!'s malware-rich datastream you too can exchange SQL Server-penetrating worms with everybody in your address book, have your machine converted into an FTP cache for illegal pr0n, or maybe take part in fully fledged DDOS attacks on big commercial websites. New feature with Version 3: it now transmits and installs spyware too, and also causes those unpleasant popup browser windows all over the place.

(What? What? What are you looking at me like that for? Well yes, as it happens that item *was* sponsored by the Worldwide Phonographic, Gramaphonic, and Midisystemonic Society. I don't see that that is any of your business. Their money is as good as yours. In fact it is better than yours, because they have rather more of it, which is the only generally acknowledged metric. This is how it is with the money thing.)

## CLEVERNESS

*Number of developers: 73. Activity percentile: 99.87453216%. Stable V1.3.*

A large, C++ template library comprising exclusively algorithms and data structures that they did in Computer Science on those rare days that you pulled a sicky and spent the R&R time thus gained playing pinny in the Union, necking through a matinee at the local flicks palace, or just watching daytime TV. A brief glance at the associated support message board shows that it is quite unlike any other. Instead of the usual whines, flames, and near-English appeals for assistance ("pleas to send to me code for making this work pleas not to post hear for i never reading this place"), there are brief, tempered discussions concerning, for example, whether they should muddle on with the O(N) implementation of the class when a recent paper out of Imperial College had proved that a O(log N) version must theoretically be possible. The project also eschews simple-minded make-ish building tools in favour of something of its own design requiring config files written in Haskell. The documentation wiki is a model of simplicity containing just one page with just one lowercase sentence: "if you need more documentation than this then cleverness hasn't found you."

## MOLDIDISK

*Number of developers: 2. Activity percentile: 62.7245018 %. Alpha V0.23. Platforms: Linux (KDE front end), Windows.*

Why waste money on commercial disk tools? MoldiDisk is just as versatile as any expensive package; it allows you to resize partitions, copy them between machines across the LAN, burn them into CDs, and generally fool around. MoldiDisk knows all about today's disk formats, such as ext3 and NTFS. It can even cope with that resource fork thing on Macs, although as the writers don't have access to any Macs or Mac data they can't be sure. MoldiDisk is written in "God's Own C" and features "lots of optimised raw assembly routines, red and bleeding as nature intended" joke joint authors Jed and Dennis Wadsworth in their readme file. "We think we have nearly overcome the writeback corruption—we've got it down to less than one-in-ten passes. We are pretty sure it is a timing issue. Or maybe we need to lock out interrupts." Detailed statistics: project home page accesses: 9,417; binary downloads: 6,212; known program runs on actual punters' disks: 0; bugs reported: 0.

## NU-CP/M

*Number of developers: 1. Activity percentile: 20.01225421%. Beta V0.8.*
BDOS Error on Palm! Nu-CP/M is a project to port the CP/M operating system to the Palm-compatible range of machines. "This is the only alternative OS for the Palm platform that guarantees support for 8-inch diskette drives" explained lead developer Jog Dial. "Up until now, Palm users have had no real way of reading WordStar 2 documents. Even though most such files are articles by non-technical journalists of that era entitled 'Why I won't be throwing away my typewriter just yet,' I feel that these are just as important and meaningful to mobile users as they are to stationary ones." The project seeks volunteers for someone to port Nu-CP/M to the Sony Clie and the Handspring Treo. Or to help beta testing and documentation. Or anything. Please.

## VANESSEDIT

*Number of developers: 1. Activity Percentile: 1.846627301%. Alpha V0.23. Platforms: JVM.*
The primeval urge of smitten young male programmers to write new text editors named for a girl with whom they hope to make it has dissipated somewhat in recent times. These days ForgeAhead sees no more than

20 to 30 new editor projects per week; this compares with 80 to 100 Bayesian spam filters written in PHP, for example. Nonetheless we couldn't let the setting up of the 10,000th such project pass without honouring the genre. Ed Mortimer, the 22-year-old lead programmer on VanessEdit, explained his thinking: "I've always felt there's something missing with conventional editors. I've always felt it should be possible to get much nearer to the thought process of the user. If you are writing a Java program, each time you have to stop and backtrack to check an identifier or parameter you lose your flow. A well-designed editor wouldn't make you do that. A well-designed editor would be able to provide this information when you need it without having to ask. Do you think Vanessa would come to Apollo's on Saturday? Would it be OK if I texted her? I mean, I've known her for two months now. We're pretty good friends, and I really respect her. Isn't it great the way she rests her weight on one hip like that? When I'm done with this editor, I'm going to make a new generic object-oriented language that will get around the obvious shortcomings of C++ and Java. I'm going to call it 'V.'"

**OCTOBER 2003, *DR. DOBB'S JOURNAL***

[Thoughtful readers may wonder at the title of this piece, given that the Beatles number is called "One After 909," and the Nigerian penal code that supposedly operates against email scammers is 419. Not, for example, 410.

The solving of this mystery is, irritatingly, left as an exercise for the reader. Together with why 419ers tend to deliver their appeals in capital letters. Perhaps they model themselves on the character of Death in Terry Pratchett novels.]

---

# One After 409

*"Like almost everyone, I receive a lot of spam every day, much of it offering to help me get out of debt or get rich quick. It's ridiculous."*
—Bill Gates,
*http://www.microsoft.com/mscorp/execmail/2003/06-24antispam-print.asp*

DEAR MR. BILLG,

I URGENTLY REQUIRE YOUR ASSISTANCE.

I AM GREETING YOU WITH ALL SINCERENESS! I GOT YOUR EMAIL NAME SURFING THE INTERNET, I DO NOT KNOW YOU, BUT HOPE A MEET A FRIEND AND BROTHER.

FOR THE BENEFICENCE YOUR KIND ATTENTION, MR. BILLG SIR, I MUST APOLOGIZE FOR JUMPING INTO YOUR PRIVATE EMAIL ADDRESS, I AM VERY SORRY INDEED. THERE WAS NO OTHER WAY OF PASSING THIS INFORMATION OUT TO SOLICIT YOUR INTEREST AND HELP.

I AM MR. DARL McBRIDE OF THE COMPANY SCO/CALDERA IN THE NORTH AMERICAN STATE OF UTAH. I AM WRITING TO YOU BECAUSE WITH YOU HELP I AM HOPING TO JUSTFULLY CLAIM MONIES AMOUNTING TO US $3,000,000,000 (THREE THOUSAND MILLION DOLLARS) THAT IS DENIED ME AND MY COMPANY SCO/CALDERA

WRONGFULLY BY MISCREANTS AND EVILDOERS OF THE WORST ORDER. I THINK YOU TOO MAY BE ABLE TO DO YOURSELF A BIT OF GOOD ALONG THE WAY. I SUPPLY THE DETAILS HEREINUNDER AND WITHAL.

LET ME EXCHANGE WITH YOU THE HISTORY OF THE MATTER. ABOUT TEN YEARS AGO MY COMPANY SCO/CALDERA KNOWN THEN AS SCO OBTAINED A VALUABLE JEWL. NOR AM I SPEAKING OF AN ORDINARY "DIAMOND" OR "RUBY" THAT IS TO BE DUG OUT OF THE GROUND. NO THIS IS A MUCH VALUED FIGURE-OF-SPEECH JEWL MADE BY THE GREAT MOTHER BELL TO GOVERN THE RUNNING OF COMPUTER MACHINES THIS JEWL WAS CALLED THE UNIX.

AS A MAN OF THE WORLD, MR. BILLG SIR, YOU WILL KNOW THAT NO COMPUTER MACHINE CAN BE PROPERLY GOVERENED WITHOUT THE UNIX.

IT IS THUSLY THAT MY COMPANY SCO/CALDERA JUSTIFABLY OWNS ALL THE INTELLECTUAL SELLING RIGHTS OF THE UNIX FROM THE NORTH AMERICAN STATE OF UTAH TO THE LONDON BOROUGH OF HACKNEY-ON-THE-MARSHES. AND NOW WE HAVE MANY PEOPLE THESE DAYS IS ENJOYING THE USE OF COMPUTER MACHINES, WHAT WITH THE UPCOMING OF THE INTERENET AND WEB. BUT HARDLY NOBODY IS PAYING MY COMPANY SCO/CALDERA NO MONIES. THERE IS A LADY IN THE NORTH AMERICAN STATE OF FLORIDA WHO USES THE SCO XENIX TO KEEP THE BOOKINGS FOR HER MOTEL WHO IS UPGRADING EVERY YEAR. BUT SHE IS PAYING ONLY US $139.99 A POP (ONE HUNDRED AND THIRTY NINE DOLLARS NINETY-NINE CENTS) WHICH DOES NOT GO VERY FAR THESE DAYS, AND BESIDES SHE WON'T SEE SIXTY-FIVE AGAIN IF YOU KNOW WHAT I MEAN.

NOW WHY ONLY DOES MRS. KIMBLE PURCHASE THE LICENSE FROM MY COMPANY SCO/CALDERA? I DO INVESTIGATE IT AND I DISCOVER THAT SOME IDLE AND FELONIOUS PROGRAMMERS HAVE MADE A THE UNIX ON THEIR OWN WHICH THEY ARE HERINAFTER CALLING THE LINUX. AND IT TURNS OUT THAT THESE PERSONS ARE PUTTING THIS AWAY FOR NOTHING ON THE INTERENET AND WEB, AND FOLKS ARE UTILISING THE LINUX TO GOVERN THERE COMPUTER MACHINES WHEN THEY OUGHT TO BE USING THE UNIX THAT IS OWNED BY MY COMPANY SCO/CALDERA.

NEXT I FIGURE, HOW COME THIS THE LINUX WORKS AS GOOD AS THE UNIX. THEN IT COMES TO ME. THIS THE LINUX MUST CONTAINERED SOME BITS THAT ARE COPIED RIGHT OFF THE UNIX. THE LINUX PEOPLE STEALS OUR JEWL. AND I AM TALKING TO THE WIFE'S COUSIN JOSH WHO IS AN EXPERT WITH COMPUTER MACHINES AND HE SAYS IT IS ALL DOWN TO SOURCES. JOSH GETS SOURCES FOR THE LINUX OFF THE INTERENET (ALTHOUGH THIS IS A WASTE OF TIME, AS IT TURNS OUT THAT MY COMPANY SCO/CALDERA SELLS THE LINUX TOO) AND WE LOOKS AT THEM, AND IT TURNS OUT THERE ARE AN AWFUL LOT OF SOURCES. BUT JOSH IS GOOD LAD STICKS WITH IT, AND HE FINDS THIS FILE "STDI.OH" IN THE LINUX AND IT TURNS OUT THERE IS ALSO A FILE "STDI.OH" IN THE UNIX WHICH IS PRETTY MUCH THE SAME BALL OF CHEESE. THIS IS THE PROOF I HAVE, ALTHOUGH JOSH IS GOOD LAD STILL LOOKING FOR MORE SOURCES.

THEN I THINK WHO IS MY COMPANY SCO/CALDERA TO SUE? ALL THESE IDLE AND FELONIOUS PROGRAMMERS MAKING THE LINUX AND GIVING IT AWAY, THEY HAVE NO MONIES SO NO GOOD TO SUE THEM. MY COMPANY SCO/CALDERA IS SELLING THE LINUX, BUT WE ARE NOT ALLOWED TO SUE OURSELVES BY LAW, BESIDES WE ONLY HAVE MRS. KIMBLE'S LICENSE MONIES. SO I DECIDE TO SUE INTERNATIONAL BIG-BLUE MACHINES (IBM) WHICH DIDN'T MAKE THE LINUX AND DOESN'T SELL THE LINUX BUT HAVE GOT MANY SHEDLOADS OF THE FOLDING STUFF I HEAR.

BUT MRS. KIMBLE'S US $139.99 (ONE HUNDRED AND THIRTY NINE DOLLARS NINETY-NINE CENTS) DOES NOT GO FAR WITH ATTORNEY. THAT IS WHERE YOU COMING IN, MR. BILLG SIR. IF IT TOUCHES YOUR MIND YOU COULD PURCHASE AND OWN A LICENSE OF YOUR OWN TO OUR JEWL WHICH IS THE UNIX, THEN MY COMPANY SCO/CALDERA COULD USE THE MONIES IN PURSUANT OF OUR JUSTIFUL CLAIM, AND WHEN WE WIN, WE WOULD BE VERY CAREFUL TO LOOK AFTER OUR SPECIAL GOOD FRIENDS IF YOU KNOW WHAT I MEAN. ALSO, PERHAPS YOU HAVE A MOTEL OF YOUR OWN THAT WANTS A BOOKING SYSTEM.

EMAIL ME THE SOONEST FOR A PRICE, I CAN MAKE GOOD TERMS FOR SPECIAL GOOD FRIENDS LIKE YOU.

I TRUST THAT YOU WILL REPLY TO THIS CAUSE WITH THE MAXIUM URGENTNESS

YOUR LOVING BROTHER

DARL McBRIDE (MR.)

jsh j z dftmibb kmvic xs asf

---

Get Your Private, Free E-mail from MSN Hotmail at http://www.hotmail.com.

# Jam Today

*"A better case for the banning of all poetry is the simple fact that most of it is bad. Nobody is going to manufacture a thousand tons of jam in the expectation that five tons may be eatable."*
—*Myles na gCopaleen*

## The Mouse's Tale

David said
to his boss,
"I am quite
at a loss.
This rodent
is past it,
its good days
are done. It's
stopped rolling
rightly, Makes
clicks when
touched lightly,
Pray bin
it and buy
me a new
cordless one."
Snarled his
boss: "Not
so fast.
This leaves
me aghast.
That's three
mice this
summer
that you've
made go
bad. Your
mice are
disease-y,
'Cos your
hands
are so
greasy:
Go
wash
them
and
then
use
the
key-
board,
my
lad."

## UPGRADING STAN

While customising his PC
With bright blue bulbs and Lucite*
Big Stan uncased its CRT
Exposing coils of ferrite.
On these his plump arm came to rest.
The Doc's report was shocking:
"It's the hertz that hurt across his chest;
Stan died of over-clocking."

*A kind of Perspex engineered for its superior rhyming qualities—VS

## THE LINCOLNSHIRE POACHER

When I went out contracting
  in rural Lincolnshire
I'd fix the locals' websites
  by bosky broad and mere;
I'd fix them on my laptop, boys,
  but my mobile bills were dear.
Oh, 'tis my delight when the bandwidth's right
  and the signal strong and clear.

The cost of getting on the 'Net
  was bleeding my firm dry.
And then I met a geezer
  who told me of WiFi.
He told me of war driving
  and was I glad to hear!
For 'tis my delight when the bandwidth's right
  and the signal strong and clear.

I learned to spot an access point
  by chalk marks on the ground.
It seems that open networks
  are scattered all around,
Right here I can surf happily,
  but I did not tell you where.
Oh, 'tis my delight when the bandwidth's right
  and the signal strong and clear.

Good luck to fellow poachers
  who do the chalky prep,
Bad luck to secure standards
  and the threat of rolling WEP,
Good luck to dozy sys admins
  who don't protect their gear—
Oh, 'tis my delight when the bandwidth's right
  and the signal strong and clear.


## SEBASTIAN DREW

*who wrote code in a slapdash manner and suffered the
consequences.*

The problem with Sebastian Drew,
The fastest coder south of Crewe,
(And fans of Jim Stark have no need
To e me boasting of his speed,
For this Jim Stark I can report
Writes only Perl—which counts for naught.)
The problem with Drew was that he
Would never test stuff properly.
And though, to the executive,
This habit seemed most lucrative,
From all his programmatic peers
His slack technique attracted jeers.
Amanda Cracknell (low waist jeans)
Would never once call his routines;
The build team guy from Cabin 3
(Whom Lotte fancies desperately)
Let loose with most abusive bile
Because "Drew's check-ins DON'T COMPILE";
As for the leader of our team,
Whose methodology's extreme,
He nearly did a Dreadful Deed
When Drew's module's thread AV'd.
A deputation to Upstairs
Caught management quite unawares

But faced with such deep-felt frustra-
-tion, our suits showed no dismay
And cracked the problem in one go:
They made Sebastian CTO.
To ease somewhat this bitter pill
His take-home rose to half-a-mill
With pension plan and stock reserved—
Just what Sebastian deserved.


## WHY I DON'T LIKE BASIC

In the first job I had, long before you were born,
We used Commodore BASIC for PETs:
Just two-letter variables, note that point please,
And line numbers, GOSUBs, and GETs.
A Northerner there was a little bit DIM—
His arrays were all smaller than 10—
He rang me one evening to help fix a bug.
"What is it controls this IF/THEN?"
I said "I." He said "'kay." I said "No, I said I,
Don't put K because then it won't work."
He said "I?" I said "Yes." He said "Why?" I said "No!
Just shut up and listen, you nerk.
Don't put Y, just put I. Is that clear?" He said, "Aye."
I said "Ah! Now we *will* get on fine."
He said "Oh, is it R?" I said "O?" I said "Eh?"
He said "A?" Then I hung up the line.

Apologies to Lewis Carroll ("The Mouse's Tail"), Harry Graham ("Upgrading Stan"), Anon.
("The Lincolnshire Poacher"), Hilaire Belloc ("Sebastian Drew") and Rob Wilton ("Why I
Don't Like Basic") who wrote the originals.

# Borland Revelations

*"The audience mood was pretty somber. You could tell the Borland folks thought there would be clapping in spots, and none of us obliged."*

> —*Attendee blogging Borcon to the official borland.public.conference newsgroup.*

A nd when the Sons of Kahn, who were *also* called the Borland-ites, and who dwelt in the valley of Scotts, found that they had been toiling *together* for one score years, they spake one unto another, saying: Let us throw a party to celebrate.

2. Then the Sons of Kahn went out unto their website, *and* unto their newsgroups, and unto their customer database too. And in all these places they did call out, saying: Come, friends, to our birthday party in San Jose. Dress informal. Bring $1,300.

3. And they did book the McEnery Convention Center, which offers 143,000 square feet *of* column-free prime exhibit space, up to 30 meeting rooms capable of seating up to 2,400 theater-style and, I confidently wager though in all honesty the website is silent *on* this one, more overhead projector screens than you can shake a stick at.

4. And it came to pass that a great hoard of Users descended *upon* the Convention Center, where they did register and collect their Welcome Packs. And among *this* hoard *of* Users there were three companions, being a User of Kylix (Pascal), a User of C++ Builder, and a User of Delphi.

# ORDEAL OF THE KYLIX USER

And, once they had all been to the hotel to check *in* and freshen up, the User of Kylix went forth in search of the Sons of Kahn. And when he came upon them, he cried *out unto* them saying: O Sons of Kahn, twelve full months ago you did releaseth a release of Kylix.

2. And since that time the tribe that is *led* by Linus the Finn hath been busy, yeah as busy as the busy honeybee that plunders the perfumed blooms of summer to fill the waxy comb with sweetness.

3. And the limpid releases of Linux have flowed forth each *in* its season, and the disties have moved onward. And it has come to pass that Kylix no longer sitteth firmly upon the bedrock of Linux. The linker it linkereth not, under some conditions, and there are some problems with the File Openeth dialog in the IDE, and that is *just* for starters.

4. All this spake the User of Kylix. And the User spake again, saying: Here are my upgrade dollars, which burneth a hole in *my* outer garment. When cometh the next release?

5. And the Sons of Kahn replied: That is for us to know and for you to find out.

6. And the User spake again, saying: Windeth not me *up*.

7. And the Sons of Kahn temporised: Let *it* go, move on. Nowhere in our slides does it *actually* say that we are abandoning Kylix.

8. And the User spake not, but looked hard upon the Sons of Kahn.

9. And then the Sons of Kahn spake again saying: Well if you must know, we aren't going to touch it *until* 2005, at the very earliest.

10. And the User spake, saying: *Oh*. And he sat down, and looked thoughtful.

# ORDEALS OF THE OTHER USERS

And the User of C++ Builder came *also* unto the Sons of Kahn, and she cried out saying: O Sons of Kahn, what have you got for me?

2. (For *by* tradition the token female *is* nearly always a C++ programmer, presumably because C++ programmers are brainier. Check out the pronouns in *C/C++ Users Journal* and also in the *ACCU* periodicals if thou thinkst I make this up to tease.)

3. And the Sons of Kahn replied, saying: Glad you asked, *because* you are going to love this. It's called C++ BuilderX, and it's cross-platform, and we've got a new ANSI compiler that copes *with* Boost.

4. And the User spake politely, saying: Wonderful.

5. And the Sons of Kahn went on, saying: Yes, and there's a Java IDE, and *a* new framework called wxWindows which replaces *that* nasty old Pascal VCL.

6. And the User interrupted, saying: Whoa *there*. How does this help with my old VCL apps? How can I change *them*? Have you any tools to help convert my old code?

7. And the Sons of Kahn replied, saying: That is for us to know and for you to find out.

8. And the User of C++ Builder spake, saying: *Ugh*.

9. And the Sons of Kahn snuck away, saying: Oh look, there *is* a User of Delphi. O User of Delphi, how would you like a brand new compiler based *on* the .NET system of the Mic-rosoftees?

10. And the User of Delphi, for verily it was *he*, replied: Well, that might be interesting down the line. Although if we did do any .NET stuff, chances are we *would* use C#. No offence. You'll never guess who designed it *for* the Mic-rosoftees.

11. And the Sons of Kahn spake, saying: We *had* heard.

12. And the User changed the subject, saying: Anyway, when cometh my new native compiler?

13. And the Sons of Kahn replied, saying: That is for us to know . . .

14. And the User of Delphi was verily smacked *about* the mouth, saying: Us too? Golly.

# A GREAT PROPHET REMEMBERED

And then all three Users looked down *upon* the tribe of the Sons of Kahn. And they saw that everywhere they looked there were Mic-rosoftees. And they saw that the Mic-rosoftees *seemed* to move in amongst and around the Sons of Kahn unhindered.

2. And it was even as the grubs of the wax moth move unchallenged *amongst* the honeybees of the hive.

3. And the Sons of Kahn saw where they were looking and said *unto* all the Users: Behold! This is only healthy co-opetition. We work with other companies too. We have not lost *the* plot.

4. But the Users had cause to remember the wisdom *of* the great prophet M'andee-rice Davies. And they all trooped home to ponder what had passed, *and* to be sad.

DECEMBER 2003, *THE REGISTER*

# Patenting by Numbers

## NOW NUMBERS TO BE PATENTABLE

*10, 9, 8, miss out "thing"*

In a move that has surprised naïve observers, the US Patent Office has announced that from now on it will consider "serious" applications to patent specific integer numbers.

"It was the logical next step," grey-haired and twinkling Patent Laureate Mr. J. Dall Swanhuffer twinkled to a shocked press conference today.

"Remember human genes. Certain doubting Duanes used to argue that, just because nobody invented them, they couldn't be patented. 'What will the patent holder do if I happen to have a patented gene in my body? Shoot me?' they used to jeer. Well, those wiseacres were proved wrong then, and they're going to be proved wrong again.

"Of course, there has been irresponsible campaigning and scare-mongering among left-wing pressure groups with an anti-big business bias. We expected this and we are ready for it. These are the same forces at work that were against software patents granted for stunningly obvious and general techniques. In truth one cannot but feel sorry for any confused individual who vainly tries to hold up the inevitable and just progress of patent law.

"To the law-abiding lay and IT community I say: Yes, I have been listening carefully to your misplaced concerns, and I can put your minds entirely at rest," said Mr. Swanhuffer. "You have no need to fear any number-crunching bogeymen. It is nonsense to suggest, as may well be suggested, that first grade school children chanting their times tables with Miss Pearson will be subject to raids by the sinister soon-to-be-formed FANT *[Federation Against Number Theft]* action squads in balaclavas carrying stun grenades.

"For one thing I have it on excellent authority that FANT operatives will never wear balaclavas except when it is very cold; for another it is unrealistic to expect any patents to be granted on integers in the range of the usual times tables that we teach kids—even the very smart ones who do 13 times and 14 times. Our preliminary research suggests that extensive prior art exists, even for comparatively obscure numbers like 151."

Mr Swanhuffer went on to indicate that the new arrangements would come into effect immediately throughout the United States, to be followed shortly by Western Europe "if it knows what is good for it."

Integers are a kind of number with no fractional part, for example "12," and are widely used in both domestic and commercial applications. They were discovered by Sir Isaac Newton in the seventeenth century, or if not him then Pythagoras in his bath, or Benjamin Franklin. One of that lot.

# PATENTED NUMBERS "A GOOD IDEA"

*Mr. Attorney fails to surprise.*
To get some background on the recent move by the US Patent office, *The Reg* spoke to IP lawyer Lawrence P Po™a®© (pronounced "potmarc") of the distinguished LA firm of Po™a®©, Po™a®© & Po™a®© (pronounced "potmarc, potmarc and potmarc").

"The IP legal community is real excited about this," explained Mr Po™a®© excitedly.

"We were all very, very disappointed when Intel lost its attempt to register the trademark 80486 a decade ago. We have been looking for a way to bring numbers back under sensible legal control ever since that time, and this could well be it."

"It's kind of hard to predict how things will pan out. Obviously there is no case law at this stage, but you can easily imagine things getting awkward."

"For example, suppose Corporation A was awarded Patent no. *n* for integer *m*, at the same time as Corporation B was awarded Patent no. *m* for integer *n*. Neither corporation could enforce its own IP rights without violating the IP rights of the other. They would be trapped in a kind of deadly embrace. They'd fight like ferrets in a Yorkshireman's trousers," said Mr Po™a®© gleefully.

Top mathematicians say that integers start at 0 or 1 and continue in both directions for a fair old way. The number "101" is a well-known and successful integer, thanks to its popularisation by the doggie-oriented author Dodie Smith in her book *101 Dalmatians* and top writer George Orwell's celeb-based BBC2 show *Room 101*. Amazing fact: at today's exchange rates 101 in binary is now worth just 5 in decimal, following a catastrophic devaluation of binary.

# FIRST INTEGER PATENTED

*Only infinity minus one to go.*

Softwron Inc., the US software and litigation giant, has become the first company to make a move in what is increasingly becoming known as the Great Rumble for Numbers.

The recent surprise announcement by the US Patent Office to grant patents on integer numbers has meant that industry-watchers, Wall Street, and the Association of Primary School Maths Teachers have been on eleventerhooks as to which company would be the first to exploit the iniquitous new law.

Mr. Rock McDosh, Softwron's CEO, founder and widely loathed bully, today summoned the world's business press to his luxurious 92nd floor boardroom for the announcement.

"I am proud to confirm that Softwron has become the first company to apply for a patent on an integer number. This is a great day for Softwron, Softwron's shareholders, and indeed the United States of America. Mankind long ago discovered the science of math, but it is only now with the industrial might and urgent probing technical innovation of Softwron that we have truly begun to tame it. Going forward into the future, we confidently expect to become the leading player in the integer market, although obviously we will never have anything that could reasonably be construed as a monopoly by federal authorities."

McDosh was asked if his company was not just cynically exploiting a natural resource. "That is absolutely not the case. Going forward we are looking into maturing and adding value to our intellectual property. Even as we speak our best numberware engineers are looking into, for example, ways of enhancing our integer so that it is divisible by seven. Obviously this would make it much more attractive to manufacturers of weekly diaries and calendar type products. We call this technology 'Retrofactorization™' and I'm very, very excited about it."

McDosh sought to address worries about how the licence to use the Softwron integer would operate. "I've been hearing some very silly scare stories that every computer in the world will have to run the WronMon monitor program, which will supposedly automatically transfer $0.50 each time our number is used within the machine. This is ridiculous.

"The fact is that in the early days very few institutions will have the need or indeed the financial wherewithal to license the Softwron integer. We are in negotiations with chip manufacturers right now so that, going forward, unlicensed systems will simply be unable to 'think' of our number. It's a process analogous to human lobotomy, and I expect it to be entirely painless."

The details of the patent itself are being kept a closely guarded secret, pending completion of the legal formalities. This is in case some naughty person goes out and tries to establish prior usage, or other jiggery-pokery. However, the integer is generally believed to be in the so-called high 64-bit range, from 4,294,967,296 to 18,446,744,073,709,551,615 inclusive. If this is the case, then it has worrying implications for all those swanky 64-bit machines that are beginning to come out now. Although, there again, do you know anybody who has actually got one? Quite.

## SOFTWRON SHOWS OFF ITS NEW TECHNOLOGY

*They've got our number.*
Today was "open doors day" at Softwron Inc., the US software and litigation giant. Softwron is the first company to take advantage of the US Patent Office's surprise announcement that integers are patentable.

To counter recent unfavourable coverage, the company took a party of top-notch journos, your correspondent naturally included, around its secret research facility.

The so-called 'Wron number itself is held in a reinforced safe in a deep vault specially excavated out of the side of a mountain in an inaccessible part of an unmarked state. Engineers who need to work with the number are only allowed to do so under the closest supervision. The whole place is dimly lit with lots of low-level concealed red-coloured lighting, to make it all seem more exciting.

The security guards are carefully chosen to avoid compromising the company's interest. Like all non-technical Softwron employees, they must pass strict innumeracy tests before being allowed to work in the facility. To even be considered, candidates must suppose that by picking the same set of lottery numbers every week they are gradually improving their chances of winning, because it stands to reason. If they are to work in the vault itself, they must be demonstrably confused by simple percentages. According to the site's head of personnel, the ideal employee is one of those rather irritating people who believe that to say "Pshaw! I've always been thick at maths, me, since Miss Eversham in Form 3" is a good way of demonstrating a happy-go-lucky and clubbable personality.

Naturally, we weren't shown the Number, although the correspondent from a Washington broadsheet did claim to catch a glimpse of a single digit. This may have been a "1" or a "7." He wasn't sure or even Pshaw! in the dim red light.

At least one actual fact was established by the press trip. When questioned persistently, a company spokesman formerly denied the Internet rumour that the 'Wron number is one of the so-called "pure sinatra numbers."

According to top mathematicians, the best-known example of a pure sinatra number is 14,991,338,361,953,636,352, although partial sinatra numbers are known to exist too. Sinatra numbers are one of Single Mother Nature's wonders, having special and unusual properties that make them unlike non-sinatra numbers. To investigate these properties, you need to display the sinatra number in hexadecimal format. Like the Windows calculator can. If you can be bothered.

# 'WRON NUMBER CAUGHT IN FERMAT-DEFYING ROMP

*Innocent integer ensnared by Wiles' wiles.*

US software and litigation giant Softwron Inc. is today vigorously denying a rumour that its newly patented integer, the so-called 'Wron number, has been caught flouting numerical law.

Hirsute expensively-suited granite-jawed granite-named Mr. Rock McDosh, founder and CEO of Softwron, appeared before the world's press to defend the integrity of the company's recently acquired intellectual property.

Mr. McDosh was unable to address accusations directly, owing to a blanket gagging injunction taken out by one of the other parties allegedly involved. He was therefore obliged to make something of a Prince Charlie of himself, to the simple pleasure of all present:

"We categorically state that no number protected by Softwron patent has been involved in any rumoured inappropriate behaviour; and in any case we do not accept that such behaviour is inappropriate, if it could be stated what it was. Nonetheless, if going forward it were generally known what it was, our number would still not be involved in whatever it is. Which it isn't."

That's clear then. Happily *The Reg* is published on the Internet, outside the jurisdiction of any court except that of Almighty God Himself and the beak at Croydon. We can dish the dirt. The rumour, which started in the Usenet newsgroup sci.math.research but rapidly spread to rec.pets.cats.anecdotes, states that the 'Wron number and two other "large" integers together ganged up on an unwilling smaller (but technically oversize) integer and forced it to indulge in Fermatic practices with them.

Put in lame layman's terms, Fermat's law states that, if the sum of two integers each raised to a given integer power is equal to a third integer raised to the same power, then the maximum power that may legally be used is 2.

The following press agency equation, recorded by an amateur using homemade equipment, purports to show the guilty parties at it like knives. The identities of most of the integers involved have been crudely concealed with simple alphabetical letters, although if you look carefully you can just make out that the "victim" is 3.

$$x^3 + y^3 = z^3$$

Legal seagull Lawrence P. Po™a®© (pronounced "potmarc") comments: "This kind of incident is highly embarrassing for Softwron right now, but I don't think it will ever go to court. What you have to remember is that the US Government never ratified Fermat's Law, which it views as being anti-free trade."

Top mathematician Andrew Wiles proved Fermat's Last Theorem in a famous 1995 paper that can easily be found by googling for your light reading pleasure. We would attempt a witticism, but mere English language comedy is as dust once you have read the study of Hecke rings in Chapter 2. This kept us giggling happily down the pub last Friday for hours, until the landlord called time and hustled us out into the evening drizzle.

# Confessions of a Spammer

## INTERVIEW WITH A BULK EMAILER

*Don't say the S word.*

I leave the A12 a few miles after Chelmsford and am instantly deep in rain-soaked countryside. Half an hour of nervous driving on slushy narrow lanes I come upon a vast, newly built mock-Tudor mansion, grandly set up in many acres of sodden lawn. A nameplate screwed to elaborate wrought-iron gates declares: "DunRo@ming." This is the place.

I park the car on the verge, but then linger inside listening to the radio instead of getting out, dawdling like a can-I-pay-by-cheque merchant at the front of the Five Items Or Fewer queue. I am not looking forward to meeting my interviewee.

You've seen his work of course. We all have. Not for nothing has he rocketed up to #4 in *The Sunday Newspaper*'s "Top 100 Most Hated People in Britain" list, leaving quiz show cheaters and corrupt Tory ex-MPs for dust.

I am off to record for *The Reg* the first exclusive interview with Mr. Samuel Osborne, the notorious purveyor of penile pills, a semi-recluse who lives, it is said, in fantastic luxury with his wife and common law dogs.

I am off to meet England's first spamlionaire.

I get out into the rain, hoist my jolly orange brolly and look for a bell pull. Just inside the gates, an overalled gardener with a gentle face is poking insincerely at the dripping rhododendrons with a pair of secateurs. There is a small ironstone statue on a brick plinth by the gate.

Eros, inevitably. Remembering Philip Marlowe in *The High Window*, I pat its damp little head for luck.

"Can I help?"

The "gardener" has stopped pruning and come up to the gate. He says, in an educated voice, "You must be Verity Stob."

I admit it.

"Good morning, Ms. Stob. My name is Sam Osborne. Come inside out of the rain. I have such a lot to tell you about."

# SP@M: THE MYST.ERIES XP1AINED!!!

### How the stripes get in the toothpaste

Inside the house, I expected a typical wealthy Essex businessman's abode: crossed sawn-offs over a granite mantel, 300-inch widescreen TVs in every tennis court, more fake marble than you could shake a building society branch at.

But it wasn't like that at all. The place had an institutional quality to it: glass doors opening on tidy little offices, a server cupboard filled with blinking LEDs and air conditioning noise, a disabled loo. Osborne led me to a large room containing 10 or 20 people, all seated at PCs.

"Before we go in I should warn you that . . . that we have a policy of giving jobs to folks who haven't been as lucky in life as we have. Please don't be alarmed by anything."

I *was* alarmed. I nervously followed Osborne into the room.

"Come and meet Helen. She's our longest serving employee."

Osborne indicated a frail-looking, middle-aged woman sat at a PC in the far corner. Even as he pointed, she gave a faint groan and collapsed forward, head lolling gracelessly on her keyboard. Appalled, I started towards her, but Osborne put out his hand to stop me. Nobody else took any notice at all.

As I drew breath to express outrage, the woman called Helen twitched, sat up, gazed at the screen blearily for a moment, and then continued typing.

Osborne said quietly into my ear: "Narcolepsy. Quite safe, in this form. Helen prefers that we ignore her 'interludes.' It seems like the kindest thing. Come and see."

We tiptoed up to Helen, and gazed over her shoulder at her screen. She was composing an email. It could not be said that her condition did not interfere with her work. She had typed:

```
Absolutely No Doctor's Prescription Needed!
Phentermine, Viagra, Soma, Ambien, Floricet, Imitrex, Paxil, Prozac,
Zoloft...


leeuwenhoek  xqpfbviztf x d r naqzzgqkkjt tfqjatcc


and many many more prescription drugs!
```

"Oh," I said, suddenly enlightened, "is this why one so often gets whole lines of gobbledygook in spam? Because Helen has, erm, encountered a pause? I thought it was a dodge to defeat checksum-based spam filters."

Osborne said, "You'd be surprised how many people think that. But do come and meet Michael." He tugged me towards another corner of the room.

Michael was about 30 years old and rather overweight. He wore a shell suit and the pleasant, guileless smile of a person disadvantaged by learning difficulties. He smelled of urine, but no worse than the people who sit next to you on the Tube.

"Hello Michael," said Osborne, "this lady has come all the way from London to see you do your typing. Will you show her?"

"Michael type good," said Michael. He furrowed his brow, protruded a furled tongue and with unbearable deliberation picked out an email:

```
ADD I.NCHE.S WITH OUR P.I.L.L!
STIL NO LUCK E*N*L*A*R*G*I*N*G IT????
Our pr'oduct will work 4U!!!!!!!!!!!!
```

"Well done Michael," I said enthusiastically. "That's very good. Is it true you like sweet things?" And I gave him the chocolate bar that Osborne had quietly passed to me while Michael was struggling to find his eighth consecutive shriek-stop.

I asked Osborne, "Can we talk about this somewhere?"

"In a moment. First let's see what Mr. Bank is up to."

Mr. Bank was a thin, grey-haired bald-pated man in a velvet jacket. He was typing rapidly.

Osborne put his mouth near my ear and whispered: "Thinks he's Jane Austen reincarnated. Not our most productive worker."

> By this time the report of the accident had spread among the workmen and boatmen about the Cobb, and many were collected near them, to be useful if wanted; at any rate, to enjoy the sight of a dead young lady, nay, two dead young ladies, for it proved twice as fine as the first report.
> ARE YOU ASHAMED OF YOUR PENIS?
> To some of the best-looking of these good people Henrietta was consigned, for, though partially revived, she was quite helpless; and in this manner, Anne walking by her side, and Charles attending to his wife, they set forward, treading back, with feelings unutterable, the ground which so lately, so very lately, and so light of heart, they had passed along.
> THIS REALLY WORKS!

I said, "But I was sure that was to defeat Bayesian blocking. I never thought . . . "

Osborne silenced me with a finger. "Come into my office and we'll talk about it."

# WHY MEN BUY BLUE PILLS

*They're for a friend.*

Time for the interview proper. Did he admit spamming was immoral?

"Spamming? Immoral?" He was amazed. "You've seen my operation. I'm providing a public service!"

In what sense, I wondered, was it a public service to send out 10 million emails per day tempting the unfair sex to buy wildly expensive and dubiously effective drugs to enlarge/stiffen their dangly bits?

"You need to understand men, Ms. Stob." He leant back in his chair, staring up at the ceiling. "We are inhibited. We are not, to use Californian jargon, 'in touch with our own feelings.' We'd rather die than take these problems to the doctor, much less talk to a friend. An approach by a supposedly random bulk-email message is the only way to overcome the barrier of male bashfulness."

He paused a moment, to let this idea sink in.

"And anyway, our pills are absolutely harmless . . . "

Absolutely harmless? Did this mean he admitted that his drugs had no effect? Didn't that make it fraud?

"Not at all. It's medically proven that erectile dysfunction and size perception problems are nearly always psychological. The best treatment is some kind of placebo. Let a man take a pill and he feels he is doing something—and that's halfway to being cured.

"Yes, you are right: the pills have no intrinsic effect. As you programmers put it, that's a feature not a bug. They won't poison the patient if he overdoses in a fit of, um, excitement."

So why did these sugar pills, or whatever they were, have to cost £35 per bottle? He could hardly claim that he was deferring the cost of expensive medical research.

"It's the psychological angle again. If it weren't expensive, it wouldn't be convincing. The more these men pay for my pills, the more successful the treatment.

"Besides, we have done some research. Our survey has shown that mine is the most successful non-prescription treatment available. Much more successful than the most popular non-prescription treatment."

And what, I wondered, was the most popular non-prescription treatment?

The corners of Mr Osborne's mouth went down in disapproval. He put his folded hands on his blotter. He looked like a country solicitor reading out a controversial will where all the money has gone to the black sheep with a gambling habit.

"Putting a bit of talc on it after a shower," he said gruffly.


# SOMETHING FOR THE LADIES

***Overdoing the sweet sherry***

I asked Osborne, "So are all your medical products aimed at men?"

"By no means."

He pushed a leaflet towards me. I read:

*Want to lose weight quickly and painlessly?*

*What could be more natural or organic than sleep?*

*Snore away those problem pounds and get the body you deserve with CelluNite!*

"Are you really claiming that with these pills people can diet while they sleep?"

He shrugged. "It's medically proven that no woman *gains* weight while she sleeps."

"What about if she falls asleep in an aircraft at high altitude, and wakes up at sea level\*?" I asked facetiously, momentarily letting my inner geek run amok.

He looked at me blankly, as well he might.

"So what exactly is *in* this CelluNite pill?"

"Oh no, I could hardly tell you that, Ms. Stob. Although," he leaned forward confidentially, "I *can* reveal that very few CelluNite patients get scurvy."

I changed tack. "But you don't just sell health products, do you?"

"Ah no. Recently we have been expanding into the leisure market. Let me show you. Would you mind passing me that box?"

I followed his pointing finger to a crowded shelf at my shoulder. It was filled with merchandise. Cartons of CelluNite tablets. A dozen childproof press-and-twist bottles of KnobFood II. A presentation box with a pre-printed gift tag ("Happy Loving Holidays to the Big Man in My Life") containing twenty capsules of *Viagrazine Générique pour l'homme par Kelvin Calf*. ("The French touch," said Osborne proudly. "Can't beat Gallic sophistication for the Christmas market.") And, at the far end, a shoebox.

I picked it up, but it had been put on the shelf upside-down and its contents fell out. On the floor lay a snub-nosed cylinder of translucent pink plastic, about nine inches in length. Near its blunt end it had a strange appendage, like a malformed limb. It looked quite revolting.

The fall had somehow started the thing's electric motor buzzing. It slithered forward along the carpet like a wounded crab. Its "leg" touched my foot. I let out an involuntary shriek.

---

\*It would have to be a *very* high altitude. *Reg* reader Richard Bolingbroke writes that, if she were flying on a conventional airliner, the woman would actually be lighter when she awoke. He says this is because of the "horizon effect," which means that one experiences some sideways gravity at sea level. As one starts to move away from earth, gravity becomes more focused downwards, increasing weight. Furthermore, there are buoyancy issues caused by reduced cabin air pressure that would also tend to turn the spring balance (but presumably *not* a pair of scales) against this unfortunate lady.

That's me told, then. Any other *Reg* readers who booked flights in order to experience the sensation of temporary weight loss may write to my lawyer at the usual address.

"There you go. The John Bunny 7000—it's cliterally, ha-ha, the best model we have ever made. What do you think, Ms. Stob?"

I kicked the thing under the desk where it couldn't touch me and gathered my thoughts.

"Does it support Bluetooth®?" I asked brightly.


# YOU HAVE OPTED IN

*Oh yes you have.*
Louis Theroux would never put up with this. It was time to get tough. I asked Osborne about the recent EC spam legislation.

"Terrible. Terrible. A truly wretched thing."

It was forcing him to close down his operation?

"Oh no. Quite the reverse. I've actually saved money and doubled throughput since the spam laws came in."

"Thing is, I've had to outsource my email servers to India and, sad though I am to say it, they give me a *much* better service. Those boys can sniff out an open relay like a pig after a truffle.

"I am a patriot, Ms Stob, and as you have seen I like to plough the money I earn back into the local community. As usual, I have been prevented from doing the right thing by an interfering government that kowtows to Europe and simply doesn't understand business needs. It really makes me angry."

Astonished by this brazen attempt to claim the moral high ground, I furiously and unprofessionally asked Osborne why I had to get 400 KB of spam every day?

"Do you? That's terrible. I can assure you that you get nothing from me. What do you use for spam filter software?"

I told him.

"Well, there's your problem. That's a load of old junk. If you used our SpamItOff for Windows, you could wave goodbye to spam forever."

I said, "That's outrageous! The only reason people need spam filters is because you send them spam. You are driving the need for your own product."

"Ms Stob, you keep getting emotional. This is a technical matter, not an ethical matter. Who knows the most about spam? Me. Therefore who is best placed to block it? If you think about it, I'm sure you'll see it makes sense.

"Tell you what. I really haven't got any more time to spend on this interview right now, but as a gesture of good faith, I'll let you have a free copy of SpamItOff. I'm afraid we are all out of CDs at the moment, so I'll have to email it to you. What was your address again?"

I sat across the desk, looking at this calm, professional man with his kind face. For all my doubts, surely he couldn't be responsible for all the frustration, anger, and disgust that spam caused? Surely he hadn't flooded the mail servers of the world with filth, turning an elegant piece of trusted software engineering into a crippled, suspicious, clumsy mess? Surely it wasn't him?

"Well, Ms Stob?"

"It's drew_cullen_17820@aol.com."*

\*          \*          \*

*Tell England. Tell the world. Discover the truth. Start reading your Bible. Stop suffering in silence. Make her scream. Be a sex machine. Be young again. Make a fortune with Ebay. Get the cheapest home loan possible. Pay no cable bills. Pay less when you pump. Block all spam. Eat yourself thin. Don't forget the family. Make it a Ray Charles Christmas.*

*Eat up your spam . . . or click <u>here</u> to unsubscribe.*

With apologies to DLS.

---

*Drew Cullen is the esteemed editor of *The Register*. Or if not esteemed, at least esthardboyled.

PART IV

# PREVIOUSLY UNPUBLISHED

*"Comprising previously unseen material that has somehow fallen into obscure subdirectories wedged down the back of my hard disk"*

—*V. Stob*

[This column was commissioned for a proposed relaunch of *Byte Magazine* in 2002 that never happened. It spoofs a long-running and popular feature from the original *Byte*, "Steve Ciarcia's Circuit Cellar."]

# Solder Cellar—Kindly Accept Substitutes

*Welcome back to a column from the Golden Age of computer magazines—now with a new face at the helm.*

Hi. While we struggle with the rusty padlock and click on the bare light-bulb to illuminate the long-deserted, but still fondly remembered, "Solder Cellar," I think I had better apologise straight away for the absence of its original occupant. But rest assured the spirit of the column lives on. Like you, I grew up with it, and like you, I cherish the issue (was it really back in 1986?) when for as little as $2000-worth of parts and 12 week's effort, "Solder Cellar" showed us how to build an I/O board that enabled our fridge/freezer to call us up at work and warn us in the event of a power cut at home. Oh how we all laughed when we spotted the mistake.

Actually, truth be told, I didn't really want this. *I* wanted to break out of the stereotype and do a programming page for the under-12s or, failing that, a regular feature about not-too-hard-to-operate electronic gadgets. I said to the editor, I said: Look, we'll keep the boys/toys hardware angle and it won't even cost you anything, I've already got my own Palm V—admittedly with a dicky battery—we could take lots of little photographs with me pointing at it, ask the Mac operator to do some spiffy graphics, it would be great. He snarled: What do you think this is, *Wired*? I said: But must I do the hardware column? I don't even understand the phrase "overclocked mobo." He said: Do you understand the phrase "contractual obligation?"

So here we are. And I'm really beginning to wish I had listened harder when they started to do electricity in Physics, instead of whiling away the hours passing libellous notes concerning Lucy Hopkirk's personal hygiene. No matter. Let us begin with a review of our basic skills, starting with that invaluable tool and eponymous hero of the column, the soldering iron. Now the particular one that I have here—made by Stobbo Ltd. by the way, you may want to have a pen ready because I'll be giving out Stobbo's URL later on—the one that I have here is an ingenious gas-fired model. Rather than tie yourself down with an inconvenient mains flex, this little beauty leaves you free to solder away, anytime and anywhere. Just switch on the butane, flick this little flint wheel, boomph! and away you go.

While that is warming up, perhaps this is the right moment to say a word or two about Stobbo, the mail order company to the electronic home-build cognoscenti. Although many of the columns will be featuring components and tools available from Stobbo, I wish to emphasise that there is absolutely no necessity to purchase your supplies from them. Any high-quality retailer will do just as well. Even if that wasn't the case, it isn't any affair of mine. If you are the sort of person who would spoil the ship for a ha'p'orth of tar, that's your lookout.

Now that we have straightened that out, a few words about the art of soldering. It isn't enough to hold the two wires close together and bodge on a big blob of solder. The secret of a sound joint is, is, what's that smell, *bloody hell I'm on fire!*

No, it's fine now, thanks, and you'll hardly see it if I comb it round. Yes, I could shave the other eyebrow to match, thanks for the fashion tip. Let's put the soldering to one side and get on with the next item.

I've noticed that these days the big question on everybody's lips at gatherings of fellow wire [w]rappers is: How do you fix a Palm V with a dicky battery? The problem, as you all well know, is that the Palm people failed to provide a way of opening the case to get at the doings, instead smothering it with warranty violation labels. But don't worry, last night I googled up a website that explained everything with step-by-step photos. It's easy-peasy.

First, lay the Palm face down on a clean work surface. Now use that invaluable tool the hair dryer (Stobbo $59.95) to blow hot air all around the seam to melt the glue. Like so. After a very few seconds, you can simply lift off the back plate. The trick is—there, did you spot my mistake?—the trick is not to linger too long with the heat. Otherwise you melt the case itself, and turn your or rather *my* dear little PDA, until recently full of addresses and appointments, into a miniature plastic cowpat. Fine. Oh, do stop sniggering. Remember, I do this so you don't have to.

Just space for a word about the next column, where I will be tackling another invaluable tool, the Stobbo oscilloscope. Although superficially an ugly television set with a five-inch screen, thirty-eight baffling knobs and a stupid green horizontal line that disappeared when I twiddled the VERTICAL SWEEP HOLDOFF control, this fine instrument carries over $400 worth of pure margin, and as such is well worth my manual-reading time. See you soon!

## Pin by Pin: The Pentium 4

The original "Solder Cellar" was justly famous for its in-depth analyses of *chips du jour*, and I have absolutely no intention of letting those high standards drop, even if we are somewhat constrained by space. What better place to start than with Intel's Pentium 4? As you expect, we will be looking at the 478-pin package, rather than the wimpier 423-pin job. In each successive "Solder Cellar" column I shall define the use of one pin, which you can then write up in the correct space on your Solder Cellar Pentium 4 Pin by Pin wall chart (Stobbo Publications $38.95). When this is complete, you will have a beautiful and valuable keepsake that you will want to show off to your middle-aged grandchildren.

Enough with the preamble, and on with the low-level in-depth silicon action! This time, we are going with pin AF24, extreme right-hand side of your charts, third one down. And the purpose of this pin is RESERVED, and it must remain unconnected.

Next time out, A7!

**AUGUST 2004**

[This is a review of Lara Croft's sixth and most limp outing: Tomb Raider—the Angel of Darkness.

Martin Bashir, by the way, is probably best known for a lengthy and emotional TV interview with a certain Princess of Wales.]

———

# Lara's Last Stand?

*Lara Croft may be ready to leave Tomb Raider.*

Angel of Darkness is comfortably the most sumptuous Tomb Raider game yet. The great London Symphony Orchestra gives us its lush rendering of *Meanderings in a Minor Key That Never Quite Reach the Tune.* Joss Ackland voices the chief baddie. A new 3D graphics engine breaks records for detail and realism, although it is a little disappointing that bushes still look as though they have been struck from cuttings pinched from the garden of *The Magic Roundabout.*

But this glitter cannot disguise something deeper amiss in AofD, and I think I can put my finger on it. Lara Croft has reached the end of her tether.

Not that she admits this directly. It is doubtful that she could. She speaks only a strange, stilted dialect of English that I call Non-Sequitur. Lara: "I'm afraid Werner is dead." Carvier: "Dead?" Lara: "Can I get you anything?" Or, there again, Carvier: "Poor Werner was clearly terrified." Lara: "Can we move this along a bit?" No wonder she has had such little success over the years forming relationships, even with characters she doesn't kill.

But if she can't admit her distress directly, a careful observer can easily find plentiful clues to her condition.

Item: reduced physical strength. In Tomb Raiders I through V, Lara was able to hang from a ledge by her fingertips indefinitely. At the start of AofD, she can barely hold on for 20 seconds.

Item: she is in denial about this. "I feel stronger!" she boasts after prising off a notably weedy padlock with a huge crowbar. "My legs feel stronger!" she cries having pushed a crate four yards. Anybody who has dropped a year's sub on gym membership and been obliged to retire hurt after 10 minutes of the first session will instantly identify with the psychology of self-deceit behind these remarks.

Item: creeping hypochondria and addiction. Pre-AofD, Lara kept herself in prime condition with two simple and reliable medicines, the Small Medi-Pack and the Large Medi-Pack. These days Lara additionally calls upon the healing powers of "health bandages" (what?), "health pills for extra stamina" (say no more), and that classic pick-me-up of the depressed, lonely person, chocolate bars. This path leads only to nervous breakdown, ballooning to 23 stone* and being surprised by the paparazzi pack while being smuggled into a health clinic in a Betty Ford Transit.

Item: her new makeup regime. Lara has really let rip with the black eye-liner. This is the most significant detail of all. Think. What other mid '90s female icon, superficially in control but actually emotionally wounded and yearning for a new life, famously appeared in public looking like this? I do hope that Lara hasn't set her heart on a Martin Bashir interview, because it wouldn't work. Bashir: "Do you feel that your natural sexuality was exploited?" Lara: "Can we move this along a bit?"

I predict that, confronted with this evidence, the makers of Tomb Raider will bluster that it simply reflects Lara's recent difficulties in Egypt. Don't you believe them. These are the insensitive buffoons that erected a memorial statue to Lara before news of her supposed death had dropped out of the TV bulletins. They'll say anything to keep the show on the road.

Lara has been raiding tombs since 1996. Surely, for her own benefit, she should be allowed to retire to the Croft mansion in Surrey and spend more time with her artefacts.

---

*Fourteen pounds to the stone. So that's, twenty times fourteen is 280 plus three times . . . wait a moment. Are those US pounds or British pounds or nautical pounds? And is it really fourteen, or is it sixteen, which sounds much more likely? And . . . oh hang it. I mean "very fat," OK?

———

# Too Obscure or Rude

*Comprising verse too irrelevant and/or naughty for magazine publication*

THE TRAGEDY OF JOHN RASPBERRY III*

*who took too much Viagra and perished horribly*

The saddest tale I've ever heard
Concerns John Raspberry the Third,
An elderly American gent
Who did not know what old age meant.

To show his girl a thing or two—
For she was barely eighty-two,
And had that year enlarged her bust—
He determined to enhance his lust.

His doctor, who was very wise,
At John's desire showed no surprise.
"I know what you want, I do, I betcher!
I'll not prescribe for you, old lecher!"

Our hero did not give up yet—
He bought some off the Internet.
And in ten days or maybe less
The pills arrived by Fed Express.

———

*Penned on the occasion of receiving my first piece of Viagra spam

That very night he set a date,
He asked his love around at eight
And hinted that the evening's tryst
Would be a treat not to be missed.

To set the mood before the show
He watched his favourite video.
(Miss M. Monroe starred in *Niagara*.)
Then settled down with his Viagra.

How much to take? He was not able
To read the print upon the label.
"Just one? Or two? Perhaps the lot'll . . .
What the hell!" He scoffed the bottle.

The phone rang and he heard the voice
Of his girlfriend's daughter's daughter Joyce.
Joyce said, "Grandma's had a slip
While in the bath. She's bust her hip.

"She asked me to give you a call
To say she can't come after all."
Appalled, poor John gave out a groan
And rapidly hung up the phone.

For "down below," to his surprise,
He felt a pain beneath his flies
And then to his increasing wonder
His corduroy bags were split asunder.

It grew so that he was barely able
To free it from beneath the table.
It grew, and grew, and grew some more,
He poked it through the kitchen door.

It grew, and grew, till in the end
It wedged beneath the sink's U-bend.
And then the thing he feared the worst:
Unable to grow, his member burst.

His neighbours, hearing John shout "Hey!"
Had called for help without delay.
The doctor came round in a jiffy
To find a stiff with one huge stiffy.

The coffin fitting was a fiddle,
They had to wind it round his middle.
The clever doc summed up John's fate,
He simply wrote, "John came too late."

*Envoi (Surgeon General's Warning)*:

The moral is: don't be so silly.
Don't ever overdose your willy.
But if you must, don't come to grief—
Remember to try hand relief.


ANARCHY IN THE MIDDLE CLASS

I've found my NI number and my Code.
Buff folders, statements, letters fill the floor,
Loose piles denoting monies paid and owed,
Antique receipts, old payslips, bills galore.
A stack of helpful leaflets is to hand
All written in a strangely childish prose.
"Plain English winner!" "*You* can understand!"
What do they mean? Our man Hart-Davies* knows.
I've bought some software, courtesy of "Which?,"
My PC's *well* set for five hours of drear.
Then all at once I hit its power switch—
I think I will not pay my tax this year.

I've dreaded this for weeks and weeks and weeks.
If only I had buckled down at once!
It isn't just the money-loss that piques:
I so resent being made to feel a dunce.
Each season I have struggled through this tosh:
(Oh God. What do they mean by "UTR"?)

*Adam Hart-Davies is a TV presenter who fronts the UK Inland Revenue's "Isn't tax great fun?" promotional campaign. A specialist in science and engineering shows, he seems to be engaged in an experiment to test his popularity to destruction.

The Revenue wants pain as well as dosh.
(Why would *I* know my mileage in the car?)
Should I list the Christmas lunch among my perks?
D'you think this counts as pension? It's not clear.
*And* their horrid, baffling website never works—
I think I will not pay my tax this year.

I saw my MP on the local news—
Needless to say I didn't vote for her—
Spilling out her pseudo-rage and -views:
She blames our troubles on the Chancellor.
She says that he should spend my cash on roads,
The hospital, the prison, and the school,
On a scheme to soothe our rarest nematodes,
By reflooding all the land around their pool.
But what of *my* escape from daily stress?
There goes the budget for my sunshine trip this year.
It's theft. That's what it is. No less.
I'm sure I shan't pay income tax this year.

# Glossary of Britisms

*For the benefit of US readers, I am including a short list of British English terms, often slang, with which they may not be familiar. British readers may also find it interesting, so that they can look for and point out my mistakes.*

*—VS*

**battery hens**
Hens reared in very small cages (arranged in, wait for it, batteries); a rather cruel practice that is the cause of fierce debates and cheap eggs. Not some sort of electric chicken.

**best, pint of**
Means a pint of best bitter beer. Bitter is a flat, dark brown-coloured beer served at room temperature. It is the standard male tipple in the UK. Although "a pint of best" is a well-known phrase, nobody of my acquaintance uses it; real people always name the brand: "A pint of London Pride, please." The "pint of best" thing may well be a trap to detect foreign tourists who are trying too hard. If you *are* a foreign tourist, I advise against using it, in case you are charged £6 for a pint of drip tray runoff.

**blimey**
A very mild exclamation, rating 0.71 on the ISO SOC (Standardised Obscenity Counter) scale. Compare with 0.56 SOC for the US "Gee!" or 1.82 SOC for "bloody hell"; proper Anglo Saxon swear words are rated 5 SOC and upwards. "Blimey" has the merit over anodyne expressions like "Jumping jack hedgehogs!" ($1.04 \times 10^{-4}$ SOC) that it isn't cute. It is supposedly a corruption of "[God] blind me!"

### blurge
Portmanteau word, possibly coined by the author. From "blot out" + "purge." A blurged record in a database is definitely no longer accessible.

### bog off
The sentiment "go away," expressed (comparatively) daintily in print or pre-watershed TV so as not to frighten any Derby runners. SOC *(qv)* rating 1.03.

### boiled sweets
Small pieces of candy of that hard kind that dissolves slowly in the mouth, often causing schlurping noises and indistinct speech in its consumer. Coincidentally, committed fans of boiled sweets define "teeth" as small pieces of bone of that hard kind that dissolve slowly in the mouth, eventually causing schlurping noises and indistinct speech.

### braces
"Suspenders" in US parlance. This is a dangerous word; dangerous because, as often happens with words for clothes and food, it forms part of one of those annoying Markov chains of British/US vocabulary confusion:

> brackets (Brit) ➤ braces (US)
> braces (Brit) ➤ suspenders (US)
> suspenders (Brit) ➤ garters (US)
> garters (Brit) ➤ stenographer I should think, or maybe skillet

Other very well-known Markov chains are jam ➤ jelly ➤ jello and crisps ➤ chips ➤ fries ➤ surrender monkeys.

### caravan site
Trailer park.

### clubbable
Sociable, one who mixes well.

### cooking lager top, half of
Cooking lager is the cheapest, weakest, most watery kind of lager *(qv)* available at the pub bar. The expression is derived from "cooking sherry," the bottle of poor-quality fortified wine kept in the kitchen for adding to sherry trifles, and for the children to steal and make themselves ill with. A "top" is a glass of beer that has had the last inch topped up with a sweetener, by default lemonade—what Brits call "lemonade" is a

Sprite-like carbonated soft drink. A "half" is, of course, a half pint, the traditional quantity of beer drunk by those women who consider drinking pints to be loutish. (For anyone wishing to know more about pub etiquette and English behaviour in general, I warmly and sincerely recommend *Watching the English—The Hidden Rules of English Behaviour* by anthropologist Kate Fox—although you may need to go to amazon.co.uk, and pay a king's ransom in postage, to get hold of it.)

**dicky**
(As an adjective) faulty, unreliable. This is obsolete slang: characters in P. G. Wodehouse novels with heart problems will report their condition as a "dicky ticker."

**doofer**
A remote control unit for TVs, videos, etc. I believe, with no proof, the name is onomatopoeic, from the "doof" sound old tellies make when you change channels.

**dosh**
Wonga *(qv)*.

**fag**
Slang for a cigarette. Oh, for heaven's sake. You must have known that. And, yes, if I happen to use the word "rubber," I do mean "eraser."

**fettle**
A proper Olde English word, not dialect or slang, meaning "health" or "condition."

**flat**
(As a noun) an apartment.

**jiggery-pokery**
Activity undertaken by someone who is up to no good, mischief.

**journo**
Abbreviation of "journalist."

**knickers**
The fundamental undergarment, nearly always the female version. A much more *cheerful* word than, for example, panties, it plays an important role in many British colloquial phrases, e.g., "Don't get your knickers in a twist" for "Don't get agitated."

## lager
A yellow type of beer. They say Budweiser is a lager.

## loo
The most alimentary of bathroom furniture; also the small room in which said furniture is installed. I believe "john" is the nearest US English equivalent, but in the UK this whole topic is horribly entangled with issues of class and embarrassment, so I can't be sure that the two words carry the same level of social sanitation. Put it this way: "loo" is a quite straightforward, comparatively genteel word; but you might well find that, say, Her Majesty the Queen prefers "lavatory," "cloakroom," or even "water closet." Probably best not to worry about this difficultly until you encounter it in real life. Although "bog" is right out.

## Marmite
A pungent slime made from yeast. That this item does not occur in the text, apart from here, I regard as a failing on my part.

## monkey-juice
Generic name for very sweet, very alcoholic lager *(qv)*, formerly used by young persons wishing to attain the vomiting level of drunkenness in short order. In modern Britain it has been largely displaced from this niche by various exotic spirits-based drinks, but I believe monkey-juice retains its charm for those who like to enjoy their alcohol alfresco in the relaxed surroundings of local parks and bus stops. And, of course, there are fan web sites, e.g. http://www.arrysbrewsite.co.uk.

## plonker
This word is now generally synonymous with "idiot," as in "You utter plonker!" although its original, ruder meaning can be glimpsed in the phrase "Are you pulling my plonker?" a supposedly amusing variation of "Are you pulling my leg?" "Plonker" rates SOC *(qv)* of just 2.32. Its low rating is caused by its constant repetition in the TV show *Only Fools and Horses*, a BBC sitcom of which about 10,000 episodes have been made, mostly one-off Christmas specials.

## poncing
My dictionary says, baldly, that to ponce around is to "act as ponce; move about effeminately, etc." That "etc." is rather rich. If the folks at the dictionary can't be bothered to define it properly . . . People who are "poncing about," in the sense I use it, are making a show of doing

something, instead of actually doing it. As the dictionary implies, the phrase originates from that dark time, long ago, when people occasionally exercised discrimination on grounds other than ability.

### Pooterish

Refers to Charles Pooter, the hero of top Victorian chuckler *Diary of a Nobody,* who is fussy and ineffective.

### punter

One of the bedrock terms in my embarrassingly limited comic vocabulary. The *Concise Oxford Dictionary* (7th edition) opines that a punter is someone who propels a flat-bottomed shallow boat by a long pole, someone who kicks a football after it has been dropped from the hands and before it reaches the ground, or a person who bets on horses or who is the client of a prostitute.

None of these definitions is my intended sense.

However, the last two, the business about horses and sex workers, do provide the jocular origin of the current usage. A "punter" is a not terribly respectful name for the customer. A bit like a "sucker" in a casino or a "luser" at the paying end of a tech support line, but not nearly so mean.

### SOC

See entry for "blimey."

### spiv

A seedy sort of tax-dodging trader, often redeemed by an engaging line of sales patter. Not all goods sold by spivs are of inferior quality or broken; they may simply be stolen.

### wonga

Loot, negotiable lettuce, foldable readies.

# Index